Mount Rainier National Park
Tales, Trails, & Auto Tours

Also by the same authors and illustrator:

Humboldt Redwoods State Park:
The Complete Guide

Redwood National & State Parks:
Tales, Trails, & Auto Tours

Mount Rainier National Park
Tales, Trails, & Auto Tours

Jerry & Gisela Rohde
Illustrations by Larry Eifert

MountainHome Books
• 1996 •

Copyright © 1996 by Jerry and Gisela Rohde

Illustrations © 1996 by Larry Eifert

Library of Congress Catalogue Number: 96-75512

International Standard Book Number: 0-9640261-1-2

Manufactured in the USA on acid-free, recycled paper by Thomson-Shore, Inc., Dexter, Michigan 48130

Body text in Book Antiqua, anecdote text and captions in CG-Omega, titles in Book Antiqua and Goudy Extrabold-MT, map text in Shannon

MountainHome Books
1901 Arthur Road
McKinleyville, CA 95519

Contents

Maps

Preface

"I find people are not interested in facts. The greater appeal is to the heart."

— Carl Sharsmith (1903–1994), Yosemite
National Park ranger for over 60 years

On a sunny late summer day, after two weeks of doing research for this book, we needed to leave the park and return home. Yet we found time for one more trail that morning, around Naches Peak, and then we stayed a little longer to circle Tipsoo Lake, where the grass had yellowed and the shrubs already blushed red with fall. It seemed we wanted to stay forever — wandering through the meadows and the forests, beholding the wildflowers and the trees, meeting the marmots and the pikas — knowing, all the while, that above us all gleamed the Mountain.

The place had captured us — had, in fact, done so decades earlier, when Gisela visited the park with her family on weekend outings from Seattle, and when the peak appeared to Jerry, before he had ever set eyes on it, shining in the moonlight within a wondrous dream.

So we came to the Mountain, as often as we could, coming to know it as well as we could, and then we wrote about it, sharing all that we could. Facts you'll find within these pages, but more than that, we hope, you'll find what we did — a place to love with all our hearts.

We are deeply indebted to the many people who helped us create this book:

Larry Eifert, Nancy Martin, Ben Bennion, Allan Borden, Norma Kirmmse-Borden, Murray Morgan, John Duffield, Bill Dengler,

Kathleen Jobson, Donna Rahier, Loren Lane, Carl Fabiani, Dinni Fabiani, John Hoffman, Marty Vaughan, Virginia Panco Squires, Gary Fuller Reese, John Thompson, Yolanda Thompson, Barbara Wilkenson, Alan Wilkenson, Pam Zeutenhorst, Marilyn Murphy, Sherry Gordon, Erich Schimps, Lincoln Kilian, Gisela Haringer, and the many helpful staff persons at local libraries and at Mount Rainier National Park.

Gisela, age 4, and
brother Bernie, 6,
at Mount Rainier

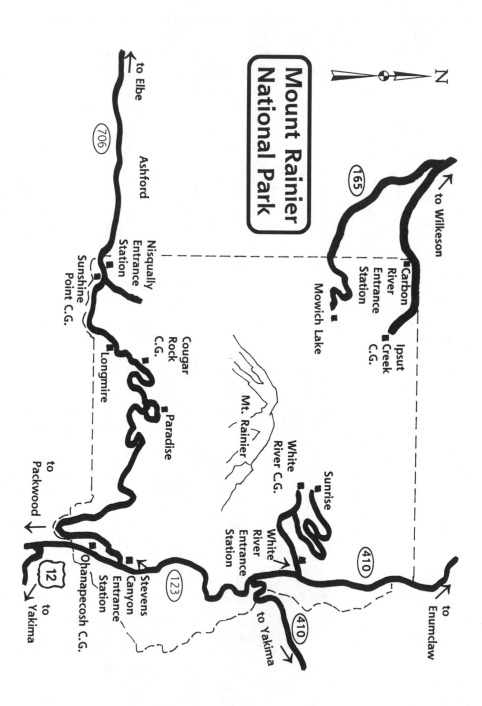

Section I:
Human and Natural History

She had been there seemingly forever, old beyond memory of the eldest elder, so old that she was traced back to the mists of myth—an angry woman, so one story went, who left her husband over in the Olympics and went south of the Sound, where she had room to spread out, finally growing so huge that she towered over everything within sight.

And thus she stood above the forest, white-topped with the snows of centuries upon her, forbidding when approached, but capable of captivating from a distance. On her slopes roamed deer, elk, and mountain goats, while a dozen different berries ripened there in fall, a harvest for the people who lived around her and grew none of their own crops.

Tacobet

Offered by her also were the waters, rushing down eight different rivers, churning through the canyons with their murky glacial melt and then slowing as they reached the low country, where they became highways for the salmon that were the peoples' staff of life.

Tacobet, they called her, with a rumbling in their chests, or Takhoma or Takkobad, if the tongue that spoke was from another tribe. "Nourishing breast," the word meant, or perhaps "the place where the waters begin," or, simply, "the Mountain." By whichever name, she was known to all the nearby peoples, a presence even when hidden by an intervening ridge or obscured by the forest or the fog. Then, as now, she filled the awareness of all who approached her, leaving an image that lingered somewhere beyond the mind's busying thoughts. And so it was that Tacobet-Takhoma might rise before a dreamer from the depths of sleep, her round, white shape released by the ever-holding, ever-*be*holding heart.

And thus the Mountain stood.

The Peak and the Park

I. Early Approaches, Early Ascents

> The weather was serene and pleasant and the country continued to exhibit between us and the eastern snowy range the same luxurious appearance. At its northern extremity Mount Baker bore by compass N. 22 E., the round snowy mountain now forming its southern extremity and which, after my friend Rear-Admiral Rainier, I distinguish by the name of Mount Rainier....

Only a day earlier had the sailors from His Britannic Majesty's sloop of war *Discovery* first seen the "very remarkable high, round mountain, covered with snow," and now, on May 8, 1792, Captain George Vancouver was naming it—not for its appearance or any other integral sense of it, but for his far-off friend, a portly, bespectacled fellow officer who had never sailed within a thousand leagues of the mountain and never would.

For the next 40 years precious few whites of any description came into the region. The group of settlers who finally showed up owed their allegiance to Peter Rainier's homeland, Mother England, as they were employees of the Hudson's Bay Company and had come to the mouth of the Nisqually River to establish a trading post on Puget Sound.

The first contingent came in the spring of 1833. Among the early arrivals at the post was Dr. William Fraser Tolmie, twenty-one years old and not long graduated from medical school in Glasgow. The distant peak soon captured Tolmie's interest, and by late August he had wrangled permission from the chief trader to make a ten-day excursion toward the mountain for the ostensible purpose of collecting medicinal herbs.

Tolmie and five local Indians promptly made for the Puyallup River, struggled up its canyon for a while, and finally crashed overland through the forest until they reached the Mowich. Arriving at

3

Hessong Rock

that river's forks, Tolmie picked out the snowiest of the surrounding mountains (later named Hessong Rock) and with two of the Indians went up. The next morning Tolmie repeated the climb, stared eastward at the great peak, which "appeared surpassingly splendid and magnificent," and then headed back to the trading post.

In addition to gaining his close-up view of Mount Rainier, Tolmie managed to collect a "variety of plants," and, as he later discovered, rupture himself. As consolation, the doctor could at least claim title as the first white man to closely approach the peak.

Eventually countless others would share Tolmie's interest in Rainier, but for many years visitors came in a trickle, not a torrent. No whites again paid much attention to the mountain until 1842, when Lieutenant Charles Wilkes, United States Navy, stared longingly at its snowy summit while surveying the Puget Sound area.

Wilkes, who never got closer than Nisqually Prairie, did attempt to triangulate the height of the peak, which he determined to be a mere 12,330 feet. Had he been as inaccurate with his navigation, his ship surely would have lodged on some unexpected sandbar, but the erroneous estimate stood as the mountain's official elevation for over 40 years.

While Wilkes's surveying duties kept him *away* from Mount Rainier, another party of surveyors found their work took them *to* the peak. While searching for a wagon passage over the Cascades they made the first known attempt of the mountain, climbing for two days up its slopes to an elevation where they estimated the crusted snow lay 50 feet deep.

Two years passed before their work bore fruit. Then in 1853 one of the surveyors, John Edgar, laid out a route over Naches Pass, northeast of Rainier. In October of that same year 35 wagons (out of a train of 36) survived the rigors of the rugged gap and made their way to Fort Nisqually. One of the party's leaders was James Longmire, who was to link much of his later life to the mountain.

Yet another survey, this one in 1855, may have led to the first successful summit climb. If so, the feat was accomplished by two anonymous surveyors who were trying to determine a reservation boundary for one of the recently concluded Indian treaties. The only report of the event came more than 60 years later, when the pair's Yakima guide, the aged Chief Saluskin, gave an account to a local historian. According to the Indian, the men made their ascent and returned to camp in a single day; at the summit they found "ice all over top, lake in center, and smoke or steam coming out all around like sweat-house."

The residents of 1850s Washington Territory, knowing nothing of Saluskin's story, still awaited the first ascent of the peak. Their anticipation extended beyond the decade as the only contestant climber, Lieutenant August V. Kautz, turned back at the 14,000-foot level in July 1857. No serious efforts were reported during the 1860s, and it was easy to wonder if Rainier's summit might forever elude conquest.

All that changed in 1870, when a determined duo of Washingtonians joined forces with a member of the British Alpine Club to assault Rainier's heights.

Stevens and Van Trump Triumph

The three climbers who left Lackamas Prairie on August 9, 1870, carried with them, in addition to a pair of flags and an array of equipment, some impressive credentials. Edmund Thomas Coleman, the lone Englishman, had made several ascents in the Swiss Alps and recently reached the top of Mount Baker. General Hazard Stevens was the son of Washington's first territorial governor and a wounded Civil War veteran who had himself garnered the Congressional Medal of Honor. Philemon Beecher Van Trump was neither medal winner nor mountaineer, but in compensation he held a deep and eloquent love for the peak, writing of

> ...my first grand view of the mountain...revealing so much of its glorious beauty and grandeur, its mighty and sublime form filling up nearly all of the field of direct vision, swelling up from the plain and out of the green forest till its lofty triple summit towered immeasurably above the picturesque foothills, the westering sun flooding with golden light and softening tints its lofty summit, rugged sides, and far-sweeping flanks—all this impressed me so indescribably, enthused me so thoroughly, that I then and there vowed, almost with fervency, that I would someday stand upon its glorious summit, if that feat were possible to human effort and endurance. (Van Trump, in Haines, pp. 31-2)

James Longmire, who had earlier explored the area south of Mount Rainier, agreed to serve as the party's initial guide. He took the climbers far up the Nisqually, then veered off southeast towards the Upper Cowlitz Valley and commenced searching for a knowledgeable Indian who could lead them the rest of the way. On Skate Creek Longmire found his man: a broken-handed Yakima named Sluiskin (not to be confused with Chief Saluskin of the reported 1855 summit climb), whose disability derived from a soldier's musket ball at the Battle of the Grande Ronde. Sluiskin rejected Stevens's suggestion that they continue along the Nisqually, for he had a better idea—cross over the rugged Tatoosh Range that rose between them and the mountain like an upturned saw blade.

Two-thirds of the climbers made it. Left behind was Coleman, who had long lagged anyway. After losing his pack, the aggrieved

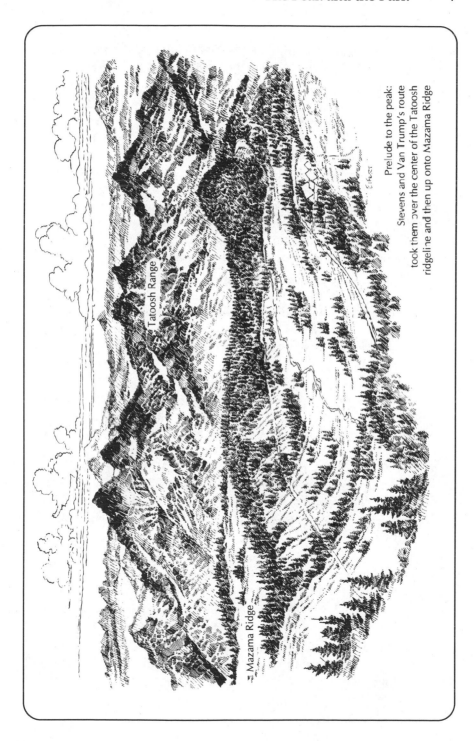

Tatoosh Range

Mazama Ridge

Prelude to the peak:
Stevens and Van Trump's route
took them over the center of the Tatoosh
ridgeline and then up onto Mazama Ridge

alpinist bedraggledly returned to the Bear Creek base camp, while the others heaved sighs of relief and headed onward.

Sluiskin's roller coaster route led across the Tatoosh ridgeline at the Pinnacle Peak saddle, dropped down to the canyon of Clear (later renamed Tatoosh) Creek, and then ascended onto meadow-filled Mazama Ridge. At timberline they made a high camp, where Stevens and Van Trump named the nearby waterfall for their guide. Sluiskin by this time was in low spirits, convinced that if the climbers challenged the summit they would probably either fall to their deaths, be crushed by falling rocks, or have a wind gust sweep them away. "But if by some miracle you should survive all these perils," he morosely continued, "the mighty demon of Takhoma will surely kill you and throw you into the fiery lake."

Bolstered by this cheery prognosis, Stevens and Van Trump started their ascent on the morning of August 17. Although it was before dawn, Sluiskin had already set off on a hunt. The climbers passed him several thousand feet up the slope, where the guide, who was staring intently at the mountain, gave the pair no more than a glance.

Stevens and Van Trump ascended the Cowlitz Cleaver at a good pace, but then slowed when traversing the rock-bombarded ledge on the Gibraltar cliff. That passage completed, they made fast progress on the glacial ice that lay above, cutting steps with Coleman's ax. After crossing several small crevasses, they needed their rope for a last, larger breach in the ice. Fatigue and a strong wind then again slowed them; the gusts were so great that the pair dropped to their hands and knees, inching their way forward some 50 yards. Here they reached an intermediate summit, which they promptly dubbed "Peak Success."

After raising their flags on their alpenstocks and giving a wind-smothered three cheers, the pair continued upward a few hundred feet to the true top of Mount Rainier. Stevens and Van Trump had finally reached the summit; now all they had to do was defy Sluiskin's prediction and live to tell about it.

Doing so wouldn't be especially easy. It was too late in the day to descend to their camp; moreover, an Arctic blast was buffeting them, they had no blankets or heavy clothing, and it would get much colder after dark.

Hazard Stevens, left, and Philemon Beecher Van Trump at the Washington State Historical Society, commemorating their ascent of the Mountain many years after the event

The old volcano saved them. Its crater, which lay just below the summit, was riddled with steam jets warmed by the subterranean heat. Stevens and Van Trump built a stone shelter around one of the larger jets, and there they huddled through the night, nearly scalded on one side and fairly frozen on the other. The next morning, August 18, Stevens left an inscribed brass plate on a mound of rocks (they had scratched out Coleman's name), and then he and Van Trump made their way down the mountain. Van Trump fell when nearly back to camp, sliding 40 feet onto some sharp rocks and gashing his thigh. Damaged but undaunted, he limped the rest of the way with Stevens's help.

Sluiskin returned as the pair finished dinner; he stopped at a distance and studied the weary climbers. Finally deciding they were indeed alive and not apparitions, he joined them, suddenly pleased and full of praise.

Van Trump's injury slowed their return. Coleman was found at the base camp, by now nearly ready to begin his own solitary assault on the mountain, and the three mountaineers then headed for the Sound. A week after their ascent, they rode into Olympia aboard James Longmire's one-horse carriage, their two flags flying jauntily from their alpenstocks. The capital welcomed them as conquering heroes, which was exactly what they were. The summit had finally been surmounted, and Mount Rainier had gained, in Philemon Beecher Van Trump, a champion who would sing its praises for the next 45 years, doing more than any other individual to insure that the peak was protected as a park.

After waiting eons for the first climbers to reach its summit, the mountain then saw a second group succeed only two months later. Not surprisingly, they were surveyors: Samuel Franklin Emmons and A. D. Wilson of the Corps of Engineers gazed down from the peaktop on October 17. The energetic pair returned to camp the same day, but their seventeen-hour round trip was only the beginning of a much longer adventure. Lacking provisions, Emmons and Wilson turned east, crossed the Cascades, and headed toward the Indian Agency at Fort Simcoe. Their eventual arrival there — nearly starved, their clothing no more than shredded rags — was a far different finish than Stevens and Van Trump's triumphal entry into Olympia.

Over the ensuing years, the brass plate that Stevens had placed upon the peak lay like a lodestone, drawing not only summit climbers and scenery viewers, but also the routes for them to travel. Roads, trails, and even rails slowly inched their way through the forests and up the canyons until they arrived at Rainier's lower slopes.

The rails came first, laid into Carbon River country in 1877, courtesy of the Northern Pacific Railroad as it reached the coal fields at Wilkeson. There, for a time, the tracks ended, but a trail built by NPRR geologist Bailey Willis took travelers south and east to the foot of the peak; now climbers could advance upon Rainier from the northwest. The route received a boost in 1884 with the opening, some 30-odd miles away, of the ornate Tacoma Hotel. Owned by the rail line, the facility soon offered guided tours to the mountain, conveniently taking the travelers over the NPRR's tracks to Wilkeson. There the excursionists hired professional guides, such as local hotel owner George Driver, who led them on horseback towards Mount Rainier.

NPRR office building, Tacoma

Meanwhile, the older Nisqually approach saw activity of its own. James Longmire again braved the rigors of the route in 1883, accompanying P. B. Van Trump, George Bayley, and W. C. Ewing to the slopes of the mountain. At Mashel Prairie, west of today's Eatonville, they picked up an Indian guide, Soo-to-lick, known to the whites as Indian Henry; he deviated from Sluiskin's earlier course, taking the party all the way up the Nisqually. The 63-year-old Longmire, who at the last moment joined Van Trump and Bayley in the climb to the top, made a portentous discovery on the return trip—while searching for his strayed horse near the banks of the upper Nisqually, he came upon an enticing collection of mineral springs. Longmire decided to develop the property into a resort and the following year built a crude trail up the river canyon to the site. Travelers could then take regularly scheduled, summertime "Indian pony" trips from Yelm Prairie to the springs, stopping over at Indian Henry's farm and Kernahan's Ranch along the way. In 1893, with a hotel, bathhouse, and several other buildings in place, Longmire and a crew of ten laborers widened the path into a rough approximation of a road; now wagons and other vehicles could reach the springs from Kernahan's, nine miles to the west. Three years later, summer stages began using the route.

Longmire's Springs; hotel at far right

Conifers, not coal, brought a second rail line toward Rainier in 1904, when the Chicago, Milwaukee & St. Paul Railway pushed through its branch line, the Tacoma Eastern Railroad, to a timber-rich terminus at Ashford. The train company quickly saw the advantage of transporting mountain worshippers as well as wood, and thus the following year the "National Park Limited" sped some 3,500 visitors to the park. The two-and-a-half-day wagon trip of a decade earlier now took only seven hours over the clacking tracks.

Pleasantly seated, with nothing to do but stare at the spectacular scenery, train passengers were a world away from the discomforts of the earlier, trail-bound trips. George Bayley, who instigated the 1883 climb that led to the discovery of Longmire's Springs, would have vouched for that.

Tough Traveling to Mount Tacoma

When Bayley set out for the mountain with W. C. Ewing, James Longmire, and P. B. Van Trump, he no doubt expected the hard part of their trip to be the final climb to the summit. The ascent indeed proved daunting, but no more so, it turned out, than the trying approach to the lower slopes of the peak.

Bayley found the group traveling a "fair" wagon road for the 25 miles between Yelm and "Mishawl" (Mashel) Prairie. After they'd spent the night in Indian Henry's barn and induced their host to guide them, the men

> were early in the saddle, and trouble began almost immediately. The woods were on fire around us, and we occasionally found ourselves hemmed in by flame and blinding smoke; smouldering trunks lay across the trail and half-burned stumps left treacherous pitfalls in our way. (Bayley, in Schullery, pp. 83-5)

Bad as this was, conditions soon became worse:

> Nests of yellowjackets were met with every few hundred yards, their revengeful inmates swarming out upon us with relentless fury. The horses were stung to frenzy, and snorted, kicked, and finally stampeded in reckless madness, until brought to a standstill by a barrier of logs, where they crowded together, trembling with terror. Nor was this a temporary experience, but was repeated at intervals of ten minutes throughout the day. We were thus in constant danger of having our brains dashed out against the trees by the maddened beasts. The pack animals seemed to suffer most, and kicked off their packs with charming regularity about every hour. (Ibid.)

Camp, when it came some 17 miles later, offered no relief:

> We all needed rest and refreshing sleep, but were denied either, for no sooner had we unpacked our animals than we were assailed by small black gnats and ravenous mosquitoes. The gnats were simply irresistible; one could not breathe without inhaling them; they buried themselves in one's flesh, burning like so many coals of fire; they got into every article of food, without however, improving its flavor....The mosquitoes stung and poisoned every exposed portion of our bodies. (Ibid.)

The next evening "the gnats were, if possible, more numerous than on the previous night," and the insatiable insects then accompanied the party throughout the following day, congregating "in increasing numbers to partake of our supper, and cause us another miserable, sleepless night." So it was that "on the morning of the fifth day, a more haggard, gaunt, blear eyed company never sat down to a breakfast of bacon and beans."

Thus annoyed nearly beyond endurance, it was an easy decision for James Longmire, despite his 63 years, to join Bayley and

Van Trump in attempting the summit. After plodding for three days through the insect-infested forest, climbing the peak must have seemed like a picnic: just tumbling rocks, gaping crevasses, and freezing winds—but, mercifully, no mosquitoes.

II. First a Forest, then a Park

If George Bayley told his friend, the author-preservationist-naturalist John Muir, about the rigors of reaching Mount Rainier, the warning had little effect. In the summer of 1888, Muir, along with landscape painter William Keith and several others, engaged P. B. Van Trump as guide and headed for the slopes. Once on the mountain, they spent a night at "a sheltered pumice patch" subsequently named for its locator as "Camp Muir," and the next day made it to the top. The trip provided material for an article by Muir in which he ruminated that:

> The view we enjoyed from the summit could hardly be surpassed in sublimity and grandeur; but one feels far from home so high in the sky, so much so that one is inclined to guess, that apart from the acquisition of knowledge and the exhilaration of climbing, more pleasure is to be found at the foot of mountains than on their frozen tops. (Muir, p. 458)

Like most of Muir's writings, the account attracted a wide audience, but it took a summit-climbing schoolmarm to create the sort of publicity that truly put the mountain on the map.

Fay's Feminist Feat

In the late 1880s the young teacher at the Yelm school, Fay Fuller, made the acquaintance of P. B. Van Trump. She attended several of the famed mountaineer's lectures and, fascinated by his stories of Mount Rainier, twice had him give talks to her class. As Fuller later put it, "his enthusiasm made me want to go up."

She went part way in 1887, climbing to the 8,700-foot level above the Paradise snowfields. That only whetted Fuller's appetite for a full-scale ascent, and in the summer of 1890 she eagerly accepted the Van Trump family's invitation to accompany them to the mountain.

Fuller arrived at Paradise to find a climbing party camped nearby; when she told the group of her hope to attempt the summit, they promptly offered to let her come with them. So it was that two mornings later Fuller found herself leaving Camp Muir in the company of Reverend E. C. Smith, Robert R. Parrish, W. O. Amsden, and a last-minute addition, Len Longmire. She was well prepared for the ascent:

> Before departing I donned heavy flannels, woolen hose, warm mittens and goggles, blackened my face with charcoal to modify the sun's glare, drove long caulks and brads into my shoes, rolled two single blankets containing provisions for three days and strapped them from the shoulder under the arm to the waist, the easiest way by far to CARRY A PACK, shouldered one of Uncle Sam's canteens, grasped my alpenstock and was resolved to climb until exhausted. (Fuller, in Schullery, p. 131)

Lacking an R.E.I. to equip her, Fuller's outfit required some improvising. Her "flannels" were a skirt and set of baggy dark-blue bloomers designed by her dressmaker; with no women's boots available, she bought a pair of the sturdiest boys' shoes she could

Fay, second from right, on the way

find. The alpenstock was fashioned by the local blacksmith from a shovel handle and a bit of metal.

Thus prepared, Fuller marched along with the men. According to Len Longmire, she refused any assistance, but Fay herself admitted that at one dangerous passage her companions tied a rope to her and, with two of them in front and two behind, helped her across.

The party encountered a few difficulties on the way up—Parrish accidentally pitched his pack down the Nisqually Glacier, Smith was hit a couple of times by bounding rocks—but by 4:30 P.M. the five climbers stood atop the summit. For Fuller, "It was a heavenly moment; nothing was said—words cannot describe scenery and beauty, how could they speak for the soul!"

The late hour made a descent dangerous. Like Stevens and Van Trump, the group elected to spend a steamy night in the crater.

Fuller suffered little more than a severe sunburn in the aftermath of her ascent. Soon she was back in Yelm, where she expanded on her duties as social editor of her father's Tacoma paper, *Every Sunday*, by writing a detailed account of her climb up the mountain. Not all readers approved of her accomplishment, however; her immodest attire was bad enough, but her unchaperoned, overnight sojourn beside the steam vents in the company of four males proved absolutely scandalous.

Others were less concerned with propriety than with proof of her feat, doubting that a "mere" woman could accomplish what was nearly impossible even for a man. One skeptical male climber subsequently got his comeuppance when he attained the summit, later admitting to Fuller, "I guess you actually did get to the top. We found hairpins there."

Climbing the mountain was but the first of Fuller's many activities that confounded conventionality. Soon she was training Tacoma's 20-member Women's Guard in march and rifle calisthenics and wearing her bloomer outfit to ride horseback on a man's saddle, rather than using the side saddle then favored by women. In addition, she took a job with her father's competitor paper, the Tacoma *Ledger*, covering the rough-and-tumble waterfront beat. Fuller later put that experience to use when she became the country's first female port collector.

> For all that, it was reaching the summit of Rainier that seemingly left her most satisfied. As she wrote at the conclusion of her *Every Sunday* account, "I have accomplished what I have always dreamed of and feared impossible."
>
> Few men could have said as much.

Following her climb, Fuller wrote tirelessly of the mountain, adding her efforts to those of Van Trump and others, but as the peak became more publicized, it also began to suffer the effects of increased popularity. Cyrus A. Moser, special agent for the Department of the Interior, investigated the area's timber conditions in 1891-92; he found not only huge areas of cutover lowland forest but damage on the mountain itself, where for amusement campers at Paradise had burned small clusters of conifers at night.

Prompted by Moser's report, President Benjamin Harrison established the Pacific Forest Reserve in February 1892; it included Mount Rainier and substantial surrounding area. By then, however, preservationists were talking of protecting the peak more completely — as a national park.

The idea had surfaced nearly a decade earlier when two foreign visitors, the German geologist Karl Zittel and the British author James Bryce, visited Rainier's northwest side and subsequently recommended that the peak be granted park status. P. B. Van Trump revived the notion some eight years later and soon others took up the cause. During 1893 and 1894 five organizations — the Geological Society of America, the American Association for the Advancement of Science, the National Geographic Society, the Sierra Club, and the Appalachian Mountain Club — proposed that Congress create a national park for the mountain. Supporters waded through the usual political quagmire for three years and then — action! A bill to create the park was approved by both houses and forwarded to President Grover Cleveland. He failed to sign it but did change the name of the existing federal area to the *Mount Rainier* Forest Reserve.

Preservationists were not impressed. Back they went to Congress where, after two more years of work, another park bill passed. It was signed by President William McKinley on March 2,

1899, although a last minute amendment replaced the park's proposed name, "Washington," with "Mount Rainier." The change soon proved to have considerable consequences.

What's in a Name?

"I am opposed to applying the names of men, even great ones, to mountains, rivers, glaciers, or any of the sublime things in nature."

—P. B. Van Trump, when told of a suggestion that his name be given to one of Rainier's glaciers

What's in a name? In the case of Mount Rainier/Tacoma, more than a century of controversy.

The seeds were sown over two hundred years ago, when Captain George Vancouver, who himself would eventually have a pair of Northwest cities bear his name, fatefully named the highest peak in the region for his admiral friend, Peter Rainier. This may have confounded the local Indians, who'd called it Tacobet, Takhoma, and similar things for centuries, but they were not consulted.

Early settlers seemed undecided as to who had it right. Dr. William Fraser Tolmie, the first white to come near the mountain, compromised by calling it "Tuchoma or Mount Rainier," although he also indicated that certain Indians sometimes referred to the peak as "Puskehouse." The posthumous publication of Theodore Winthrop's *The Canoe and the Saddle* in 1863 brought "Tacoma" into print as the spelling for the native people's preference. Twenty years later, the Northern Pacific Railroad, whose branch line ran up the Carbon River, announced that it would henceforth use this name in its guidebooks and other publications. Residents of Tacoma, as would be expected, were delighted with the connection thus forged between the great mountain and their small but growing city.

Their joy lasted less than a decade. Seattleites, unnerved by the advantage their competitor down the Sound gained from the name association, campaigned for the retention of Rainier. The controversy was duly referred to the United States Board of Geographic Names, and in 1890 that august body came down in favor of the status quo. Unanimously. It seemed the final word in the dispute.

But Tacomans still had plenty to say. A "Justice-to-the-Mountain Committee" soon solidified around newspaperman Sam Wall (whose leadership qualifications included having once shot a rival editor for implying that Wall was pro-Seattle). Committee members busily sought out sympathizers; among their recruits were Colonel John Puget, who indicated he preferred Tacoma over the name his great-granduncle had bestowed, and journalist Carl Snyder, who sniped at poor Peter Rainier, calling him a "nautical nobody."

Peter Rainier,
Admiral of the
Blue, Royal Navy

Despite their efforts, Tacoma boosters suffered a second setback in 1899 when the nautical nobody's name was given to the new national park. The Justice-to-the-Mountain Committee railed against this additional injustice and continued its work. More converts joined the cause, and in 1917, with their anti-Rainier allies ranging from Will Rogers to Theodore Roosevelt to Mary Roberts Rinehart, the protesters were granted their most cherished request—a rehearing before the Board of Geographic Names. Once again, however, the decision was to retain Rainier. Perhaps trying to silence the pro-Tacoma gadflies for good, the Board's secretary added a stinging rebuke:

> No geographic feature in any part of the world can claim a name more firmly fixed by right of discovery, by priority, and by universal usage for more than a century. So far as known, no attempt has ever been made by any people in any part of the world to change a name so firmly established.

Pro-Tacoma camper

It was a crushing blow to the Justice-to-the-Mountain Committee, which accordingly disbanded. Loyalist members, however, reorganized as the Mount Tacoma Club and soon had unexpected success. Miraculously enlisting the support of Seattle mayor Edwin J. Brown, the club in 1924 secured a joint resolution from the U.S. Senate to change the peak's name to Mount Tacoma. The resolution was shipped off to the House Committee on Public Lands, which acted on the measure in January, 1925: Four committee members favored "Tacoma." There were five abstentions. And nine votes upheld the status quo.

After that, only the most dyed-in-the-wool Tacoma diehards held out any hope for success. One person who did was Minnie Mitchell, the erstwhile secretary of the Mount Tacoma Club. Ousted from her job after clashing with the trustees, Minnie spent the rest of her life trying to change enough minds to finally change the peak's name. She worked virtually alone, corresponding with a small circle of supporters while badgering the British Museum and the Royal Geographic Society to locate the aging atlases, maps, and geographies that she was certain would show her beloved landform as "Tacoma." After Mitchell died in 1941, a plane dropped her ashes on the slopes of Minnie's still-misnamed mountain.

Other pro-Tacoma protesters maintained Mitchell's tradition after her death, approaching the Board of Geographic Names almost annually with requests to rename Rainier. Then, in the 1990s, like an eruption from a new vent in the long-forgotten volcano, the controversy again bubbled to the surface. Its cause this time: baseball.

The trouble started when the Seattle Mariners acquired the minor-league Tacoma Tigers as their farm team. The new owners thought they could stimulate local sports interest by turning the Tigers into the Rainiers, thus resurrecting the one-time name of Seattle's earlier-day entry in the Pacific Coast League. Sweetening the situation was a deal to provide the Rainier Brewing Company with an exclusive contract on beer sales at the games. For old-time Tacomans, it was too much. They refused to call the Rainiers anything but the "Suds" and some of the fuming fans even boycotted the ballpark. One local wondered wistfully if a rearoused Minnie Mitchell might be "contemplating a postcard campaign from the cemetery."

As their suffering continues, Mount Tacoma advocates can at least take heart in the information provided by one of Peter Rainier's descendants, who, when visiting the park, indicated that the admiral's French Huguenot family pronounced their name "*Rainy*-er," as in "more rain." That, as anyone who's observed the mountain's weather will attest, is indeed an apt description for the peak.

III. Founded, but not Funded

The mountain, whether called Rainier or Tacoma, finally had its park, but there were strings attached—purse strings—and they were drawn tightly shut. To get the park bill past powerful "Uncle Joe" Cannon, chair of the House Ways and Means Committee, proponents had promised they would make no funding requests as long as Cannon remained in Congress.

Thus for three years the site was a park in name only, unsupervised, and without a budget. Then, in 1902, Grenville F. Allen, the superintendent of the Mount Rainier Forest Reserve, was given temporary charge of the park but no funds with which to administer it. A dribble of dollars came the following year to pay a pair of seasonal forest rangers, and Tacoma Congressman Francis W. Cushman, who had not participated in the bargain with Cannon, pushed through a $10,000 allotment for connecting the county road at Ashford with the Paradise area.

In 1906 Mount Rainier received its first true park ranger, Oscar Brown; his credentials included having been part of an Enumclaw climbing party that 15 years earlier placed a tall flagpole upon the mountain's summit. Brown soon set to work building a cabin for himself at the Nisqually Entrance. By 1910, when Edward S. Hall took charge as Mount Rainier's first permanent superintendent, the park had also acquired three abandoned miner's cabins, built a cabin and barn at Longmire, and was working on a cabin at Carbon River. Construction continued on the Paradise road, and in the fall of 1911 the route was ready to receive an important visit.

"Taft is Mired on Mountain"

They came in a caravan sixteen cars strong, crossing the prairies and foothills, as per instructions, at "all possible speed"—which meant some 35 miles per hour. Spectators crowded the crossroads along the route; at one point a small boy raised an American flag, and the large figure in the second vehicle responded by removing his cap. After two hours the column arrived at Ashford and then passed Mesler's sawmill, where the family had built an arch of autumn-tinted maple leaves. The excursionists bowed their heads and cheered as they passed under the display.

Lunch at Longmire was an important event, for the man with the cap, President William Howard Taft, had not attained his 326-pound bulk by skimping on food. As one of the Tacoma papers reported:

> The President seated himself at the head of the table and tucked a big white napkin in his collar. His appetite had been whetted by the ride in the cool morning air and he plunged into the plate of fried chicken in real earnest. When the President arose the luncheon placed before him had completely vanished.

Taft paused only once in his attack on the victuals; a tiny hand had touched his, and he looked down to see the two small sons of ranger Sam Estes peering up at him.

"Why hello!" the President exclaimed. "Glad to see you!"

And setting down his fork for a moment, he grasped each boy's hand in his and left the little brothers with a lifelong memory.

Then it was back in the cars for the final climb to Paradise. A brief stop at the Nisqually Glacier was followed by a longer stay at scenic Ricksecker Point. Binoculars in hand, the President stepped to the very edge of the overlook, where he stumbled slightly and lurched into a newspaperman, nearly pitching the hapless reporter down the precipice.

Taft takes in the view
at Ricksecker Point

Two miles ahead the caravan encountered mud. Soon the pilot car had sunk in to its radiator. Like cavalry riding to the rescue, a group of mounted park guides conveniently arrived and used their horses to pull the vehicle free. Taft offered to help push, claiming his weight was worth the effort of several teams, but the President remained in his auto instead, where, serving as ballast, he helped the car motor through the mire unscathed.

Nearly all the other vehicles, lacking Taft's tonnage, became stuck. The horses kept busy all afternoon removing the autos from the muck; meanwhile, the President merrily continued on to Paradise. There Taft enjoyed the sunset from Camp of the Clouds and then returned in the gloaming to Ashford, where he boarded the Tacoma Eastern's special train for Tacoma. Behind him, on the switchbacks above Longmire, four stranded cars waited until daylight to be salvaged.

After he had boarded the train, Taft jovially announced, "I've had a tip-top time, and enjoyed the trip from start to finish. That little experience in the mud," he added nonchalantly, "was nothing to get excited about."

It wasn't until 1915 that Taft's mud-plagued motor route opened to regular traffic. Paradise at last had its road, and that

One-way traffic
above Narada Falls, 1917

same summer the park got a peak-encircling path, a 93-mile-long route that soon became known as the Wonderland Trail. The first "around the mountain" hike had been made only four years earlier, by J. B. Flett and C. A. Barnes Jr.; other similar treks followed, and with enthusiasm for a loop trail running high, the park duly completed the final connecting segments on the east and west sides of the peak. The Mountaineers outdoor club inaugurated the new circuit, bringing along more than a dozen cooks and packers, a commissary and pack train, and over a hundred hungry hikers. Staying at 14 different camps along the way, they managed to both reach Rainier's summit *and* complete the loop in a mere 22 days.

Mount Rainier's improved accessibility was accompanied by an increase in publicity, prompted, in no small part, by a pair of picture takers who tirelessly promoted the park.

When Magic Lanterns Lit the Mountain

The audience waits expectantly, staring at a white sheet suspended between a pair of alders. Behind them, a kerosene lantern is lit, there is some shuffling as a painted photographic plate is slipped into place, and then the improvised screen comes alive with soft-hued colors: the lupines and lilies of Paradise, spreading across a rock-strewn meadow; the gray spires of the Tatoosh Range, poking into a pale blue sky; Mineral Lake, encircled by dark green firs.

The man who shows the slides is both knowledgeable and enthusiastic; he may hold up a copy of his book, *Our Greatest Mountain and Alpine Regions of Wonder*, which onlookers can purchase later for 25¢. Now, however, there are the magnificent "magic lantern" pictures, and their taker and maker, Albert Henry Barnes, is busy attaching a string of words to each image.

Barnes, who in his 44-year life managed to be photographer, painter, mountain climber, author, *and* lecturer, found in the magic lantern a system for showing the wonders of Washington's greatest attraction, enthralling early visitors with a mixture of high-elevation artistry and an aging, albeit amazing, technology of slide projection first used in the 1650s. Soon movies would eclipse such shows, but Barnes would not be there to witness the change; he died in 1920, just as the magic was poised to leave the lantern.

Mount Rainier was also blessed with a second photographer-promoter. Like Barnes, Asahel Curtis lectured beside the magic lantern, enthralling viewers with selections from his 500 slides of wildflowers. The brother of the famous Indian photographer Edward S. Curtis, Asahel carved out his own creative niche by documenting the development of the Pacific Northwest through a series of publicity photos he sold to several railroads; his stately, sepia-colored shots of the peak and its surroundings most noticeably graced the travel brochures of the Chicago, Milwaukee & St. Paul Railway, which had recently run its Tacoma Eastern branch line to Ashford. Like his brother Edward, Asahel was an accomplished climber, and in 1917 he briefly traded in his photographer's smock for an alpenstock, serving that summer as the Rainier National Park Company's first chief guide for the mountain. Later, as one of the leaders of the Mountaineers, he worked for years to protect and enhance the park.

Little remains today of Barnes's work, although some 2,000 of his glass negatives are preserved at the Maryhill Museum that was founded by one of his patrons, financier Sam Hill. Curtis, who died in 1941, left a larger legacy—a collection of over 60,000 negatives that includes both his own shots and those of other photographers. Together, the two men brought the image of Mount Rainier to a generation of mountain lovers, leaving memories that lasted far beyond either of their own lives—or that of their magic lanterns.

By the 1910s, visitors to the park found several tourist facilities waiting to serve them: Longmire's Springs featured the family's crude hotel and the Tacoma Eastern's National Park Inn; Paradise had its Camp of the Clouds; and Indian Henry's Hunting Ground offered the Wigwam Hotel. A fixture at the latter was aging P. B. Van Trump, who regaled visitors with tales of the mountain, cared for weary climbers, and for a time served as a seasonal ranger; he finally quit the park in 1914, just two years before his death.

Van Trump's presence at times seemed a solitary sparkle upon the mountainside, for the high country camps were generally drab affairs, known to provide rough, unappealing accommodations for a captive clientele of climbers and alpine excursionists. Stephen T. Mather, the deputy Secretary of the Interior in charge of the national parks, learned of the situation during his visit to Mount Rainier in the summer of 1915 and immediately set out to find a remedy. Convening a collection of business leaders from Seattle and Tacoma, he miraculously managed to effect a temporary truce in the bitter Rainier/Tacoma name dispute and have the group form the Rainier National Park Company (RNPC), which, as arranged by Mather, was given an exclusive contract as the park's concessionaire. By the following summer the RNPC was busy building the Paradise Inn, while Mather was preparing to take charge of the newly formed National Park Service. With the RNPC and Mather combining efforts, the park soon had better facilities *and* better funding.

Paradise Inn

IV. Cecil B., Silver Skis, and the Three C's

The Paradise Inn opened on July 1, 1917, providing the mountain with a new magnet to lure tourists. Instead of enduring the rustic rigors of a ridgetop tent camp, visitors could now enjoy the stylish accommodations of a modern hotel, relaxing in a lobby framed and furnished with glossy Alaska yellow-cedar. The end of World War I aided the boom in attendance, and Labor Day 1919 drew the largest crowds in the park's 20-year history; anticipating the throng, the park borrowed some 500 army blankets from Fort Lewis to supplement the RNPC's supply.

The visitors that summer came not just from around the Sound, but from across the nation: more than 400 representing the Washington State Bankers' Association, over 200 affiliated with the West Coast Lumbermen's Association and another 78 from the Massachusetts Forestry Association, and even a 125-person contingent from the estimable Brooklyn *Daily Eagle*. If people so chose, however, they did not have to pilgrimage to the peak to behold its many splendors — thanks to the miracle of motion pictures, Rainier's stunning scenery could be viewed by non-travelers at their local theaters.

A Mountain for the Movies

Three o'clock on a fall afternoon. A large party has gathered on the Nisqually Glacier. Three guides and eight rangers are with the group, and one of these, chief guide Heine Fuhrer, peers anxiously at the gathering clouds. He approaches the party's leader, advises him that they should go back, and is promptly ignored. A short time later, Fuhrer repeats his warning: "We must leave here not later than 3:45." Again there is no response.

The minutes speed by. Suddenly an icy blast sweeps across Rainier's flanks, and the group is pelted by the beginnings of a blizzard. Now everyone races for safety as the storm roars down upon them; three of the women are carried the last stretch by the men.

A scene from a thrill-a-minute movie? Almost. Only in this case it is the film makers themselves who become part of the drama, as one of Rainier's mood swings disrupts Cecil B. DeMille's shooting of *The Golden Bed*. The storm rages throughout the night, scattering and shattering some $22,000 worth of film and equipment that the crew left on location when they fled. Decisively walloped by the weather, DeMille admits defeat and departs for Hollywood the following morning.

The daunted director was not the only one to have movie troubles on the mountain. In 1937, an April blizzard snowed in Sonja Henie and Tyrone Power as they tried to finish scenes in the Scandinavian skater's second movie, "Thin Ice." Still, the setback had its rewards for the leading couple; reputed to be "real-life sweethearts," they no doubt found extra time to snuggle at the Paradise Inn.

Other, less-illustrious performers also plied their trade beneath the peak, creating such now-forgotten matinee favorites as *Raw Country* and *Wings of the Storm*, whose titles indicate that the mountain may have been up to more meteorological mischief.

One star had no difficulty adapting to Mount Rainier's weather. Balto, the sled dog made famous by his 1920s run to Nome with a supply of diphtheria antitoxin, came south to the park for the filming of his life-saving exploit. Production manager W. H. Ely announced that he was actually *hoping* for a storm so that he could accurately reproduce Balto's dash through Alaska's wintry wilderness.

As DeMille and his cohorts could assure him, Ely would not have long to wait.

"Tin pants" sledding at Rainier

By the time Balto arrived from the frozen north, the park was under the supervision of Major Owen A. Tomlinson, who had recently gained recognition for his own achievements in the far-off, sunny south. Appointed Civil Governor of the specially organized "wild tribe" provinces in the Philippines, Tomlinson was instructed to persuade the resident headhunters to pursue another, less-disruptive pastime. This the major duly accomplished, convincing the Ifugaoes of northern Luzon to take up basketball—a more socially acceptable activity that still allowed the islanders to handle a round object.

Tomlinson failed to locate many cagers among the crags of Rainier, but his long tenure as superintendent, which lasted until 1941, found the park filled with other sporting enthusiasts. His first summer saw a hillclimbing contest, sponsored by the Tacoma Motorcycle Club, draw 300 riders and their machines to the slopes; the following winter brought the park's first extensive snow recreation as Longmire offered not only a thousand-foot toboggan run, but rides on a four-horse bobsled, Russian-style sleigh, and dogsled. Skiing was also available, having been part of the park's winter activities for more than a decade.

The Silver Skis

Christmas week 1912 found a party of Tacoma Mountaineers, led by A. H. Denman, bound for the National Park Inn at Longmire while "proceeding through the deepening snow on various kinds of misfit snowshoes and footgear." In the party was Olive Rand, who "struggled along on two lanky slabs of wood, with turned-up ends and a pair of simple loops for harness which quite failed to keep the runners straight, or for that matter, to keep them on her feet at all." Rand "explained that the slabs were skis and that she had, in a misguided moment, borrowed them."

So passed the first recorded use of such equipment in the Pacific Northwest. Despite Rand's inauspicious experiment, the lure of steep slopes and heavy snowfall proved compelling, and by 1915 instructor Thor Bisgaard had a sizable ski group schussing down the side of the mountain. The following year saw the start of an annual Fourth-of-July ski tournament; Scandinavians dominated the

Paradise skijumper

jumping contest, with world amateur champ Nels Nelson soaring a record 240 feet from the top of Alta Vista in 1923.

Thrilling as the midsummer ski jump might be, the event was easily eclipsed by the first Silver Skis Race, held on April 22, 1934. The course itself was a challenge—down from Camp Muir to McClure Rock, then past Panorama Point and Alta Vista to finish, 3.16 miles later and 4,662 feet lower, just above the Paradise Inn— but what elevated the race to the realm of the incredible was the decision that all sixty contestants would start together...and thus share the slopes simultaneously.

The prospect of mountainside mayhem proved irresistible; newsreel crews and radio announcers pushed their way up to Paradise, jostling with the largest crowd ever to pass through Longmire in the wintertime. By 1:30 P.M. a throng of spectators was waiting expectantly when, far above, starter Otto Sanford dropped his red flag in front of the line of apprehensive racers.

The result exceeded expectations. Skiers crisscrossed haphazardly in front of each other, slammed into one another, and bounced wildly over rough spots in the snow as they thrashed and crashed their way down the mountainside. Out of the tangle, two contestants emerged unscathed—weekend skier and cross-country runner Don Fraser and pre-race favorite Carlton Weigel—to vie for the lead at McClure Rock. At first Fraser was in front, but a short-wave report from Panorama Point indicated that Weigel had gone ahead. The rest of the skiers, their minds more on survival than success, were strung out far behind.

Fraser regained the lead at the bottom of the Panorama run. Coming down Alta Vista, the pair had to pole through the slushy afternoon snow, and here Fraser's cross country training kept him ahead. At the finish line, it was still Fraser—by a ski length.

Forty-two of the other contestants struggled down the slopes to the finish, with Jack Hillyer lurching across on one ski. Despite the chaos at the start, there was only one noteworthy injury, a broken jaw suffered by Ben Thompson when he collided with another competitor.

Given the chances for disaster, the race participants had been lucky. But there were enough close calls and general confusion that the rules were changed for the 1935 race to eliminate the pandemonious, plural-skier start that so nearly brought the first contest to an early conclusion.

The Silver Skis Race continued for years in its safer, saner, duller form. Other competitions were added, and Tacomans thrilled when one of their own, "flaxen-haired" Gretchen Kunigk, easily won the women's open in February 1938. It was not as exciting as Fraser's finish in the 1934 race, but it did show that female skiers had come a long way since 1912...and Olive Rand's "two lanky slabs of wood."

Skiing, while perhaps hard on the participants, was at least easy on the environment. Not so with some of the other activities offered at Paradise during the 1930s: much of the flower-strewn valley was ripped up in 1931 for a 9-hole golf course, and for a time the motorcycle run continued to cut through the fragile foliage of the hillslopes. Soon both desecrations were mercifully discontinued.

Pressure on the Paradise area eased with the opening of park facilities at Sunrise in 1931. Unfortunately, the new site included 200 housekeeping cabins, all located in the middle of a fragile meadow.

On the links at Paradise

During the 1930s, as a Depression-bound public sought out the mountain for recreation and relaxation, the park also saw an invasion of active young men who came to work instead of play.

The Three C's Rated Straight A's

The country never saw anything quite like it, before or since. It came like a whirlwind out of the desert of the Depression, and, in the near-decade of its existence, brought a garden of beautiful, well-built buildings, bridges, and trails into bloom. It was the Civilian Conservation Corps (CCC for short), and its legacy still endures at Mount Rainier and hundreds of other national forests, recreation areas, and parks.

The CCC was probably the most inspired, most popular program of Franklin Delano Roosevelt's New Deal. Only five weeks after FDR's first inauguration, droves of unemployed young men were lining up for enrollment, and in just three months a quarter million of them were at work in 1,300 camps scattered across the country. It was soon apparent that the government, desperate for solutions to the country's economic collapse, had found a win-win-*win* situation: untrained workers were learning job skills from experts, the young men's needy families were receiving the major part of the paychecks, and the country was getting a lot of high-quality construction work for next to nothing.

Rainier's CCCers at work

Mount Rainier benefited big from the program. By the summer of 1934, over a thousand CCCers were working in the park at six camps and had already compiled an impressive list of accomplishments:

Camp Tahoma Creek—Company 930, from western Washington: developed the Longmire campground; cleared 75 acres of blown-down timber; built two miles of new trail and reconstructed 27 miles more; completed pine beetle control work; built a new saw mill; put in various lawns and did other planting at Longmire.

Camp White River—Company 1229, hailing from New York City: cleaned up 10 miles of road into Yakima Park (Sunrise); stretched 40 miles of telephone wire; performed pine beetle control work; reconditioned 44 miles of trail and built five new miles; improved the campgrounds at White River, Tipsoo Lake, and Yakima Park; and removed lots of logs and debris from Fryingpan Creek and the White River.

Reports from the other four camps were similarly impressive.

Mount Rainier's CCC projects modernized and reconditioned many parts of the park. Today, a number of these aging improvements still remain; a showpiece is the 1933 patrol cabin at Ipsut Creek, which was constructed so expertly that no chinking was required between its logs. Several of the attractive residences at Longmire were also CCC-built, as was the stone-walled trail shelter at Summerland and the A-Frame ski tow structure at Paradise.

The park obviously profited from the CCC's efforts, but the workers also benefited from their tours of duty in the park. Not only did they gain valuable job experience while living at one of the loveliest places on the planet, they also from time to time received more immediate rewards, such as on Thanksgiving 1939, when the Longmire camp served up the following menu:

> Shrimp Cocktail; Olives; Roast Young Tom Turkey
> Giblet Gravy; Oyster Dressing; Snowflake Potatoes
> Cranberry Sauce; Candied Sweet Potatoes; Buttered Peas
> Hot Mince Pie; Assorted Jams; Ice Cream; Coffee; Cider
> Cigarettes; Cigars; Mints; Nuts

Building those cabins, trails, and shelters sure worked up an appetite.

V. Modern Times Come to the Mountain

CCC activity ceased with the country's entry into World War II, as the park operated at half speed until the end of the conflict. During the winter of 1942 Paradise Lodge housed the men of the 87th Mountain Infantry Regiment, who came to Rainier to practice their snow and ice skills; three other units trained on the mountain the following year. The nearby inn hosted its own wartime visit, an impromptu lunchtime arrival by President Harry S. Truman; Chef Harry Pappajohn managed to provide Dungeness crab cocktail and Puget Sound salmon, hastily brought up from Tacoma. The meal apparently met with Truman's approval, for afterwards he shook hands with all the inn's employees and then treated them to a few tunes on the lobby's venerable, cedar-encased piano.

Visitors came to the mountain in record numbers after the war's end, filling the facilities to near bursting. Almost all arrived by motor vehicle, for the Tacoma Eastern had ended passenger service to Ashford in 1931. One intrepid individual, however, found a unique way to enter the park.

The Piper atop the Peak

When Lieutenant John Hodgkin reached Mount Rainier's summit late in the afternoon of April 12, 1951, he was more than eighty years behind Hazard Stevens and P. B. Van Trump. Still, the 42-year-old Army Air Force pilot had reason to believe his "ascent" would enter the record books, for it was the first to have been accomplished in an airplane.

Hodgkin had taken off from an airstrip near Spanaway, assisted by a friend, George Brooks, who towed the 84-horsepower J-3 Piper Cub with his small coupe until the ski-mounted plane had enough speed to lift out of its specially made box skids. Hodgkin intended the flight to be more than a stunt; his plan was to show that his type of lightweight aircraft was suitable for high altitude flying and mountain rescue work. He had considered trying Mount Hood, but weather conditions there were unfavorable, so he chose Rainier instead, which was more than 3,000 feet taller and would certainly provide him with his test.

The Piper passed the first part of its exam with flying colors, easily cruising onto the saddle between Point Success and Columbia Crest. Hodgkin shut off the engine to savor his triumph, and then discovered he had made a mistake; when he tried to restart the plane he found the spark plugs had frozen solid.

Evening was nigh. Hodgkin realized that like Stevens and Van Trump, he would have to spend the night atop the mountain. To stabilize the stalled Piper in the rising wind, he drove pieces of plywood into the snow and then roped the plane to them. A 40-mile-per-hour gale kept him at the controls all night as he "flew" the tethered craft with the wind currents, trying to prevent it from being blown away.

Hodgkin ties down his Piper for the night

Meanwhile, word of Hodgkin's flight (and plight) reached the park, and at 2:30 A.M. a rescue party headed by Assistant Chief Ranger Bill Butler started up the slopes. A note was airdropped to Hodgkin, telling him to sit tight until the rangers arrived.

The pilot never got the message. Morning found him chilled by a night of zero-degree temperatures and tired from his tied-down flight. After hours of futilely trying to start the engine, the abashed aviator pushed his plane towards the upper Tahoma Glacier, hopped in, and took off in a powerless glide. The Piper Cub rose for a moment, touched back on the snow, and then, bolstered by a headwind, stayed aloft. Hodgkin tried diving the plane to start the engine. No luck. Finally, he swooped down onto frozen Mowich Lake and made a dead stick landing.

Later in the day a B-17 rescue plane located Hodgkin at the lake and dropped him supplies and gasoline. The next morning the lieutenant was busy taking the engine apart when District Ranger Aubrey Haines hailed him. Hodgkin looked up and inquired, "Have you got a wrench?"

Haines didn't, but he took Hodgkin to a nearby patrol cabin, where they rerigged a pair of wire splicers to remove the plane's spark plugs. After cleaning the plugs, Hodgkin made a practice run on the lake. Then, with Haines's OK, he took off and belatedly returned to Spanaway.

Butler and the other rescue-party rangers struggled up the mountain for twelve hours Friday, reaching the summit about a half hour after Hodgkin left. Instead of the pilot and his Piper, all they found were several containers of emergency equipment, dropped by the rescue plane.

Although the public and even Butler and his crew expressed admiration for Hodgkin's courage, various officials were not impressed. His army superiors confined him to his quarters at the McChord air base, while the park had him brought before U.S. Commissioner Earl Clifford.

The hearing might have gone better for the pilot had not his attorney, Earl Mann, contended that Hodgkin did not land on the mountain itself, as charged, but only on its covering of snow, "a moving and transitory part of the Park landscape, which would end up melting and flowing beyond the Park boundary."

"You'll have to do better than that," replied an unsmiling Clifford, who admonished Hodgkin to "straighten out your thinking," and then slapped the pilot with an *in*transitory $350 fine and a suspended six-month jail sentence.

The fine was nearly half the $795 Hodgkin asked for his plane when he'd recently tried to sell it. Now, however, he was thinking about taking the Piper Cub off the market. After all, it was somewhat of a celebrity, keeping company with a select group of climbers—and no other aircraft—that had made it to Rainier's summit.

Hodgkin's airborne antics notwithstanding, Mount Rainier in the 1950s was settling into a sort of middle-aged maturity. The park now contained a host of substantial (but aging) buildings, while such ill-conceived irritations as the golf course and three tracts of housekeeping cabins were merely a memory; moreover, with the completion of the Stevens Canyon Road in 1957, Paradise and Sunrise were finally linked. Adding to the park's growing stability was a seasoned staff that included one especially steady ranger.

Bill Butler:
the Rescuer of Rainier

The headline caught his interest, so the young man, just off the train from Tennessee, bought the Seattle paper. It was a big investment—he was bound for Alaska and had only twenty dollars left—but what he read changed his life and, thanks to the decision he was about to make, would save the lives of many others.

Bill Butler, erstwhile sports star and student leader at Chattanooga's McCallie School, scanned a story about the "Greathouse Accident."

A climbing party descending from Mount Rainier's summit had plunged into a crevasse above Gibraltar Rock. Ranger Charlie Browne took to the slopes in a summer snowstorm to search for the victims, followed by a rescue team that rode on horseback to Camp Muir. Four of the climbers survived the fall; Browne soon found one of the others, Edwin Wetzel, dying. Five days later the ranger recovered the body of the sixth member of the party, apprentice guide Forrest Greathouse, from deep within the crevasse.

Perhaps it was a connection Butler made with Greathouse, who had been a football coach in Seattle, or it may simply have been the seeming nearness of the mountain, towering above the forests to the south, but for some reason the young Tennessean decided to forego his Alaska adventure and head for the gleaming white peak.

Butler set off on foot, thinking he'd arrive at Mount Rainier in but a few hours; instead it took him two days, going at a good clip, just to reach its lower slopes. There he found refuge for the night in an abandoned cabin, an old door he had pulled from its hinges his only blanket. Once in the park, Bill took work as a laborer at Longmire. He fought fires when necessary and spent the winter shoveling snow off the community's roofs to keep them from collapsing. Two years later, in 1931, he became a temporary ranger.

Ill-fated climbers—Forrest Greathouse, far left; Edwin Wetzel, second from left

Early that summer Butler had his first taste of action. A climber died in a fall near Gibraltar Rock, and Charlie Browne led a party to look for the body. When Browne turned back because of altitude sickness, Butler was placed in charge. The searchers found the victim deep in a crevasse. Lowered on ropes, Butler and longtime guide Swede Willard had to chop the frozen body out of the ice so it could be pulled to the surface. The schoolboy from Tennessee had come of age on the mountain.

Butler's first great love was Rainier, but after six years on its slopes he found another—Martha Botten, a college student and summertime waitress who shared Bill's enthusiasm for skiing and alpine scenery. Only when it came to dancing did their interests diverge; Martha would polka with a passion, while her newfound boyfriend preferred to boycott the ballroom. Once, while she fox trotted through the evening at the Paradise Inn, Bill did some solitary outdoor footwork, tramping all the way to Little Tahoma Peak while making the first-ever moonlit ascent of the 9,360-foot rock.

Bill and Martha were married that fall. To furnish their cabin at Paradise, Butler bought his new bride a sofa, which the dutiful husband then carried two miles up the snow-covered mountainside.

Hardly had their honeymoon finished when Bill was called out on the most dangerous assignment of all, a wintertime rescue. Delmar Fadden, a teenager from Seattle, was reported by his brother as missing on the mountain after apparently attempting a January ascent of the summit. A search plane found his body, frozen to a ridgeside, seventeen days later; Butler was among a select group of mountaineers sent in to bring Fadden's remains back. Descending with the corpse, another climber slipped on a forty-five-degree slope, entangling Butler and the body and sliding them all toward a gaping crevasse. Bill desperately clawed for a hold with his crampons, which finally caught and brought the men to a stop—six feet from a drop to near-certain death.

Two months later, Bill and Martha, skiing down from Paradise, found the trail obliterated by an avalanche. Three sets of ski tracks vanished into the snow; Butler located a nearby emergency phone, summoned help, and then probed for the victims. Bill and the rescue party managed to bring two of the three buried skiers out alive.

It was, for a park ranger, all part of a winter's work, but Butler's mountainslope heroics attracted the attention of some high-placed administrators. Later that year, a direct order from Franklin Delano Roosevelt made Bill's ranger position permanent, giving him civil service status without examination—the only time the requirement had been waived.

Additional recognition followed: in 1939, an official commendation from the Forest Service, whom he assisted in an avalanche search on Mount Baker, and then a Distinguished Service Certificate from the Navy *and* the National Parks' Distinguished Service Medal in 1947 for locating the wreckage of a Marine Corps troop plane on the Tahoma Glacier. Grateful parents of the crash victims sent Butler a reward check; Bill returned the letter, unopened. He did, however, accept the award of a one-step promotion—which increased his salary by $2.41 a week.

It probably seemed like big money to a man who had landed on Rainier with only twenty dollars in his pocket. Besides, he was still busy saving lives and climbing on the mountain, and that, for Bill Butler, was reward enough.

Butler retired in 1963, after more than 30 years at Rainier. He left just as a bureaucratic juggernaut jolted the park, threatening some of the mountain's most popular landmarks. Called "Mission 66," it was a ten-year, billion-dollar program meant to significantly upgrade the national park system by 1966; as a decidedly mixed blessing, Mount Rainier was designated the project's "pilot park."

First came a study that suggested "removing all overnight facilities from Paradise Valley and placing them outside the park." Part of this was accomplished by razing the lodge, but an outraged outcry managed to save the picturesque, albeit dilapidated, inn. Rising from the ashes of the lodge was an otherworldly visitor center that delighted sci-fi buffs but befuddled more tradition-bound observers. The inn, for its part, received a belated facelift in 1980-81, allowing its more conventional styling to provide a continuing counterpoint to Mission 66's nearby modernesque monument.

In 1962 the mountain served as a training area for an ambitious project: the first American ascent of Mount Everest. Except for

Visitor center, Paradise

high-elevation lack of oxygen, Rainier approximated Himalayan conditions, even providing a howling nighttime storm that swept one sleeping team member and his tent to the lip of a yawning crevasse before he was rescued. When the expedition successfully scaled Everest the following year, it was Rainier guide Jim Whittaker who placed the flag on the summit.

Paradise experienced a 1,122-inch snowfall during the 1971-72 season, a world record; it was one of three winters during the 1970s when the snows exceeded a thousand inches. The decade closed with a September 1979 storm trapping KYYX-FM disc jockey Terry MacDonald and two guides atop the mountain. Eight feet of snow fell on the trio, who had made the climb as a charity promotion. The blizzard-bound MacDonald raised some $26,000, more than enough to offset the $5,000-plus cost of the rescue effort, which saw a Fort Lewis helicopter finally pluck the men from the peak.

In June 1981 a huge icefall on the Ingraham Glacier killed 11 members of a large climbing party; Jim Whittaker and his brother Lou led an unsuccessful search for the bodies, which were buried by some 70 feet of ice. The tragedy, ranked as the worst in U.S. mountaineering history, is memorialized by a haunting photograph in the Paradise visitor center, taken by Jonathan Laitone shortly before the avalanche swept him to his death: light from the rising sun colors a vast panorama of clouds, ice, and snow to create a magical, early morning moment on the mountainside. "People ask why people climb mountains," Lou Whittaker said at a special service for the victims. "Look at that photo. There's your answer."

During the early 1990s some two million tourists visited the park each year. A century earlier, in 1893, a grand total of 174 hardy travelers completed the grueling wagon trip to the mountain's only accommodation, the Longmires' rough-hewn hotel. The intervening decades have brought differences in more than just numbers: Modern-day motorists, if so inclined, can leave Seattle or Tacoma in the morning, visit both Sunrise *and* Paradise, stop to lunch at any of several pleasantly situated picnic areas, and be back home that same night. Climbers can don an array of high-tech equipment, avail themselves of an expert guide service, and (if all goes well) share the summit with dozens of other successful peak scalers. Campers can amble from their Winnebagos or rainproof tents to nightly naturalist programs that feature taped music and big-screen slide shows. In these and many other ways, Mount Rainier has changed greatly since the days of Stevens and Van Trump, of Fay Fuller and John Muir, of the Longmires and Indian Henry, but for those who behold the annual blooming of her flower-filled parks or the seemingly eternal whiteness of her gleaming glaciers, she is merely — and magnificently — what she has always been — the Mountain.

On the Skyline Trail, Paradise

Molten Rock and Massed Ice: The Mountain and Its Glaciers

Nowadays, geologists tell us that Mount Rainier originated from a series of volcanic eruptions. In earlier times there was a more intriguing explanation: She resulted from a marital dispute.

Tacobet's Troubles

Long ago there was a man-mountain, either the one we now call Mount Baker or a peak in the Olympics, who had woman-mountain troubles. The man-mountain was married to at least two women-mountains—and they did not get along. One of them, usually called Tacobet or something similar, was both big and quarrelsome. She proceeded to grow larger and larger while becoming no friendlier. Finally Tacobet ran out of room; she then left the scene of domestic strife and settled down in the open area southeast of the Sound. Removed from the cramped confines of her former mountain-family, she finally had space enough to expand and relax, filling a great flat place that had heretofore lain vacant. Thus ensconced, Tacobet became the biggest mountain in the entire Northwest, subject now to only occasional fits of temper, at which time she would shoot off some fire from her top—just to remind the other mountains she was still someone to be reckoned with.

So went the account according to early-day Indians from Puget Sound. Modern mountain experts, more focused on rock formations than family relationships, tell a different story, one that traces the origin of Tacobet/Mount Rainier back some 50 million years.

45

The region that is now western Washington was at that time nearly flat, its surface cut by streams and seacoast and covered with swamps. As the watercourses flowed towards the ocean they dropped part of their cargo en route—ton upon ton of sand and clay that settled into the swamplands and mixed with peat from the local plantlife. Layer after layer of these deposits bedded upon each other, like residents of a cramped condominium, until they formed a mass some 10,000 feet thick. Time and pressure converted the material into sandstone, shale, and coal, leaving a collection of rocks called the Puget Group.

Geologic grandeur:
Eagle Peak, left, and the
Nisqually River Valley

Two or three eyeblinks of eternity and it is now only about 38 million years before the present (B.P.). The coastal plane, which had previously sunk beneath the Pacific, is fighting its way upward. A series of volcanoes erupt under the ocean; their accumulations of lava gradually emerge from the water as islands. At about the same time, explosions of steam below the surface shatter molten rock, which flows as a fragment-filled mud across much of the ocean floor, and the Ohanapecosh Formation is formed.

The clock ticks onward. More eruptions occur about 25 to 30 million B.P., covering parts of the area with hot pumice that hardens into the welded tuff known as the Stevens Ridge Formation. Next come eruptions of the Fifes Peak Formation — basalt and light gray andesite — followed by a bit of uplifting, compression, and folding. Then, around 12 million B.P., extrusions of molten rock push up through older formations and solidify as the Tatoosh Pluton, a light-colored, gray- and black-flecked granodiorite.

After that the Cascade Range begins its gradual rise toward full, 6,000-foot mountainhood, all the while being channeled and eroded into a rugged convolution of ridges and peaks, valleys and canyons. Finally, about a million years ago, the mountain that will become Rainier slowly emerges, rising as a series of large andesite lava flows from a crack in the earth's crust. Like Tacobet's temper, the peak eventually begins cooling off, and its top, as befits one of increasing age, grows white with the glaciers that form around the now-frozen summit.

The eon inches forward, and the mountain lapses into a mild, middle-age deterioration of explosion, collapse, and erosion, losing perhaps 1,500 feet from its top. Mudflows (sometimes called lahars) and avalanches scar its slopes, reaching a sort of climax some 6,000 years ago: a huge rockfall sweeps down from near the summit and spreads across the Paradise area, leaving a colorful mixture of orange-yellow clay and rock that still decorates the meadows; about the same time, another avalanche rips away the northeastern part of the mountain's cone between Steamboat Prow and Little Tahoma Peak. This slide triggers a large lahar into the White River Valley, but it is soon surpassed by the enormous Osceola Mudflow, which streams down the same drainage, covering the future sites of Buckley and Enumclaw with a 70-foot coating of geologic guck.

Kautz Creek

Then, around 600 B.P., the Electron Mudflow pushes through the Puyallup River Valley, burying a Douglas-fir forest that grew where Orting stands today.

Status as a national park has not stemmed the mountain's penchant for slipping, sliding, and flowing. A 1947 lahar filled Kautz Creek, taking out the road to Longmire and leaving a forest of dead trees that still stands starkly near the streambed. One canyon to the west, debris runoffs in Tahoma Creek have rampaged intermittently since 1967, finally forcing closure of much of the park's Westside Road. The destructive culprits here have been "jökulhlaups," sudden floods of rock, water, and mud that break forth from the glaciers up canyon. Rockfalls also occur frequently; notable was the 1963 diminishment of Little Tahoma Peak, which whiled away a December afternoon by dropping pieces of itself onto the Emmons Glacier.

Although these activities were unsettling for those who happened to be near the mountain at the time, for most residents on the Sound such events were little more than Sunday paper feature filler. The Tacobet of tempestuous youth was gone; what Washingtonians now had was Mount Rainier, a stately matron of snow-clad stability. Then, in 1994, came an unsettling government-sponsored report from the National Research Council, informing us that the mountain has not mellowed as much as we thought. In prose as chilling as a night on the summit, the council announced that:

> Mount Rainier poses a significant hazard to life and property in heavily populated areas surrounding the volcano, particularly in the Seattle-Tacoma metropolitan area. The most likely hazards include edifice failures, glacier outburst floods, and lahars, with or without volcanic eruptions.

If that were not enough, the council found another reason to worry — the existence of an active fault, only recently recognized, that crosses through the Seattle area and is capable of generating an earthquake at least as severe as the 1989 "event" that devastated San Francisco. Such a quake, according to the report, "could trigger a catastrophic collapse of a portion of Mount Rainier's volcanic edifice." The council concluded its study by recommending a "Mount Rainier Hazards Information Network," an "emergency response plan," and "risk mitigation measures."

Scientists who studied the peak a century ago, blissfully unencumbered by such concerns, were less interested in assessing Mount Rainier's stability than its size.

Measuring the Mountain

When the Mazamas climbing club set out from Camp Muir on the morning of July 27, 1897, most of the party wanted only the challenge of scaling the peak. One exception was a handsome young man with a neatly trimmed moustache who carried a long leather tube strapped to his back. For Edgar McClure, Professor of Analytical Chemistry at the University of Oregon, the ascent was a business trip, and when he arrived at the summit later that day, he unloaded his cargo and went to work.

Inside the tube was a second container, a hand-made wooden case McClure himself had built, and within that was the object of his interest, a standard mercurial barometer, constructed by James Green of Brooklyn, New York, and numbered "1612." This particular barometer had a history of highly specialized use; for the last 30 years it had measured mountaintop atmospheric pressures to help determine the elevations of several Cascade Peaks. Number 1612's impressive resume included measurements made atop Mount Hood in 1867 and 1870, Diamond Peak in 1891, Middle Sister in 1894, and Mount Adams in 1895. For the Rainier calculation, McClure had refilled the barometer's tube, distilling the mercury himself, and then carefully checked the vacuum to make sure the seal was perfect.

McClure exposed the barometer to the peak's frigid air, waited until the instrument chilled to the ambient temperature, and then, at precisely 4:30 P.M., took his reading: 17.708 inches. At the same moment, barometric measurements were being recorded at several locations of established elevation in Washington and Oregon; when adjusted for latitude and temperature and then compared with one another, the readings would allow McClure to extrapolate Mount Rainier's altitude.

Fifty-five years earlier, Navy Lieutenant Charles Wilkes determined the mountain's height to be 12,330 feet. He did so (very imprecisely, it turned out) by triangulation, which, unlike barometric measurement, relies on trigonometric calculations based on a nearby point of known elevation. Subsequent triangulation work revised Wilkes's figure, and in 1884 the U.S. Geological Survey listed the elevation as 14,444 feet. The USGS triangulated new measurements in both 1895 and 1896, which yielded altitudes of 14,532 feet and 14,519 feet, respectively, while Major E. S. Ingraham, using the barometric method, came up with 14,524 feet. McClure's results were eagerly awaited, for if they were close to the other recent figures they would confirm Rainier's status as the highest peak in the United States.

McClure completed his readings, and ten minutes later most of the Mazamas began their descent. Eight of the group, including the indomitable Fay Fuller, had elected to spend the night in the crater;

McClure Rock

EIFERT

the rest reached Camp Muir by 9:30 that night. Here the climbing leader, photographer Edward S. Curtis, made a fateful decision. Days earlier, Curtis had surveyed the group and commented, "It will be a grand trip, but there are too many inexperienced people in the party. I fear that before we return some accident will happen which will bathe the trip in gloom." Now, however, in the glow of the successful summit ascent, he ignored his forebodings and relaxed his control over the group: anyone who wished was allowed to proceed down the moonlit slopes to Paradise.

Among those electing to continue was McClure. Earlier in the day, he had remarked that if he brought his barometer back intact, it would be the first one to return from the mountaintop unbroken. Now he was carefully cradling the case as he and Ella McBride scouted a route for a small advance party.

The pair came to a rocky point called The Sphinx. McClure told McBride he would work his way down a short cliff. "Don't come down here"; he called up a moment later, "it is too steep." McBride turned away. Almost immediately she heard the sound of a fall; she looked back, but McClure had vanished down the mountainside.

Word of the accident was carried to Paradise, where a party set out by lantern light to search for McClure. They found the 35-year-old professor's battered body near the base of a 200-foot slope; he had crashed head first into a mass of rocks and was then propelled into a pile of boulders. Nearby were the broken remains of barometer #1612.

Carrier pigeons were sent to Tacoma with word of the tragedy. The stunned Mazamas held a service for McClure and then placed his body on a pack horse for its journey down the mountain. The next night, two more of the group's climbers almost lost their lives near the spot of McClure's fall. The Mazamas soon cut short their outing and departed; The Sphinx, the rocky outcropping high above their vacant camp, would now be called McClure Rock.

McClure's work was unfinished, but one of his colleagues, mathematics professor E. H. McAlister, completed the calculations and announced the result: 14,528 feet—extremely close to the last three measurements.

Based on this figure, Rainier retained its ranking as the country's highest peak. Then a revision dropped the mountain's elevation to 14,363 feet, more than a hundred feet lower than Mount Whitney. A new topographic study of Rainier, begun in 1910, promised to yield more precise figures. F. E. Matthes supervised the U.S. Geological Survey's work for its first two years, making measurements from McClure Rock and three points in the Tatoosh—Eagle Peak, Stevens Peak, and Pinnacle Peak. His work was completed in 1913 by Claude H. Birdseye, who led two trips to Mount Rainier's summit; on the first, the survey party was caught in a summer blizzard and survived only by taking refuge in the ever-protective crater. Birdseye and his crew, their fingers and ears "badly frozen," descended temporarily to a lower camp but were back at the peaktop three days later to finish their calculations.

In January 1914 the USGS announced the results of the Matthes-Birdseye measurement—Mount Rainier's roller-coasting elevation had risen to 14,408 feet. Although an improvement, it was not enough to dethrone Mount Whitney, which was listed at 14,501 feet. Rainier-boosters reacted petulantly; Mazamas president H. H. Prouty sniffed that "A few feet signify nothing. No California mountain masked behind the Sierra can vie in majesty with this lonely pile that rises in stately grandeur from the shores of

Triangulating from Pinnacle Peak

Puget Sound." He may have been right, but it was Whitney's, not Rainier's, name that was in the record books.

So the situation stood until 1952, when a German scientist took some new measurements on Mount Rainier and concluded that the peak might be 50 or 60 feet higher than its official listing. That was enough to bring back the Geological Survey, which performed a recalculation in 1956. This time, rather than repeating Birdseye's struggling ascent, the surveyors were airlifted to the summit in a recently-designed Bell 47-G helicopter. It was soon apparent that a new altitude record had been set—but not by the mountain. It was the 47-G, which had climbed higher than any other similar aircraft.

Based on the new measurements, Rainier's elevation was, however, increased two feet, to 14,410. If it kept growing at that rate, the mountain would have passed Whitney in another 1,950-odd years, but the question became moot in 1959, when Alaska's admission to the Union brought with it 20,320-foot Mount McKinley.

The altitude derby was irredeemably lost, and even the most inveterate mountain measurers then had to rely on Prouty's "stately grandeur" when indicating Rainier's importance. In the end, the various figures given for the peak's height were, of course, nothing more than mere statistics, and if any number is to provide lasting significance, it should no doubt be the one James Green gave to a particular mercurial barometer—"1612"—which, along with Edgar McClure, met its end on the mountain.

The mountain that was born of fire eventually became a peak encased in ice. More than a score of glaciers now surround Rainier's summit, their milky white mantle clothing the mountainslopes throughout the year. From a single viewing they appear immobile, impassive, fused to the rock beneath them in a bond of unyielding permanence. Seen over time, however, they display their true selves — rivers of ice — moving, slowly to be sure, but always moving, carrying immense quantities of crushed rock and frozen water over the slopes, sometimes advancing toward the valley floors, sometimes retreating toward the mountaintop, forever following an ancient rhythm that pulses through the ice and stone.

The glaciers came as soon as the lava-hot dome cooled enough to permit it, for Tacobet had risen from the earth in the middle of the Ice Age. From time to time the mountain's eruptions rent the frozen fabric that then blanketed much of the continent, but eventually the persistent, icy covering spread itself across even the top of the peak. When the last intense glacial period ended about 10,000 years ago, some of the ice rivers stretched 40 miles into the valleys. Since then, the size of the glaciers has fluctuated; the Nisqually, for example, almost touched the first road bridge that spanned its canyon, but nearly a hundred years later the shrunken ice mass sits upslope more than half a mile above the early-day crossing site. Around the mountain to the northwest, the Carbon Glacier conversely staged a mini-advance in the 1970s, when rocks discharged from its downward movement crushed the vegetation below its base.

Throughout the park is evidence of the glaciers' work. The course of the upper Paradise River, scooped and scoured by ice, hangs above Sluiskin Falls in the trademark fashion of glaciated valleys, just as the river's next section perches above Narada Falls. To the southeast, Snow Lake is cradled in an ice-crafted bowl, called a cirque, beneath the resistant rock of Unicorn Peak. Such glacially built mountain lakes — tarns — dot the park; the Chinook Pass park entrance offers arriving motorists a stunning downward look at one of the loveliest, tiny Tipsoo Lake. From Sunrise, observers can peer into the vast emptiness of the Emmons Glacier's enormous basin, where a river of rock lies below the always grinding ice. Whether comprehended or not, the effects of the glaciers are

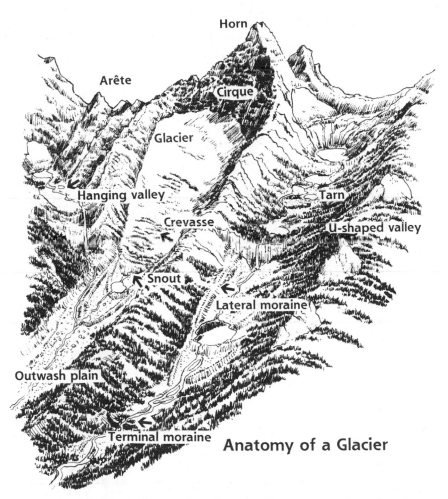

Anatomy of a Glacier

everywhere present, hastening the heartbeat even when they leave no imprint on the mind.

Rock wedded to ice, Tacobet/Rainier continues her course through the centuries, calmer now than she once was, but still capable of calamity and chaos. Beneath her cool white dome she only *seems* to be asleep.

Plants Below the Peak

For generations, Rainier's great white dome has beckoned like a beacon, calling travelers, adventurers, and simple admirers to approach and behold at close range the magnificence so strongly promised from afar. Once at the mountain, some feel compelled to climb it, others merely to observe its icy grandeur, and others to explore the places far below the summit slopes. Those who visit the latter locations soon find themselves within a world of immediate enchantment—a wonderland of meadows and forests, filled to overflowing with dozens of different flowers, trees, ferns, and shrubs. The dazzling enormity of the peak is then hidden or but a background—foremost are the colors, shapes, and scents of the plantlife that covers so much of the lower mountainsides. Here the eye widens not with the sublime, but with the beautiful, and each new turn in the trail, each new bend in the road, fulfills yet another anticipation.

So be prepared when visiting Rainier; all that glitters is not ice and snow! The drop of dew upon the hemlock bough, the azure glimmer of a sun-struck gentian—these and a thousand other similar sights are there for the seeking, each speaking its own soft message: *There is more to see than the majestic summit of the mountain – if you will but look among the gentler places…where the plants in all their guises have come to make their homes.*

The park's varied vegetation resides in four distinct habitats, each of which is arrayed at numerous locations around the mountain. These plant communities and some of their more interesting residents include:

Low-Elevation Forest

The riverbottoms and nearby benchlands in the Carbon, Nisqually, and Ohanapecosh drainages contain collections of dark-colored conifers that rise above various ferns, devil's club and other

56

leafy shrubs, and a host of pale-blossomed flowers. The trees grow tall and thick-trunked, their foliage often forming nearly unbroken canopies. Thus shaded, and soaked with moisture, the ground-bound rocks and logs are frequently blanketed with heavy coverings of bright, yellow-green moss.

Hikes that feature striking sections of lowland forest include: Carbon Glacier (p. 268), Ranger Falls - Green Lake (p. 266), Trail of the Shadows (p. 223), Silver Falls (p. 248), Grove of the Patriarchs (p. 251), and Deer and Chinook Creeks (p. 253).

Douglas-fir *(Pseudotsuga menziesii)*

An imposing tree, the Douglas-fir is difficult to miss with its massive trunk and deeply furrowed, dark brown and orange-red bark. Although to the south it assumes subordinate status to the towering coast redwood, in the Cascades the Douglas-fir reigns supreme, sometimes reaching 300 feet in height. One account from 1895, confirmed by the local sheriff but otherwise widely discounted, reported a downed specimen that measured 417 feet in length. More substantial testimony about the Douglas-fir's great size comes from the records of lumber mills at the base of Rainier: ships' masts 130 feet long; roof beams measuring 150 feet, needing three railcars to carry them; a single 225-foot-long log, nearly 50 feet in circumference.

In both quantity and range, Douglas-fir dominates Pacific Northwest forests. It is, moreover, the primary commercial timber tree on the continent, although in earlier times it was often ignored by loggers as a substandard wood; to sell its lumber to a reluctant public, it was sometimes marketed as "Oregon pine." Indians had long recognized Douglas-fir's value, using it for such implements as harpoon shafts and salmon weirs and its pitch for healing (wounds) and sealing (canoes, etc.). Not a true fir, its scientific name means "false hemlock."

Western Hemlock *(Tsuga heterophylla)*

Its effect is subtle, but sooner or later the western hemlock gains attention with its dense foliage—masses of tightly packed needles, arranged on gracefully spreading limbs like billows of bright green fog. The tree's top topples over in a characteristic droop, although

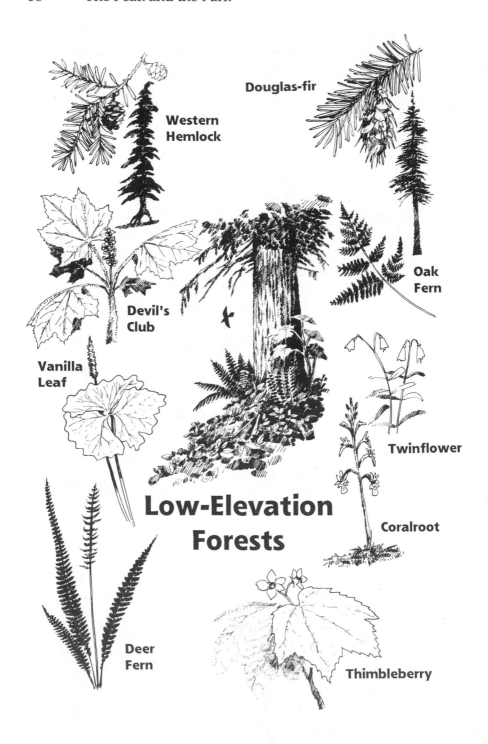

Western Hemlock

Douglas-fir

Devil's Club

Oak Fern

Vanilla Leaf

Twinflower

Low-Elevation Forests

Coralroot

Deer Fern

Thimbleberry

it is seldom visible, since the western hemlock frequently finds itself obscured by its taller companion conifers, the Douglas-fir,
western redcedar, and Sitka spruce. Given enough time, however,
the hemlock will outlast these dominating big brothers, for its thick
canopy shades out the competitors' seedlings while its own shade-
tolerant seeds are left to sprout and prosper.

Foresters shunned the hemlock for years before deciding it
made acceptable lumber, but the native peoples long used the tree
for many purposes: its tannin-rich bark served for hide tanning and
to create several dyes, including one of reddish tint for mountain
goat wool and basket materials; its durable wood was carved into
spoons, bowls, spearshafts, and other implements; its pitch and
bark became medicines to treat injuries, colds, and bleeding. Skirts
and headwear were crafted from hemlock boughs, presaging the
tree's later use as a fiber source for rayon. Humble though it may
be, the western hemlock has compiled an impressive list of uses.

Thimbleberry (*Rubus parviflorus*)

Many a section of woodland understory is filled by the large,
light green leaves of the thimbleberry; adding to the foliage's effect
is a speckling of bright white flowers that sparkle among the shadows like small stars. All Northwest Indian tribes ate the fruit, but
its seediness made it less appealing than certain other berries. Pioneer women rubbed the fine-haired leaves against their cheeks; the
slight irritation that resulted produced a becoming blush that took
the place of rouge.

Devil's Club (*Oplopanax horridum*)

A shade-loving shrub with an attitude, devil's club brandishes
its thick, stickery stems beneath a camouflaging cover of enormous, deeply lobed leaves. Cone-shaped clusters of bright red berries warn passers-by to keep their distance — lest they encounter the
half-hidden profusion of prickles that await the unwary.

Devil's club, like its cousin ginseng, served Northwest native
peoples as a medicinal agent, for its roots and inner bark treated
arthritis, ulcers, diabetes, and digestive problems. Ash from its
bark, mixed with bear grease, became dark face paint and tattooing
ink, and even the spiky stems had value, serving as fishing snags

and lures. For unsuspecting white settlers, however, devil's club offered more pain than promise, as an 1865 account indicated: "Both stems and leaves are covered with sharp spines, which pierced our clothes as we forced our way through the tangled growth, and made the legs and hands of the pioneers scarlet from the myriads of punctures."

Oak Fern (*Gymnocarpium dryopteris*) and Deer Fern (*Blechnum spicant*)

Often a lowland forest floor glows with masses of the small oak fern, its lime green, triangular fronds forming a colorful carpet beneath a dusky cover of conifers. Despite its name, it does not grow near oaks, instead preferring cooler, moister habitats. Deer fern sends up two distinct types of fronds: spreading sterile ones, with some 35 to 70 paired leaflets each, that somewhat resemble those of the sword fern, and upright fertile ones that rise from the center of the plant. Deer reportedly rub their antler stubs on the fronds, an activity which inspired some native peoples to use the leaves for treating skin sores. The fronds serve as a winter food for deer, elk, and cattle.

Vanilla Leaf (*Achlys triphylla*)

Vanilla leaf brightens the forest darkness from summer through fall, as its large, three-part leaves turn from soft green to pale honey-yellow. Adding to the luminous effect is a slender spike of white flowerlets that rises from the center of each leaf. When dried, the leaves smell sweetly of vanilla; they were used by North Coast Indians as an insect repellent and by white settlers to perfume their linen closets.

Twinflower (*Linnaea borealis*)

As the name implies, the flowers on this low-growing shrub come in pairs, the soft pink, bell-shaped blooms nodding opposite one another from a Y-shaped stem. The delicate plant was a favorite of the 18th-century naturalist and taxonomist Carl Linnaeus, who successfully prevailed upon a benefactor to name the species for him. The systematic Swede subsequently held a sprig of the flower when posing for portraits, and *Linnaea borealis* became a part of his coat of arms after he was knighted. Perhaps inspired by the twinflower's delightful duality, Linnaeus convinced other biological classifiers to adopt "taxonomic twosomes" — double-word scientific names for individual species of animals and plants. Within the park, twinflower accommodatingly lines many a lowland pathway, its modest situation belying its honorable pedigree.

Coralroot (*Corallorhiza* spp.)

Rising on pale pink spikes from the forest floor, coralroot seems a shadowy presence — lacking green leaves, it blends into the darkness of fallen conifer needles and damp earth. Since it is unable to produce its own food, this parasitic plant must prey on certain forest fungi that decay groundlevel organic matter. Three species of coralroot are found in the park: spotted (*C. maculata* ssp. *maculata*), western (*C. maculata* ssp. *mertensiana*), and striped (*C. striata*).

Mid-Elevation Forest

On the mountainslopes above the lower river canyons a wide band of woodland displays itself, offering a different set of sylvan plants from those found at the warmer elevations below. New varieties of conifers now provide the canopy; huckleberries and several other bushes fill in much of the understory. Lake margins and the edges of avalanche falls are often fringed with bright-blossomed flowers and shrubs, while shade-loving species bloom in the darkened forest depths.

Several hikes encounter outstanding examples of mid-elevation forest: Eunice Lake - Tolmie Peak (p. 269), Eagle Peak (p. 225), Carter and Madcap Falls (p. 228), Comet Falls - Van Trump Park (p. 229), Narada Falls (p. 232), Pinnacle Peak (p. 243), Box Canyon (p. 246), Owyhigh Lakes (p. 257), and Summerland (p. 259).

Pacific Silver Fir (*Abies amabilis*)

Seeing the silver-gray, blistered bark of this tree signals arrival in a mid-elevation forest, for in the Mount Rainier area the Pacific silver fir grows as the dominant species at altitudes of about 3,000 to 5,000 feet. To confirm the conifer's identity, look for a double layer of needles on its twigs, one flat and spreading to the sides, the other inclining forward and upward from the twig top. The Pacific silver fir's upright, stout cones mark it as a true fir (other conifers suspend their cones); like other firs, its cones disintegrate while still on the tree, leaving only a core to mark their passing. Native peoples used the Pacific silver's boughs for floor coverings and bedding. Similarly, early white explorers esteemed its foliage above all others as a sleeping mat.

Alaska Yellow-cedar (*Chamaecyparis nootkatensis*)

Fires have made this limp-limbed tree the celebrity conifer within the park. Its silvery snags stand sentinel on The Burn in Stevens Canyon, while much of the Paradise Inn and its furniture were built of yellow-cedar timbers salvaged from a fire site east of Ricksecker Point. Whites crafted the straight-grained wood into benches, tables, and roofbeams; native peoples put yellow-cedar to smaller-scale use, fashioning bows, paddles, masks, and other implements from it. Indians also used various parts of the tree medicinally — as treatment for insanity, kidney ailments, and rheumatism. Certain northern tribes, aware of its durability and perhaps sensing a spiritual quality within the wood, crafted their totem poles out of yellow-cedar. The Japanese now import it for use in their temples.

Vine Maple (*Acer circinatum*) and Douglas Maple (*Acer glabrum*)

East meets west at Mount Rainier with this pair of large, spreading shrubs, which fringe streamsides and forest margins at low to middle elevations. In some park locations the vine maple, common to westside Cascade slopes, will grow within a few yards of the Douglas maple that is normally an eastside resident. Confusion can be avoided by examining their leaves (seven to nine lobes for the vine, three to five lobes for the Douglas) and their samaras, the beautiful winged fruits that form a straight line on the vine maple and bend into a "V" on the Douglas. In fall, the leaves of each species will delight observers with their flame-colored tintings of yellow, orange, and red. Indians, thinking ahead to winter, converted the wood from both bushes into snowshoe frames.

Bunchberry (*Cornus canadensis*)

A miniature member of the dogwood family, the moisture loving bunchberry grows as a ground hugger or tree climber, usually

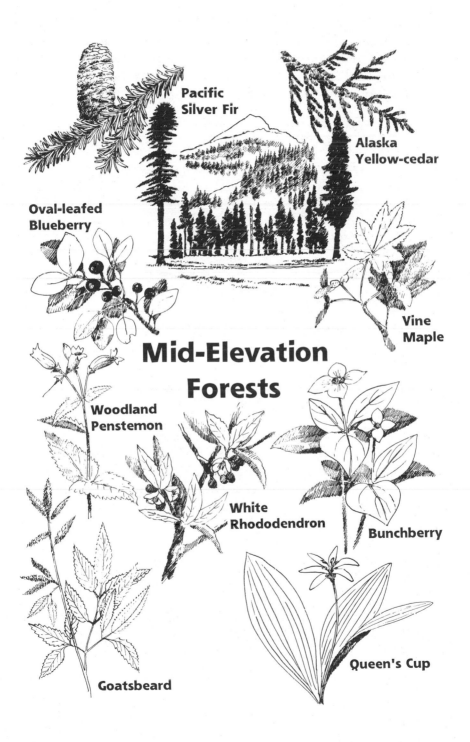

Pacific
Silver Fir

Alaska
Yellow-cedar

Oval-leafed
Blueberry

Vine
Maple

Mid-Elevation
Forests

Woodland
Penstemon

White
Rhododendron

Bunchberry

Goatsbeard

Queen's Cup

in forests but sometimes in more open areas. During early summer it produces four white, petal-like bracts above a whorl of compact, mid-green leaves; a cluster of bright red berries, bunched together on a single stalk, follow. Northwest Indians often ate the tasteless fruit with an accompaniment of grease.

Queen's Cup (*Clintonia uniflora*)

The flower of the queen's cup displays an appropriately regal bearing — an orderly rosette of flat white petals, so bright and tidy it almost seems out of place upon the needle-littered forest floor. A single blue-purple berry (inedible) replaces the flower in fall. Two or three long, elliptical leaves rise from the base of the plant; they resemble those of the avalanche lily (to which it is related). The name "queen's cup" was bestowed by a Mrs. Henshaw, a Canadian writer described as "evidently a staunch Royalist." She was apparently unaware that the scientific name honors American statesman De Witt Clinton, whose father fought *against* the British Monarchy as a Revolutionary War general.

Huckleberries (*Vaccinium* spp.)

This family of fruit-filled shrubs comes into its own during late summer and fall, tempting the tongue with a plenitude of plump, juicy berries while engaging the eye with masses of deep-tinted leaves that girdle the midsection of the mountain like a wide, wine-colored sash. These appealing plants do have a less approachable side, however, for the individual species resist easy identification; careful study of such facets as leaf shape, branch structure, and shrub height are often required to determine exactly which berry is being contemplated or consumed. The confusion is not confined to just scientific designations; common names also welter in uncertainty, with huckleberry, blueberry, whortleberry, and bilberry all having their adherents.

What to do? If you must be certain which *Vaccinium* stands beside you by the trail, carry a good field guide and prepare to be patient. The authors of this book will be of little help, for they have grouped all of the park's species together as huckleberries.

Called by whatever name, these bushes are all members of the heath family, their flowers sharing a characteristic urn shape. Most of Rainier's *Vaccinium* varieties have blue to purplish black berries; a few have fruit that is red. Nearby Indian tribes, who made the mountain a main stop in their seasonal migrations, gathered an abundance of huckleberries that they either ate fresh or dried for later use.

White Rhododendron *(Rhododendron albiflorum)*

Not the state flower, which is the pink-blossomed *Rhododendron macrophyllum*, this related species resides in Rainier's upper forests and open areas, delighting the eye with its bright, cream-colored blooms. Unlike most rhododendrons, its blossoms grow along the stem rather than at the stem end. The buds served Northwest Indians as a treatment for colds, sore-throats, ulcers, and cuts.

Goatsbeard *(Aruncus dioecus)* and Oceanspray *(Holodiscus discolor)*

In early summer, both these bushes brighten roadsides and other open areas with their ivory-white flowerlets. Oceanspray arranges its blooms in dangling clusters that taper downward, while goatsbeard places its tiny flowers in long, narrow branchlets. Oceanspray stems served native peoples as digging sticks and as shafts for spears, arrows, and other weapons; the plant's medicinal uses included a treatment for chickenpox. For its part, goatsbeard treated blood diseases, stomach pain, and smallpox.

Penstemons *(Penstemon* spp.)

A burst of bright pink upon a rockface, framed by a small mat of greenery; clusters of blue-violet flowers lining the roadside; a scattering of small purplish pincushions at the edge of the trail—most penstemons prefer dry cliffs, rock outcroppings, and other open places, shunning the streambanks and meadows favored by many of the park's wildflowers. Also unusual is the prominence of the penstemons' long floral tubes, which make the flowers most striking when seen in profile rather than in frontal view. At least eight varieties of penstemons grow in the park, with the species' habitats covering a wide range of elevations. Closely related is the lovely woodland-penstemon *(Nothochelone nemorosa)* that often colors forest openings.

Subalpine Meadows

Between the mid-elevation forests and timberline lie the gardens of Rainier — patches of subalpine meadows, or parklands, that in summertime are filled nearly to overflowing with wildflowers. Some of the plants, eager to begin blooming, poke their shoots through the still-melting snow; a few linger into early fall, when the job of coloring the countryside is taken over by the burgundy-hued foliage of the huckleberries. Trees from several sturdy conifer species speckle and sometimes surround the open areas, their green-needled limbs contrasting with outcroppings of gray rock; at most, however, they provide a forested frame for the meadows' true masterpieces: the blossoming blues, reds, yellows, whites, and purples that brighten the greenery of the grasslands like dottings from the brush of some sunny-dispositioned Impressionist.

Flower fanciers will find dazzling subalpine scenery on a host of hikes: Eunice Lake - Tolmie Peak (p. 269), Spray Falls - Spray Park (p. 272), Eagle Peak (p. 225), Comet Falls - Van Trump Park (p. 229), Nisqually Vista (p. 234), Alta Vista - Deadhorse Creek (p. 235), the High Skyline (p. 237), Reflection Lakes - Mazama Ridge (p. 240), Bench and Snow Lakes (p. 244) Tipsoo Lake (p. 254), Naches Peak (p. 254), Owyhigh Lakes (p. 257), Summerland (p. 259), Sunrise Rim - Shadow Lake (p. 261), and Frozen Lake - Berkeley Park (p. 262).

Subalpine Fir (*Abies lasiocarpa*)

How many mountain climbers, bent by their loads as they struggle toward timberline, have taken heart at the sight of these straight-trunked little trees and shouldered their packs with new-found vigor and fortitude? With its dark foliage and narrow, spirelike crown, the subalpine fir fringes the parklands, its pointed shape and somber color contrasting with the bright, free-form swatches of the neighboring berries and wildflowers. The tree's distinctive appearance derives from the shortness of its upper branches, an adaptation that protects against the stresses of heavy snow loads and driving wind; its lower limbs, which in winter are buried by a protective layer of snow, can afford the luxury of longer length. Even at timberline, where its height is reduced to some three or four feet, the subalpine fir stands proudly upright, rather than prostrating itself before the icy winter wind as some other species do.

Sitka Mountain-ash (*Sorbus sitchensis*) and Cascade Mountain-ash (*Sorbus scopulina*)

Mountain-ash produces what may be the most spectacular berries found in the park, large clusters of bright red, fall-ripened fruit that blaze forth from a contrasting mass of dark-tinted, compound leaves. Sitka mountain-ash has blue-green, rounded leaflets, while those of the Cascade mountain-ash are yellow-green and pointed. The berries, while well-liked by birds, are normally not eaten by humans but were used by one Northwest tribe as a scalp treatment for lice and dandruff.

Avalanche Lily (*Erythronium montanum*) and Glacier Lily (*Erythronium grandiflorum*)

Similar in shape and size, this pair of lilies sometimes grows closely together in the park. The yellow glacier lily often pushes its shoots through a melting springtime snowpack; its large corm is stored by small rodents for food and also eaten by black bears. The white avalanche lily is the later bloomer but still arrives before many of its other subalpine companions, frequently filling entire hillslopes with its bright white flowers.

Paintbrush (*Castilleja* spp.)

Ranged in its various hues from magenta to scarlet to orange-red to yellow to white, paintbrush is a mainstay of subalpine areas, mingling with the blues of lupine and the whites of bistort and valerian. The actual paintbrush flowers are small and greenish, but they are surrounded by large bracts that give each of the various species its distinctive color. The Makah Indians used paintbrush to trap hummingbirds, which then became charms for whaling.

Pasque Flower (*Anemone occidentalis*)

An early subalpine arrival, the pasque flower (aka western anemone) opens its cream-colored cups shortly after snowmelt; later, when other flowers reach their peak, it offers a plume-shaped

Subalpine Fir

Cascade Mountain-ash

Avalanche Lily

Magenta Paintbrush

Subalpine Forests and Meadows

Bear Grass

Western Pasqueflower

Jeffrey's Shooting Star

Broadleaf Arnica

Lewis Monkeyflower

seed head that waves in the wind and justifies its nickname of "moptop." The Taidnapam Indians made a tuberculosis-treating tea from some species of anemone, but the pasque flower is poisonous when consumed fresh.

Beargrass (*Xerophyllum tenax*)

What hiker would not be transfixed by a beargrass-filled meadow in early summer, where hundreds of creamy flower clusters seemingly float above the ground like a great, glowing cloud, brightening all that surrounds them? So, too, in the mid-elevation forests, where, torchlike, beargrass illuminates the understory with its blossom-filled balls of light. Few other plants, even at Rainier, can exert such an enthralling effect.

Although bears will indeed chew up its leaf bases in spring, beargrass could as well be called meadowvolegrass or pikagrass, since these much smaller critters are its more consistent consumers. The long, strong leaves served local Indians for their basketry; nineteenth-century naturalist David Douglas prized beargrass hats so highly that he once traded a seven-shilling blanket for three of them.

Jeffrey's Shooting Star (*Dodecatheon jeffreyi*)

A wet forest opening, streambank, or subalpine meadow often hosts masses of this delicate, pink-petalled flower, which glimmers gently in the dewy greenery. The shooting star's name refers not to its color but to its cometlike shape, with stamens pointing forward and turned-back petals following behind. John Jeffrey, for whom this species of *Dodecatheon* was named, came to the Pacific Northwest in the early 1850s at the behest of a group of Scottish gentlemen, who wanted him to continue David Douglas's botanizing. Jeffrey spent some time in the vicinity of Fort Nisqually and later went southward, where he managed to give his name to a second, somewhat larger plant, the Jeffrey pine.

Broadleaf Arnica (*Arnica latifolia*) and Arrowleaf Groundsel (*Senecio triangularis*)

These distinctive members of the aster family are two of the larger yellow flowers found in Mount Rainier's meadows, bringing

an added dimension to the reds, whites, and blues that often domi-
nate the floral displays in the subalpine parks. The arnica has wide,
opposite, and generally oval-shaped leaves, while the groundsel's
are alternate, triangular, and squared off at their base.

Monkeyflowers (*Mimulus* spp.)

A ribbon of pink winds its way along a meadow streamcourse,
cascading down the hillslope like a bright-colored cataract—the
dazzling Lewis monkeyflower (*M. lewisii*) is again at work, enhanc-
ing the surrounding greenery and catching the eye of each pass-
erby. Few other subalpine flowers create such a concentrated effect
as the Lewis, as it masses in rich-hued magnificence around the
mountain. Less dramatic but also appealing are the park's four yellow monkeyflowers and a second reddish species, the tiny
Brewer's monkeyflower (*M. breweri*).

Alpine Tundra

Above timberline lies a rocky landscape of alpine austerity,
where a handful of hardy plants manages to bloom during the few
snow-free weeks of high summer. Mats of dark green foliage are
brightened by the small blossoms of mountain-heather or phlox,
while miniature versions of lupines and daisies rise only a few
inches from the ground. Diminutive but delightful, the flowers and
shrubs of the high country wait for the watchful hiker to pause,
come closer, and appreciate.

Good spots for observing alpine tundra are: at and near Frozen
Lake (p. 263), on Burroughs Mountain (p. 262), on the Spray Park
Trail above Spray Park (p. 274), on the High Skyline Trail (p. 237),
and on the Wonderland Trail above Summerland (p. 261).

Lupines (*Lupinus* spp.)

Forming patches of pale blue-purple on the tan-gray alpine terrain, the alpine lupine (*L. lyallii* or *L. lepidus* var. *lobbii*), features
leaves covered with a silvery sheen of tiny, silky hairs. Found below timberline is the subalpine lupine (*L. latifolius* var. *subalpinus*),
which frequently forms lovely compositions with a host of contrastingly colored meadow flowers. The genus name, "lupus"
(Latin for wolf) was perhaps bestowed in the mistaken belief that,

wolflike, the plants devoured soil fertility; in actuality, lupines are nitrogen fixing and thus enhance the ground in which they grow.

Mountain-heathers (*Phyllodoce* spp. and *Cassiope* spp.)

Few sights give such a sense of the highlands as that of a rock-covering carpet of mountain-heather, its deep-green foliage dotted by hundreds of tiny, bright flowers. Four species grow in the park: the yellow *(P. glanduliflora)* is almost always found above timberline, the white *(C. mertensiana)* inhabits an intermediate range, while the red *(P. empetriformis)* and Alaskan *(C. stelleriana)* prefer lower elevations nearer to forest. The beauty of red mountain-heather once moved botanist Lewis Clark to ecological eloquence:

> These cheerful bells ring an invitation to high places above the timber line, to those serene and lofty slopes where peace and quiet enter our souls....The hiker or climber, who puts aside his pack-sack or pack-frame, to watch the cirrus overhead and deeply breathe the tonic air, knows well the subtle perfume of Phyllodoce.

Saxifrages (*Saxifraga* spp.)

Tiny, fleshy leaves; flowers with five white, distinctly separated petals — the Tolmie's saxifrage (*S. tolmiei*) is a striking specimen of the alpine tundra, sometimes holding forth as the only flower present. Common in the park, it honors Dr. William Fraser Tolmie, the Hudson's Bay Company physician who approached the mountain in 1833. Several other saxifrage species are found in the park; they variously occupy a wide range of elevations and often grow on rocks and cliffs. The genus name comes from the Latin *saxum* (rock) and *frangere* (to break), since it was believed that the plants split the stones upon which they grew.

Asters, Fleabanes, and Daisies (*Erigeron* spp. and *Aster* spp.)

While certain species of these bright-colored ray flowers grow at lower elevations in the park, the alpine varieties, with less floral competition, are perhaps the most striking. Golden fleabane *(E. aureus)* is a denizen of the tundra, splashing its yellowy blooms against the gray-brown rocks; alpine aster *(A. alpigenus)* circles its lavender petals around a central golden disc. Below timberline,

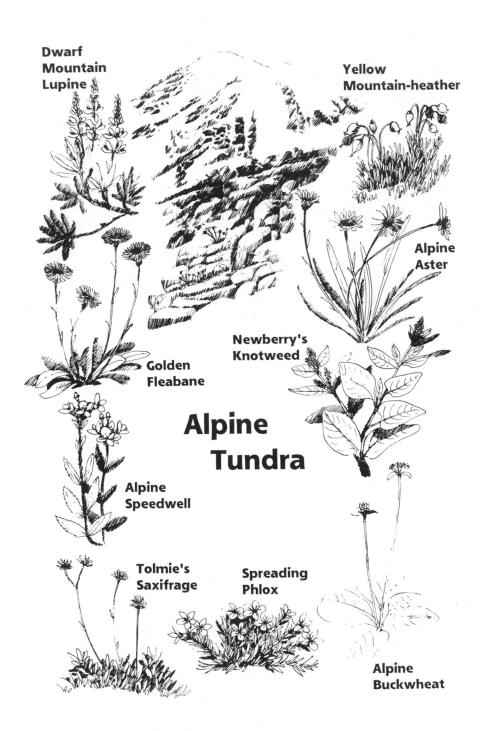

Dwarf
Mountain
Lupine

Yellow
Mountain-heather

Alpine
Aster

Newberry's
Knotweed

Golden
Fleabane

Alpine
Tundra

Alpine
Speedwell

Tolmie's
Saxifrage

Spreading
Phlox

Alpine
Buckwheat

wandering daisy *(E. peregrinus)*, Cascade aster *(A. ledophyllus)*, and leafy aster *(A. foliaceus)* are found in the meadows.

Newberry's Knotweed *(Polygonum newberryi)*

This low-growing, spreading flower is most noticeable for its leaves — a soft, slightly grayish green in early summer and pale yellow-red later — which form colorful clumps amid the rockfields of alpine and subalpine areas. Sometimes called "fleeceflower" for its fuzzy covering, the plant was named for John Newberry, a surgeon-naturalist who explored the east side of the Cascades as part of an 1858 army expedition; the Newberry Crater in California's Mojave Desert is also named for him.

Alpine Buckwheat *(Eriogonum pyrolifolium)*

The white to pinkish flowers of alpine buckwheat poke up from a cluster of gray-green basal leaves, adding to the impression of dryness their rocky alpine habitat creates. The smell of the plant, however, evokes damp areas (such as an unventilated gym locker), which justifies its sobriquet of "dirty socks."

Spreading Phlox *(Phlox diffusa)*

Its petite, five-petalled flowers cluster together as if trying to form a ground-level bouquet, nearly obscuring the mat of dark green foliage beneath; the delicately colored petals are variously found in soft shades of white, pink, lavender, and blue. Such gentle hues soothe the harshness of the plant's stone-filled surroundings, welcoming hikers who have made it to the high country.

Speedwells *(Veronica spp.)*

These small, single-stemmed plants are sometimes called brooklimes in recognition of their proclivity for growing in wet spots. "Speedwell," an old-fashioned term for good-bye, may refer to the flower petals, which fall off as soon as they are picked. Two varieties, each of which favors high elevations, are found in the park: alpine *(V. wormskjoldii)* and Cusick's *(V. cusickii)*. The blue-purple blooms of both plants often appear at pathside like flecks of a twilight sky, enticing an observer to bend lower and behold their dainty, often overlooked beauty.

The Mountain's Many Inhabitants

Late morning on the slopes above Paradise. A hiker on the Deadhorse Creek Trail pauses at the top of a hill and notices a gray rock among the wildflowers. Ready to resume hiking, he finds that the rock is now moving. Toward him.

A hoary marmot, head down, plows her way through the paintbrush and lupine, chewing up the plants like a small, fur-covered lawnmower. Only when she is within a few feet of the hiker does she finally alter course, leaving a swath of vanished vegetation in her wake. The marmot munches happily away for a few more minutes and then makes her way atop a *real* rock, where she relaxes after her meadow repast, her ample body warmed by the noontime sun.

The play and its participants vary greatly, but time and again the same script is followed: person meets critter; person watches critter; person leaves, smiling. The scene could be as stirring as that of two mountain goats, climbing the rock-shattered ridge beyond Van Trump Park; it may be as mundane as a sooty (blue) grouse, taking a dust bath in the meadow below Eagle Peak; or it might be as mysterious as a piercing "eeenk" that reverberates among the rocks below the Tatoosh ridgeline, where an alert eye will finally pick out the movement of a pika as it scurries through the scree.

The rockfields, meadows, and forests of Mount Rainier offer many such opportunities for animal encounters, for some 190 species of birds, mammals, amphibians, and reptiles live or visit there. Some, like the elusive mountain lion, are seldom seen; others, however, are all too anxious for human contact, as anyone who's had a gray jay pluck a potato chip from an unguarded lunch plate will readily attest. Here are brief introductions to a score of interesting critters, both shy and bold, that park visitors might meet:

Mountain Goat (*Oreamnos americanus*)

His profile painted on the sides of thousands of burgundy box-cars, the redoubtable mountain goat has long stirred the hearts of railway watchers, his likeness speeding down the tracks of the Great Northern far from the rocky habitat he calls home. Seeing the actual animal is another proposition, however, since they favor the rocks and cliffs of the high mountainsides where no trains and few wildlife watchers make their way. Often the most a hiker can hope for is a distant view of several white specks, their shapes outlined against a nearly sheer rockface that, incredibly, they then ascend with little difficulty.

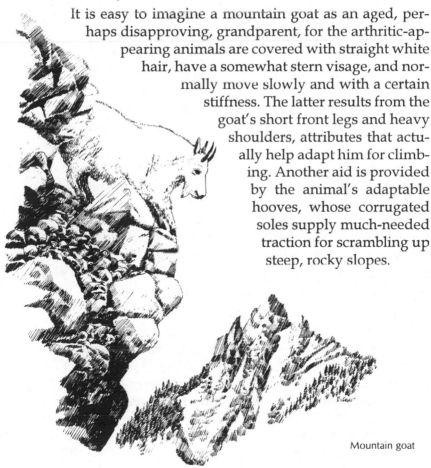

It is easy to imagine a mountain goat as an aged, perhaps disapproving, grandparent, for the arthritic-appearing animals are covered with straight white hair, have a somewhat stern visage, and normally move slowly and with a certain stiffness. The latter results from the goat's short front legs and heavy shoulders, attributes that actually help adapt him for climbing. Another aid is provided by the animal's adaptable hooves, whose corrugated soles supply much-needed traction for scrambling up steep, rocky slopes.

Mountain goat

This crag climbing creature is, however, misnamed, since he is actually no goat at all but a sort of antelope whose closest relative is the chamois of the Swiss Alps. Nonetheless, the effect of decades of usage is strong, and the mountain goat's name will probably remain unchanged, as will our image of him as the animal that always rides the trains.

Elk *(Cervus elaphus* or *C. canadensis)*

Although Olympic elk were native to the region around Mount Rainier, they were hunted to extinction there long ago. The elk that now inhabit the area are, oddly, the Rocky Mountain species, brought here for restocking. One band, from Yellowstone National Park, arrived by train at Enumclaw on New Year's Eve 1912, accompanied by Game Warden Harry Reif. After spending a few weeks in an enclosure on White River Lumber Company land, the herd was set free to roam the hills. In January 1933 a railcar load of elk from the Jackson Hole area debarked at Eatonville, paid for by Pierce County's game commission; nine years later, the Eatonville elk were going strong, having just trampled farmer Nick Koenig's crops. Bolstered by the protection afforded by the park, Mount Rainier's immigrant elk have firmly established themselves.

A male elk in summer is a striking specimen, somewhat resembling an athlete stoked on steroids; deep chested, and almost overbalanced by an enormous set of antlers, bulls will outdo even a Big Ten linebacker in outbursts of intimidating aggression. Their repertoire includes bugling (a nearly operatic activity progressing from a bellow to a shrill whistle to a series of grunts), attacking trees and brush with their antlers, and wallowing in pre-dug pits previously lined with an aromatic mixture of urine and feces.

All this is but a prelude to game day, when pairs of bull elk square off for antler clashing contests to determine who will control that year's harem of female elk. The dominant male from previous years may remain unvanquished, but time works against him. His "reward" as victor has been an energy-sapping regime of harem maintenance, contests with other bulls, and sexual activity with up to 60 females. It may be quite a life while it lasts, but it has its limitations; dominant males generally die several years sooner than their less successful competitors, victims of the virile vicissitudes of their overstimulating occupation.

Hoary Marmot (*Marmota caligata*)

Mornings are friendly in the marmot colony. The various inhabitants begin with their daily greeting ritual, going from burrow to burrow to rub cheeks and noses, touch mouths, and nibble on each other's neck and ears. Next it's time to move outside for the day's main business, sunning themselves on inviting flat rocks and grinding up the groundcover of the nearby meadows. The furry food processors can devastate a flower patch daily as they attempt to add an ample layer of fat for winter, when they will languish, nutritionless, for up to nine months. During their long underground layover, the ever-companionable marmots hibernate in heaps, their heartbeat slowing from four beats a second to only four per minute as their already languid life of summer virtually stops.

Although among the most relaxed of rodents, marmots do have periods of activity. The arrival of a golden eagle, bear, or other predator will prompt a shrill whistle from a rock-perched marmot sentinel, sending the colony scurrying for the seclusion of their burrows. Their tunnel system affords them ample protection, for it can extend over as much as five acres (the result of much unmarmotlike hard work) and includes numerous escape exits.

Hoary marmots are the largest members of the woodchuck-marmot family; the heaviest individuals weigh as much as 20 pounds.

Hoary marmot

Pika

Their common name derives from their grizzled, grayish coats, while their black-brown feet have given them the Latin descriptor *caligata*, which means "boot." An appropriate marmot monicker is "whistler."

Pika (*Ochotona princeps*)

Sharing the high country with the marmot is the pint-sized pika, a small eared, gray-brown relative of the rabbit. Like the marmot, the pika has a highly audible alarm, a shrill "eeenk!" that reverberates among the rocks and seems to come from no visible source. Close inspection of the surroundings often reveals a small, granite-colored object, immobile upon a talus slope except when vibrating with its warning call.

When not threatened by the presence of a backpacker or other unwanted visitor, pikas zip about with great industriousness, preparing for the rigors of winter, when, instead of hibernating, they remain alert, active, and *hungry*. Pikas process vast quantities of plant material in preparation for the snowy season, cutting down flowers and grasses from mountain meadows, transporting their bounty to conveniently located flat rocks, arranging the cuttings in neat stacks, and then leaving them to dry in the sunlight. Taken beneath the rocks for winter, the cuttings are stored in a sort of pika plant pantry, to be consumed during the long subalpine winter.

A colony of pikas will all inhabit the same rockfall, but individuals keep to themselves and defend their territory against intrusions by other colonists. Choicest colony neighborhoods are those at the edge of the talus slope, where access to the nearby meadows is easiest. The one occasion when pikas show a cooperative spirit is during an attack on a colony member by a weasel or other predator; the co-colonists then frantically zoom around the rockfall in an apparent attempt to distract the dangerous intruder.

Such activity, however, is more than most pika perusers can hope to see. For many hikers, it will be sound alone that alerts them to the presence of pikas—in the words of one frustrated would-be watcher, those "sharp, squeaking, querulous ventriloquial notes or cries, deceptive as to distance and locality." Unlike children, pikas seem destined to not be seen, but heard.

Chipmunks and Squirrels

Five species of these small critters scamper around the park. Both the Townsend chipmunk (*Eutamias townsendi*) and yellow pine chipmunk (*Eutamias amoenus*) have a white eye stripe that distinguishes them from the squirrels. Both also sport black stripes on their backs, but the Townsend is a larger chipmunk, much darker in color, with a distinctive white frosting on its tail. The Townsend prefers moist forest, while the yellow pine likes drier woods and open meadows. Both gather and store immense quantities of berries, seeds, and buds, which they carry in puffy cheek pouches.

The golden mantled ground squirrel (*Spermophilus saturatus*) frequents open woods and relatively dry habitats, making it more common on the east side of the park. It can be bold in begging food but if startled may bite the hand that feeds it. The golden mantled's name derives from the rich, yellow-brown coloring of its head and chest. More colorful yet is the Douglas squirrel (*Tamiasciurus douglasii*), or chickaree, which accents its gray-brown, reddish tinged back with an arrestingly orange-gray underbelly. A tree squirrel, it can dart through the forest canopy far above, chattering a noisy warning of hikers, predators, and other intruders. Late summer and fall is harvest time for the Douglas; it tears around the tree limbs, nipping off cones, and then descends to the ground, where it gathers the fallen foodstuff and carts it off for storage. An expert at piece work, it can nip between 12 and 30 cones per minute, depending on their size. Also moving between tree and ground is the seldom-seen northern flying squirrel (*Glaucomys sabrinus*), an adventurous nocturnal aviator who gracefully glides from tree perch to forest floor by utilizing large, lateral skin flaps that it stretches out, capelike, during its descent. Dietary staples are different for the flying squirrel than his cousins—a gourmet menu of underground fungi in summer and horsehair lichen in winter.

Gray Jay (*Perisoreus canadensis*)

Each summer an airborne crime wave sweeps through the park as Rainier's resident gray jays commit petty larceny at picnic sites far and wide. A single scrap of sandwich is enough to activate a squadron of the fluffy-feathered, light gray birds, who swoop into position on nearby tree limbs, waiting to pilfer, plunder, and purloin whatever is left lying about. Anyone who has seen a gray jay in action will likely call it by its nickname, "camp robber," evermore.

Clark's
nutcracker

Gray jays are close cousins of the crows, sharing with them their harsh, grating voices and a restless, rambunctious intelligence that leads to brash behavior and a life outside the law. Like other jays, the camp robber amuses himself by accurately imitating the calls of various birds, an avocation that also has a practical effect: a well-modulated hawk screech can easily send a squirrel scurrying for cover, with the seed it leaves behind now available for the gray jay's taking. Reversing roles, the camp robber often becomes victim when his cousin, the Steller's jay, burgles his buried food cache, carting off what by then may be twice-stolen goods.

Clark's Nutcracker (*Nucifraga columbiana*)

Although the Clark's nutcracker sometimes imitates the gray jay's freeloading lifestyle, she more often is compulsively industrious, ranging over as much as 14 miles of pine forest in search of seeds, shaking the individual seeds with her bill to determine their quality, stuffing a sublingual pouch full of her find, and then making a full-faced flight to bury her bounty for winter. The clever Clark's looks for landmarks, like boulders and trees, to locate the seed caches later. A single nutcracker may harvest several times as much food as she needs—up to 30,000 whitebark and lodgepole pine seeds in a single year—and the uneaten residue, often interred far from its source, will help disperse the species by germinating into treehood.

The Clark's nutcracker is a difficult bird to miss: her gray and white body, black wings, and white tail all catch the eye, as does her leisurely, crowlike flight and, contrastingly, her nervous hopping from limb to limb once she alights. Nutcrackers communicate with a cacophony of "harsh cries, some like the snarling of a cat, some high and squealing, but usually including the characteristic *kr-a-a-a*, varying in pitch and loudness."

Sooty, or Blue, Grouse *(Dendragapus obscurus)*

Broo, broop, broop, burroo, broo, broo...the sound is coming from *some*where, but it could be almost *any*where in the surrounding forest. Little wonder that our eyes can't find the source of the strange call, for this ventriloquist's voice is not meant for human ears, but rather for those of the female sooty grouse, whom the male hopes to attract with his basso booming. Having gained the attention of the object of his affections, he will then perform a distinctive dance wherein he fans his tail, inflates his yellow neck sacs (the source of the booming), raises his orange eye combs, and then struts before the favored female. If he really means to impress, the strut will be preceded by a down-and-dirty display flight wherein he drags his wings, cocks his tail, and tucks in his head. What recipient could resist such an enticing entreaty?

During the warm months, sooty grouse enjoy a varied diet of berries and bugs. They often move up the mountainsides come winter, enduring the colder weather found there while consuming the conifer needles that are then their menu mainstay.

Mountain Chickadee *(Parus gambeli)*

How deeply runs the memory of a warm mountain morning, the summer dust rising from our feet, and a lazy, lisping *tsee-dee-dee*

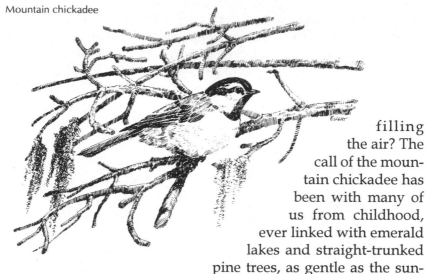

Mountain chickadee

filling the air? The call of the mountain chickadee has been with many of us from childhood, ever linked with emerald lakes and straight-trunked pine trees, as gentle as the sunlight, as soothing as a mother's whispered lullaby. The rotund little gray-bodied bird whose voice evokes these images is at home throughout the forested high country of the west, and makes Mount Rainier a favored residence. She nests in cozy tree cavities that are either naturally occurring, abandoned by a woodpecker, or self-constructed; the hole is made homey with a carpet of wood chips and wall coverings of fur, feathers, and sometimes animal feces. Food — eggs, larvae, adult insects and spiders, various conifer seeds — is gleaned from foliage and branches, with the forager nimbly swinging below a branch and plucking additional prey while hanging upside down. As curious as she is cute, the mountain chickadee will drop to the bottommost tree limbs to inspect a passing human or other object of interest.

Northern Flicker (*Colaptes auratus*)

Northern flicker. A seemingly unassuming name, but one tied to some two million years of history. About that long ago there was probably but one species of flicker in North America; then came an oscillation of climatic changes that divided a number of bird species — including the flicker — into two or more groups. When ornithologists arrived on the scene and began classifying birds, they designated an eastern (yellow shafted), a western (red-shafted), and a gilded flicker. Later experts determined that the three species interbred, and the trio was then lumped together again. Thus today visitors to Mount Rainier will find what is called the northern flicker, red-shafted *sub*species. This taxonomic tangle makes little difference to the average bird watcher, who only knows what he or she sees—a fairly large, delicately colored bird with white rump, barred brown back, and wings and tail lined with red. If spied standing rather than in flight, the flicker presents an arresting sight: a head olive-brown on top and back, gradating to gray below the eyes; a speckled chest; and, covering its lower throat, a crescent-shaped black bib; to this, the male adds a bright red mustache that streaks back from his beak.

Flickers are part of the woodpecker family, but unlike their relatives, they find most of their food (ants and other insects, seeds, and fruits) on the ground. When they do peck at a tree, it's usually to drill a nest hole or drum a message to another flicker. Affection, for flickers, is not a quiet affair; they proclaim their readiness to mate with a resonant *wick-wick-wick-wick* that fills the forest with its hollow-toned homage to love.

Rufous Hummingbird *(Selasphorus rufus)*

Of the world's 334 hummingbird species only two make their way to the Mount Rainier area, the infrequently seen calliope and a regular resident, the rufous; the latter's name is apt, for it is the reddest of all North American hummers. The rufous shares, with other hummingbirds, an attraction to red-colored flowers, using its long pointed bill to feed from several tubular species common to Mount Rainier—Lewis monkeyflower and the various penstemons and paintbrushes among them. And feeding, for hummingbirds, is serious business: as the smallest of all birds, they have a metabolic rate similar to their animal counterparts, the tiny shrews, and this means a frantic, day-long search for fuel; a hummingbird will daily consume up to half its body weight in sugar, the equivalent of a human downing about 70 or 80 pounds of Lifesavers.

The attentions of an amorous male rufous are difficult to ignore, for the swooping swain will soar and dive in an ellipse several hundred feet high, passing within inches of his beloved at high speed while creating a shrill shrieking sound with his wings. Once mated, the skyclimbing suitor becomes an indifferent spouse; the

female is left to raise the young, while the unfettered male con-
venes with his cronies for an early migration south, leaving the
mothers and their young alone in the meadows by mid-August.

American Dipper *(Cinclus mexicanus)*

If ever an avian were a born entertainer, it is the dynamic American dipper, or water ouzel. This small gray bird busies himself by
bouncing from boulder to boulder in some spray-spattered stream
channel, pausing briefly to plant his yellow feet and break into a
body-shaking, leg-flexing boogie that outdoes the best show on
Broadway; when done with his dipping dance, he will likely dunk
himself into the frigid current in search of food. Once in the water,
he often uses his multifaceted feet to walk on the creekbottom,
while at other times he swims with his wings, quickly taking flight
if the sweeping stream proves too swift—he seemingly skis over
the creekbed's gravel when in shallow spots. The dipper becomes a
diver when confronted by a lake, dropping, at times, to considerable depths; for variety, he sometimes forages on snowfields. All
told, it appears that the dipper can never be far from water, for his
flights are usually confined to spray zones over streams, and he often nests behind waterfalls.

The swimming, skiing, diving, dancing dipper is also a
singer. His effervescent,
flutelike song soars
above all but the
noisiest water
sounds, bring-
ing a second
smile to the
lips of those
listeners
w h o

American dipper

earlier delighted in merely watching him. Even the most melancholy hiker cannot help but take heart after an encounter with this rock-hopping little entertainer.

Water Pipit (*Anthus rubescens*)

Despite its name, the water pipit is seldom found by streams or lakes; instead it frequents alpine country, either in song-filled flight far overhead or striding across the tundra, its dark tail bobbing as it probes the ground for insect food; like the horned larks, pipits walk and run but never hop. Its treeless summer habitat compels the water pipit to nest on the ground, where it makes substantial structures of moss and dried plant stems, hiding them near grass tussocks or rocks. In winter, pipits form large convoys that convey them as far south as Central America.

Pacific Giant Salamander (*Dicamptodon ensatus*)

This largest of land-based salamanders is able, because of her size, to catch and consume a wide-ranging diet of forest creatures. Not limited to the fare of insects and invertebrates that are the lot of her smaller salamander siblings, the Pacific giant also ingests mice, garter snakes, and other amphibians. The undersides of logs, rocks, and forest litter serve as homesites for the Pacific giant, who helps hide herself with a camouflaged coloration of black mottling over brown to purplish skin. Unlike most other salamanders, the Pacific giant possesses a voice, but she uses it only in the most dire of circumstances, uttering a low yelp when captured.

Northern Alligator Lizard (*Gerrhonotus coeruleus*)

His name implies a warning: the alligator lizard bites, often painfully chomping down on whatever picks him up. Another defense is perhaps equally unpleasant—he will defecate all over a would-be collector's hand. It's fortunate that the alligator lizard is provided with such protection, for his stubby, weak legs make it difficult to escape predators; with such limited mobility, his diet consists of critters slow enough for him to catch, which means certain insects and snails. The alligator lizard's ever-so-humble home is made under rotten logs, rocks, or loose bark, where, sharp teeth waiting, he asks only to be left alone.

Banana Slug (*Ariolimax columbianus*)

A signature species in temperate forests, the slow-moving banana slug can be found inching its way along the needle-strewn ground, probing ponderously for fungi and plants that it will then masticate with several thousand tiny teeth. Slugs lack the protection provided by a snail's shell, but they avoid being eaten by lacing their slime with a tongue-thwarting dose of bitter, burning chemicals. Being shell-less creates another problem: the thus-exposed gastropods are prone to lose too much moisture in warm, dry weather, so they must remain in cool shaded areas, sheltering themselves under plants when additional protection is needed. Despite their various difficulties, banana slugs can survive up to six years—testimony, perhaps, to the benefits of living life in the slow lane.

Banana slug

The Tribes of Tacobet

For the Northwest's native peoples, the peak known as Tacobet was a forbidden place, guarded by a powerful, protective spirit, and anyone who ventured too high on its icy reaches would find death the result. It was different farther down the mountain, however, where the great grazing parks and encircling forests offered foods to gather, game to hunt, and grassy meadows where horses could feed. So it was that at least five tribes visited Tacobet's foothills and lower slopes, enjoying seasonal sojourns at these places of plenty that spread so invitingly below the inhospitable summit.

From the east came the Yakimas, crossing the crest of the Cascades to reach the upper Ohanapecosh River and the meadowland now known as Sunrise Park. To the south the Taidnapams made forays out of the Upper Cowlitz Valley, climbing into the Tatoosh Range. On the west and north the tribes near the Sound followed the stream canyons towards the mountain: the Nisquallys, Puyallups, and the bands later known as the Muckleshoots coming up the Nisqually, Carbon, and White river drainages.

During summer and fall the various bands occupied the subalpine open spaces that surround the mountain, living in brush shelters at temporary camps. The men busied themselves hunting deer, elk, mountain goats, and smaller game. The women and children picked berries, making juice from salmonberries and blackcap raspberries and drying the other varieties over open fires; they also gathered many of the mountain's plants for medicinal use. When the picking season was over, the Indians burned the meadow areas to kill the brush and small trees, thereby preserving the clearings.

For untold generations the tribes made their annual migration to the mountain; along with their wintertime life of fishing on the lower rivers, it was part of a well-established cycle that had brought them prosperity and relative peace. The arrival of the whites changed all that, for the early explorers carried diseases, such as smallpox and measles, to which the Indians had no immunity, and between 1775 and 1865 a series of some eight epidemics decimated the native peoples, killing perhaps three-quarters of the population. The establishment of Washington Territory in 1853 brought new trouble; pressured by Governor Isaac Stevens to give up most of their land and facing encroachment by settlers and miners, the Indians resisted, and the resulting Puget Sound War (1855-56) and Yakima War (1855-59) saw the defeat of the tribes and the death of many of their leaders. The Nisqually village of Mashel, near the confluence of the Mashel and Nisqually rivers, was attacked by white militia and all its residents massacred. Leschi, the Nisquallys' foremost fighting chief, was captured after the end of the Puget Sound War and charged with murder. Despite a compelling defense that his only killings were of enemy soldiers during combat, Leschi was eventually convicted and executed.

By the 1860s, most of the remaining Indians were residing on newly established reservations, with the vast part of their former

lands taken over by the whites. Lost, too, was much of the continuity of tribal culture, as government officials pressured the native peoples to adopt the whites' speech, dress, agriculture, and religion. Some of the Indians nevertheless managed to return to the mountain for their annual summer visits, and a few found places to live in the surrounding foothills where settlers had not yet gained a foothold.

Starting with Dr. William Fraser Tolmie, who hired the Nisqually La-ha-let in 1833, early climbers called on local Indians to show them the way to Tacobet. Later guides included Wah-pow-e-ty, who left the Nisqually Reservation to take Lieutenant August Kautz to the mountain in 1857, and the wounded Yakima War veteran Sluis-kin, who guided Stevens and Van Trump en route to their 1870 ascent.

Muckleshoot girl

In 1886 a white youngster, Allison L. Brown, accompanied a hunting party from the Yakima reservation up the Ohanapecosh Valley and onto the Cowlitz Divide; not finding any game, they went farther up the mountainside, reaching a point above the Cathedral Rocks before turning back. It is the only recorded instance of Indians venturing so high onto the slopes.

On the opposite side of the mountain another tribesman was regularly assisting travelers bound for the peak.

Indian Henry

While on their way to Mount Rainier in 1888, John Muir and his companions spent a night near the confluence of the Mashel and Nisqually rivers, staying in the barn of the well-known Mashel village leader, Indian Henry. With Scottish succinctness, Muir described his host as "a mild-looking, smallish man with three wives, three fields, and horses, oats, wheat and vegetables."

Henry, who was known to his own people as Soo-too-lick, was variously reported as being either a Klickitat, Cowlitz, Yakima, or Nisqually. His ancestry apparently mattered little to him, for he had "renounced allegiance to his tribe...[and] adopted the dress and manner of living of the whites." For a time he had lived on Skate Creek, south of today's Longmire; while there he married three women from the local village. Rather than move to a reservation, Henry, his wives, and a number of other Indians relocated to Mashel Prairie. The site they selected was near the Nisqually tribe's old Mashel village, whose inhabitants had been tragically massacred by white militia during the Puget Sound War.

Some thirteen families joined the new community, building houses of cedar logs and shakes. Indian Henry's barn became a hay-filled "hotel" for travelers to Rainier.

Henry knew a bit about the nearby peak, for he had hunted mountain goats and other game on its southwest slopes while his wives gathered huckleberries in the meadows and woods; their camping area came to be called "Indian Henry's Hunting Ground." In 1883, he let James Longmire, whom he'd guided through the foothills years earlier, persuade him to lead the George Bayley climbing party to the Paradise area. For the most part, however,

Henry was content to host mountain-bound climbers and excursionists at his farm. Besides Muir's party, such Rainier luminaries as the Longmires, Fay Fuller, and the Van Trumps bedded down in his barn.

Indian Henry died in 1895. The village at Mashel Prairie maintained itself for a time, but by the mid-1920s the last residents had left. The Indian Shaker church they had built was converted into a barn, and the village cemetery, which contained Henry's grave, became overgrown with brush. Since then, the graveyard has periodically been restored, and visitors to the spot will now find a fenced-in patch of grass and, at its center, a stonework monument to Indian Henry.

Nearby is the dusty dirt road that long served as the main route to the mountain. It is now bereft of travelers, for those who once trod it have departed as surely as has Indian Henry. Yet perhaps a sense of their presence still lingers—a tramp of tired feet, long on their weary way from Tacoma; a pause; and then a hollered, hopeful inquiry: "Have you a bit of hay in your barn for a bed?"

The answer, so long as Henry abided there, was always "yes."

Indians continued their hunting and berry picking on the mountain after Rainier became a national park. In 1905 Acting Superintendent Grenville F. Allen reported that a party of Puyallups had

Nisqually canoe ferry

visited the Tatoosh Range, and the next year he noted that a group of Cowlitz Indians (Taidnapams) were hunting between the Cowlitz and Emmons glaciers.

Late in the summer of 1915 a pair of park rangers found a band of some 30 Yakimas hunting in the northeastern section of the park. When the rangers attempted to explain that such activity was illegal, the group's aged chief produced three worn documents from his teepee, including a copy of Governor Stevens's 1855 treaty with the Yakimas. The rangers withdrew without pressing their case; Chief Ranger Thomas O'Farrell subsequently searched for the hunters but found they had departed. The Indians' leader, it turned out, was Chief Saluskin, who had reportedly guided two treaty surveyors to the mountain 60 years earlier.

Yakimas traveled to the park almost every summer. By the 1920s some still came on foot, leading heavily laden pack ponies, but most arrived by auto. Ranger Floyd Schmoe described their poignant presence:

> The men have long hair worn in two ropelike braids tied with a bit of red cloth, and the women wear deerskin moccasins. Among their berrying equipment may still be found ancient baskets woven of cedar roots and tight enough to hold water...

> While the women and children gather berries the old men sit in camp, tending the babies and looking at the mountain.

By the 1950s organized groups of Indians no longer came to the mountain, but even today, individuals and families from various tribes still make the traditional summer journey to the peak's lower slopes. There they pick berries and medicinal herbs, and, for a time at least, renew their relationship with Tacobet.

Their great and fearsome benefactor is hard to forget.

Section II:
Auto Tours

As there is more to Mount Rainier National Park than just the majestic peak, so there is more to the Mount Rainier region than just the magnificent park. Motorists will soon discover this as they approach the mountain along any of eight different routes, passing through scenic and historic settings that provide a prelude to the wonders of the park's own roads. The dozen auto tours in this section follow the various thoroughfares that run towards and around the peak, describing the communities, landscapes, and landmarks located along the way. Whether it be the coal-mine-riddled mountain slopes of the Carbon River Canyon, the early-day edifices of Elbe and Eatonville, or the waterfalls and woodlands within the park itself, the auto tours will note their presence, indicate their appearance, and tell the stories of their significance.

(Note: mileages and directions given in the auto tours are from the perspective of a motorist driving from a route's starting point to its end point. Thus, for example, a mileage given along Nisqually-Paradise Road will indicate the distance from the park's Nisqually Entrance, while a direction of "left" or "right" will be from the viewpoint of someone in a car proceeding from the entrance toward Paradise.

Within each tour, driving instructions and certain basic descriptions are given in italics, while more detailed information about particular locations is provided, under subheadings, in regular type. Short anecdotes about selected topics are framed by boxes and printed in a different typeface.)

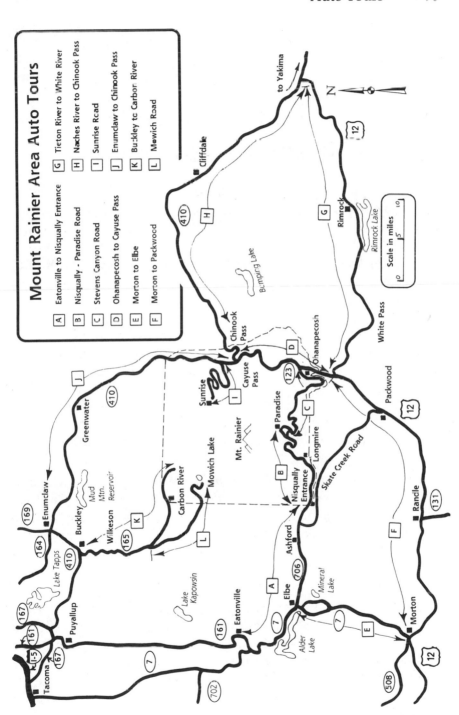

Mount Rainier Area Auto Tours

A Eatonville to Nisqually Entrance
B Nisqually - Paradise Road
C Stevens Canyon Road
D Ohanapecosh to Cayuse Pass
E Morton to Elbe
F Morton to Packwood
G Tieton River to White River
H Naches River to Chinook Pass
I Sunrise Road
J Enumclaw to Chinook Pass
K Buckley to Carbon River
L Mowich Road

Eatonville to Nisqually Entrance

"Indian Henry's Trail," "the Mount Tacoma Road," "the Mountain Highway"—with its many names and many improvements the route up the Nisqually River has long served as the premier approach to Mount Rainier, from Stevens and Van Trump's trip in 1870 to the million-plus tourists who now annually pass through the park's Nisqually Entrance. The course has always had its obstacles, from muddy mountain ridges to confining canyons to numberless yellowjacket nests, but early on it proved to be the least daunting and most direct way to reach the mountain's manifold splendors at Longmire's Springs, Paradise, the Tatoosh Range, and Reflection Lakes. In earlier days, exhausted excursionists found succor at a string of settlements—among them Eatonville, Elbe, and Ashford—whose hotels and stopping places eased the rigors of the trip. Today these towns offer attractions in their own right, preserving buildings and bits of memorabilia that document a century and more of service as *the* gateway to the park.

The auto tour starts in downtown Eatonville at the intersection of Center Street and Washington Avenue (State Highway 161). The route follows the highway through the southern end of town, passing the ruins of the Eatonville Lumber Company mill, 0.3 mile, left, just before crossing the Mashel River.

Eatonville

In the spring of 1889, young Tom Van Eaton rode up from Tacoma to where the Mashel River joined the Nisqually and asked the local Indians where the winter snows were lightest. They pointed to a valley near the rivers' confluence; the location looked good to Van Eaton, who, for $50, soon bought squatter's rights to the spot from an "old man with a long gray beard" known only as "Hank."

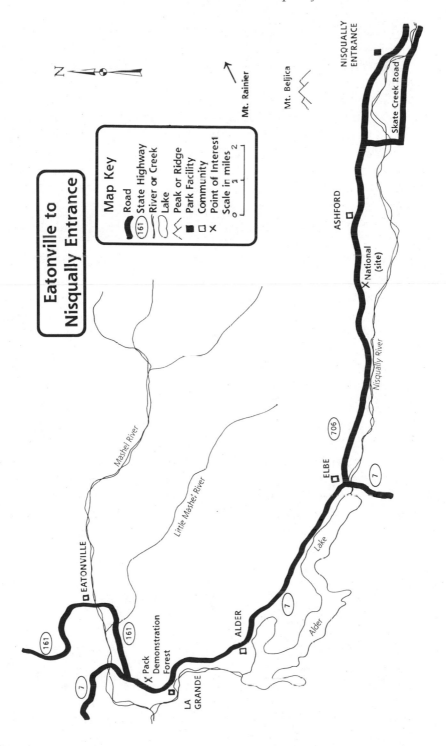

Van Eaton dreamed of developing his own town and over the next four years made a good start. He cleared a patch of "dense forest" and then, using hand-split cedar, built a house, real estate office, and store-post office; to this, Frank Groe added an eight-room hotel. Van Eaton's store at first traded chiefly with the local Indians. Later, when homesteaders became part of his clientele, he would loan them a horse on which to carry their purchases; its job done, the animal was turned loose to find its way back over the mountain trails to the store. As its first postmaster and founding father, Van Eaton graciously gave the community five-eighths of his name.

By 1898 Eatonville was ready for a school; its construction, however, posed certain difficulties. The ever-generous Van Eaton donated the land, logs, and nails, but some of the locals objected to the proposed location. The night before the raising of the new building, several dissidents stole onto the site and sawed four feet off of all the logs; undaunted, the raising party put up a shrunken but nonetheless serviceable schoolhouse. Relocated and renovated, the little structure still houses little people — it is now the Eatonville Cooperative Pre-School, situated in the town's Glacier View Park.

Prosperity arrived at Eatonville in the early 1900s. First the Tacoma Eastern Railroad came through, cutting the day-and-a-half stagecoach trip from Tacoma to the train ride's mere hour and a half. Then, in 1907, Wisconsin investors established the Eatonville Lumber Company, whose mill eventually employed some 250 workers. An improved county road was next; it was soon filled by hordes of weekend "wheelmen," bicyclists from Tacoma who would lunch at the Eatonville Hotel en route to Longmire and Paradise. By now the town was rapidly moving forward, but its antiquated fire-fighting facilities failed to keep up.

Eatonville's Fire Follies

Like many small towns, Eatonville had limited finances, so it economized as best it could. The town clerk, for instance, not only kept the community's records, but also painted the bell tower, repaired the streets, read meters, drafted ordinances, issued liquor licenses, shot stray rabbits, took away dead rats, and maintained the marshal's office. Eatonville also excelled at another way to save money—neglect the local fire department.

The town's early-day response to burning buildings was thus a masterpiece of minimalism: "when the fire bell rang, any male citizen so inclined helped haul out the hose cart and fight the fire." The department skimped on maintenance as well as equipment. In 1918 the bell tower was reported in unsafe condition; nothing was done to repair it, and two years later gale-force winds swept the structure to earth, in the process demolishing the front end of Hose House No. 1.

Eatonvillians cooling off between fires

Soon the fire department was in the news again. Responding to an alarm for a house fire, Nels Christensen and Fred Kittleman, feet flying, rushed to the station, hauled out the hose cart, and raced along the street with it. Up came Rollo Potter, panting for dear life, to lend a hand. It was a mistake; Christensen and Kittleman, charging ahead like a pair of blindered mares, knocked poor Rollo flat. An instant later the cart and its load of hoses clattered over Potter's prostrate form.

If this was an inauspicious start to the decade, things only got worse. In July 1922, a fire broke out east of town near Lynch Creek.

A crew soon dug a protective trench, but it did no good; the blaze jumped the break, trapping six of the men near a railroad track. As the flames closed in, the firefighters put their heads between the ties, where they finally found a bit of air to breathe. C. A. Nettleton meanwhile played a stream of water on them from his logging engine, occasionally turning the water into his own face when the smoke became too thick.

Thanks to Nettleton and the railroad ties, the firemen survived, but their narrow escape was a prelude to an even closer brush with disaster. Just two years later, the woods went alight near Alder, and a 40-mile-per-hour wind quickly whipped the fire north toward—where else?—Eatonville. The gale played havoc with the flames, and soon the blaze burned on two converging fronts; five hundred residents fled as the conflagration surrounded the community. The fire department, with its hose cart, was nearly helpless against the encircling inferno, but a well-placed backfire stopped the burn southwest of town. Then, as the houses on the north end of Washington Avenue were about to go, a *real* fire engine arrived from Tacoma, and, reinforced by additional equipment from Fort Lewis, rushed from hot spot to hot spot, dousing the flames. By evening, a light rain began to fall, and Eatonville was saved.

Despite its flirtation with flame-borne catastrophe, the town failed to upgrade its fire equipment, leaving the community still vulnerable. Structures turned to cinders as the City Council clutched its purse strings and clung to its hose cart; the largest loss was the Eatonville Lumber Company's mill, which went up in December 1932. By the following year, the town had suffered a series of four near-fatal house fires, including, as a grand finale, one in which the firefighters:

1) spent several minutes trying to locate the hydrant wrench;

2) couldn't open the first hydrant once they found the wrench;

3) displayed great difficulty opening a second hydrant;

4) had two lengths of hose burst after they at last got water.

Inside her blazing home, would-be victim Mrs. George Sabourin watched the farce unfolding below her; finally, giving up all hope of rescue, she leapt to safety. After the blaze the firemen failed to drain and dry the remaining hoses. Mildew ate into them, and six more burst when tested six months later.

This final debacle at last set the wheels of change turning. Slowly. The fire department expended $27 to purchase a second-hand Dodge coupe, which the volunteers themselves then converted into a fire truck. Dubbed "Mae West," it was finally ready for action by 1935. The same year, with no other money forthcoming, the firemen donated their own salaries toward purchasing a new pump. The momentum carried away the department, and only seven years later it bought a *new* engine; $100 of the purchase price was provided by—of course—the volunteers.

Then, early in 1949, came the department's greatest moment. Fire protection had improved so much that the State Rating Bureau advanced Eatonville from an eighth-class fire insurance rating to seventh-class.

The announcement, to the surprise of no one, came on April Fool's Day.

The forest that had confronted Van Eaton stretched for miles across the mountains, and Eatonville's part in harvesting it enabled the town to become "one of Washington's most important lumber-producing and log-shipping centers." All this activity had the predictable effect; the timber gradually thinned out, and by the 1940s the Eatonville Lumber Company's mill was operating only intermittently. When the mill closed for good in 1953, the town scrambled to sustain itself. The situation eventually stabilized as workers found jobs in neighboring cities while retaining their homes in Eatonville, anchored there, perhaps, by the community's "locust tree lined streets,...ivy covered school buildings," and other country charms. In fact, the town for a time even experienced a housing shortage, a circumstance that would have pleased Tom Van Eaton, seated in his real estate office, no end.

The community still preserves many reminders of the its colorful past, including such relics as Eatonville Lumber Company's mill, whose 80-foot teepee burner rusts in magnificent decay above the Mashel River, and the former clinic of Dr. A. W. Bridge, who started his famed contract medicine practice here in 1909. Far across town is the Eatonville cemetery, whose northeast corner contains the tidy, compact graves of Japanese millworkers and their families.

Where are You, Shinako Nakatani?

On August 14, 1905, S. Masuoka, a foreman at Eatonville's Goodwin Mill, was standing near the large drive wheel of the mill engine. Suddenly "his clothes became entangled in the spokes and he was carried through the air at an alarming rate of speed, fortunately coming in contact, however, with nothing solid." Masuoka attributed "his escape to his usual good luck, this being his third miraculous escape from death."

Mr. Masuoka of the many miracles was among the first Japanese workers to arrive in Eatonville. More soon followed, lured by the call of H. S. Mitchell, manager of the Eatonville Lumber Company, who actively recruited them for his labor force. The company provided the immigrants with their own section of row housing, along with a community hall that was used for both church services and wrestling matches. A colony of some 100 Japanese-Americans developed, and Eatonville became known as "Little Tokyo." The colonists were exemplary citizens; for nearly 40 years their names were unknown on the town's police blotter, with nary a Japanese ever arrested or involved in a brawl.

Then came Pearl Harbor. Six months later, a fleet of buses arrived, the Japanese compliantly climbed aboard, and none were ever seen in Eatonville again; after a brief time at the Puyallup fair grounds, they were sent to internment camps in Montana, California, and Idaho. An anti-Japanese association formed at Sumner, with a branch in Eatonville. If any of the colonists had wanted to return after the war, they didn't.

Today, little is left to mark the nearly four decades that Japanese-Americans lived in Eatonville. A yellowed page records the 1924 Fourth of July baseball game, when the Japanese team outlasted the town "regulars," 7-6; an account of Eatonville High School reveals that the 1940 class salutatorian was Miss Shinako Nakatani; a shaded section of the town cemetery, with its close-packed gravestones, testifies to the Japanese custom of burying their dead in a sitting position.

Unless protected by another miracle, S. Masuoka is long since in his own grave. But Shinako Nakatani could well be still alive. Is she perhaps somewhere on the Sound, enjoying a gray-haired grandmotherhood? Does she ever recall Eatonville and the promise of the future she must have felt as she marched at graduation?

We find no answer to these questions. The story of her life is incomplete, interrupted by a war she had no part in and by an attitude of intolerance she did not create. We ask, "where are you, Shinako Nakatani?" but hear only 50 years of silence. The burden of being born Japanese at the wrong time, in the wrong place, has swallowed her like the night.

Eatonville Lumber Co. mill

Modern-day Eatonville offers a full range of tourist services, including lodging, dining, gasoline, grocery stores, laundromat, and showers.

After running through a bit of the Mashel River Valley, Highway 161 ends, mile 3.0, at a junction with State Highway 7. Here the auto tour turns left, presently passing the handsome log and shingle entrance building, left, for the Pack Demonstration Forest.

Pack Demonstration Forest

Established in 1926 with a donation from Charles Lathrop Pack, President of the American Tree Association, the 4,300-acre facility serves as a research unit for the University of Washington's College of Forestry. It includes an interpretive center with a walk-through model of the watershed, an arboretum, a stand of old-growth Douglas-fir, several trails, and a waterfall on the Mashel River.

Highway 7 twists through the hamlet of La Grande at mile 4.0. A post office/store is the only business in town.

La Grande

French Canadians employed by the Hudson's Bay Company called the Nisqually River's deep gorge "the grand place." Its grandeur notwithstanding, the city of Tacoma built a hydroelectric plant here in 1912, converting the rush of the canyon-bound watercourse into kilowatts. A hotel and general store catered to the construction crews; later came a gas station that served Rainier-bound motorists. During World War II the La Grande Dam added its restriction to the river.

The highway then winds high above the Nisqually, passing a pullout, mile 5.1, right, that offers views of the deep river canyon and of the La Grande Dam. Another pullout, 6.6 miles, right, provides a perspective of the dark fan of concrete that is the Alder Dam. The town of Alder, mile 7.5, has a store.

Alder

Homesteaders who arrived here in the 1890s found a vast stand of red alder, the regenerating result of a fire that had consumed the area's conifers more than a century earlier. The replacement species gave the place its name when a post office was established in 1902; soon the Alder Mill Company came in and built a store and hotel. The mill closed in 1911 and burned the following year, but the diminished community continued. During the Depression, the lower floor of the Alder Odd Fellows Hall served as an odd sort of factory, in which a government-sponsored project enabled locals to convert surplus Southern cotton into mattresses. Alder was subsequently described as "a trading center for a community of mountaineers," where:

> Dressed in mackinaws, high "tin pants," and red hats, the men group about trucks, loaded with firewood and heavy logs, and chat in drawling tones. Red-cheeked women gather about the town's lone store and exchange bits of gossip. Living on mountain ranches, these people, descended from emigrants who came here from Tennessee, Kentucky, and the Carolinas, supplement a livelihood gained from their own logging efforts with a few vegetables grown on none too productive soil. (*Washington: A Guide to the Evergreen State*, p. 529)

Soon such picturesque scenes were found only on higher ground, when the low-lying village was relocated in 1943 as Alder Dam's backwater flooded the area.

East of town the road runs above the stump-stippled shore of Alder Lake and then enters Elbe, mile 13.0. Here travelers will find a store, gas, food, and lodging.

Elbe (EL-be)

Settled in the late 1880s by a predominantly German population, the budding burg was subsequently named for the Elbe River valley. The community was slow in growing; a traveler coming up from Tacoma in 1893, after passing though "the densest forest I have ever seen," found at Elbe only "a hotel, a store, a saloon and one house, of the same characteristic construction." The six-room Hotel Tourist was rough-built, and, "with the loose joints of the boards, if anybody whispered, anywhere, all in the house could hear it." The following year a fire destroyed the tiny Tourist (over the years every hotel and restaurant burned at least once), but it was promptly replaced by a 48-room log structure built by Henry and Charles Lutkens. Henry proved an adept fisherman, supplying the new hotel's table with trout pulled from the nearby Nisqually.

Large lumber interests, including the Weyerhauser Company, began buying timber from the local settlers about 1900. Storekeeper Adam Sachs then started the area's first mill in 1902, which was soon followed by several others. Business boomed even bigger when the Tacoma Eastern Railroad arrived in 1904 and started hauling out timber and hauling in tourists. Completion of a new gravel road to Mount Rainier five years later gave further impetus to the community's economy; the greatest beneficiary was no doubt Elbe *Union* editor, stage owner, and town blacksmith Levi Engle, who in 1911 added a garage to his many other enterprises. His first customer was a big one — 326-pound President William Howard Taft, bound for his visit to the park.

The garage proved a bonanza for Engle, since for a time it was the only service station along the highway to the mountain. For Labor Day, 1916, Engle had two mechanics on duty plus his wife, Pearl, who herself hand pumped over 1,000 gallons of gas by the time she finished at 1:30 A.M.

Elbe

While tourists came through town in ever-increasing numbers, Elbe's other economic mainstay, logging, diminished. By 1941 residents peered up at a "denuded mountain range," and just three years later the area's biggest employer, the mill at nearby National, shut down for good; Elbe's 1930 population of 437 dropped to 56 by the 1990s. Nowadays, the town's main attractions are based on the past: its railroad heritage is recalled by several stationary cars that house a restaurant and shops and by an excursion train, variously pulled by one of several restored steam locomotives, that travels to picturesque Mineral. Beyond the track, the Evangelical Lutheran Church (built 1906) petitely preserves the town's German religious tradition. With only six pews and some forty-odd seats, it was once reputed to be the "second smallest church in the world." The iron cross on its steeple was forged by jack-of-all-trades Engle, whose name (spelled Engel) appropriately means "angel" in German.

South of town at mile 13.3 is a junction: State Highway 7, right, continues on its way to Morton (see p. 154); our route, left, now follows State Highway 706. The road runs eastward through fields and forest, passing the turnoff, mile 16.9, left, for Mount Rainier National Park's headquarters (238 Avenue East). A rail crossing at mile 19.5, just after the Mt. Rainier Lions Club, points toward nearly obliterated National, right.

National

Little now remains to locate the once-large community of National, which for nearly 40 years was the mill town of the Pacific National Lumber Company. Started when the Tacoma Eastern Railroad arrived in the early 1900s, National eventually housed some 1,500 residents. The original sawmill burned in 1912, but the company soon built an expanded facility that specialized in cutting large logs: a record specimen, brought down from nearby Mineral, measured 225 feet in length, had a 48-foot circumference, and was 800 years old; head sawyer Jim Daly needed a steam dragsaw with an 18-foot blade to make the initial cuts. A series of three railroad flatcars transported National's biggest timbers. Using this system the mill once shipped out three beams, each measuring three feet square and 150 feet in length, for use in constructing the Ford Motor Company's factory in Dearborn, Michigan. Many similar mammoths were converted into spars, masts, and keels for ships.

When sawyer Daly moved to National in 1920, he and his family were provided a company house for $6 a month; the wage for his highly skilled job was $4.96 for a ten-hour day. Daly sawed National's timber until there was none left to cut. By 1944, with the hillsides bare and the mill owner ill, the property was sold to an Aberdeen plywood company; the mill closed, and what remained of National was later purchased by Weyerhauser. Some of the town's houses were moved to Ashford and eventually the entire community disappeared. Today, visitors will find only a vacant space to stare at, a far cry from what was there in 1940:

> The great red buildings of the mill, its rusted stacks belching black smoke and white steam, dominate the town. Crowded close together and fronting crooked, planked streets are tiny box-like cottages, painted in the same dingy red as the mill....Citizens arise in the morning, eat their meals, and go to bed by the mill whistle. (*Washington: A Guide to the Evergreen State*, p. 530)

Motoring to the Mountain

Whistleless, its buildings vanished, old National slumbers to the sound of the midday breeze that, like a lingering lullaby, now rustles the rising cottonwoods.

Ashford's business district begins at 20.7 miles; a gas station, showers, stores, shops, restaurants, and lodging accommodations line the road.

Ashford

Called Suh-ho-tas by the local Indians for the black raspberries that grew throughout the area, the designation was corrupted by early white arrivals to "Succotash" Valley. When James B. Kernahan and his family relocated here from Tacoma in 1885, their nearest neighbor lived some 20 miles away, and "Kernahan's" soon became an important stop on the trail to Mount Rainier. Travelers commented favorably on the family's "fine strawberries and raspberries," while perhaps puzzling over the absence of the corn and lima beans seemingly promised by the valley's name.

Anxious for access to the area's timber, the Tacoma Eastern Railroad established a terminus here in 1904, the same year that Walter Ashford platted the town that bears his name. The train line boosted travel to the mountain, so in 1912 the Mesler family accordingly expanded their farmhouse stopping place into an inn; in a neat division of labor, Alexander Mesler's three daughters milled the lumber for the new building and his two sons constructed it. Alexander himself apparently supervised.

Tourism gradually outpaced logging as Ashford's main activity. By the 1940s the town catered not only to park-bound travelers but also to bear and deer hunters; one local kept a string of "varmint" dogs for use in tracking such bounty animals as cougars and lynx.

Kernahan Road, mile 23.6, offers a connection, right, with Forest Service Access Route #52 (Skate Creek Road).

Skate Creek Road

This paved, two-lane road (closed in winter), runs some 23 miles between Ashford and Packwood. Midway the route passes Bear Prairie, site of the Indian village where Indian Henry once lived and where Sluiskin was engaged to guide Hazard Stevens and P. B. Van Trump on their approach to the peak. The road then winds beneath a canopy of bigleaf maple in the lush canyon of Skate Creek, providing a scenic shortcut to the Ohanapecosh section of the park

Highway 706 passes a series of roadside businesses before the auto tour concludes, mile 27.1, at the Nisqually Entrance to Mount Rainier National Park. The Nisqually to Paradise auto tour (see p. 108) begins here.

Nisqually Entrance Arch

Nisqually-Paradise Road

By far the park's most popular thoroughfare, this winding, climbing route passes through history-rich Longmire, encounters such scenic enticements as Ricksecker Point, and then concludes high on the mountainside at panoramic Paradise. Hiking trails and photographers' viewpoints abound, complemented by three picnic areas and two campgrounds. Many motorists who make the excursion to Paradise as a mere day-trip will leave, long after dusk, convinced that an entire week would be more appropriate.

Starting at the Nisqually Entrance Arch, the auto tour immediately arrives at the park entrance station.

Nisqually Entrance

A pair of picturesque structures enhance the Nisqually Entrance. Encountered first is the impressive wooden arch through which incoming traffic passes; erected in 1911 and reconstructed in 1973, it is composed of nine immense cedar logs. Just past the portal and to the right is the park's oldest building, the Oscar Brown Cabin, built in 1908 and used by the first park ranger for collecting entrance fees. Ranger Brown was no newcomer to the area, being one of the four Enumclawians who climbed Mount Rainier in 1891 and placed a tall flagpole on the summit. Brown put up the cabin himself, with the help of a horse to skid and raise the logs; an attractive ornament is the fan-shaped limbwork beneath the gable.

The route proceeds eastward through lush old-growth forest, passing Sunshine Point, 0.4 mile, right.

Sunshine Point Campground & Picnic Area

Located on the edge of the Nisqually River, this year-round facility provides a picnicking area and 18 campsites. It has no showers or flush toilets, but compensates by being located in a lovely grove of red alder.

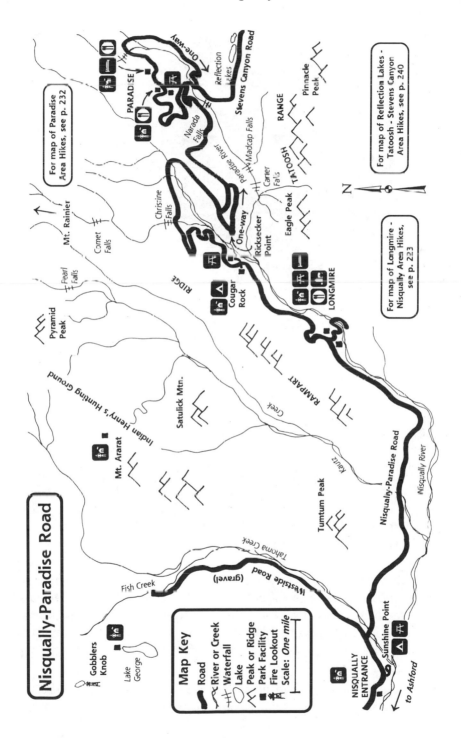

Nisqually-Paradise Road

For map of Paradise Area Hikes, see p. 232

For map of Reflection Lakes - Tatoosh - Stevens Canyon Area Hikes, see p. 240

For map of Longmire - Nisqually Area Hikes, see p. 223

One-way

Stevens Canyon Road

Reflection Lakes

PARADISE

Pinnacle Peak

Narada Falls

Madcap Falls

RANGE

TATOOSH

Paradise River

Carter Falls

Mt. Rainier

Christine Falls

One-way

Eagle Peak

Comet Falls

Ricksecker Point

N

Pearl Falls

RIDGE

Cougar Rock

LONGMIRE

Pyramid Peak

RAMPART

Indian Henry's Hunting Ground

Satulick Mtn.

Creek

Mt. Ararat

Kautz

Nisqually-Paradise Road

Tumtum Peak

Nisqually River

Tahoma Creek

Westside Road (gravel)

Fish Creek

Gobblers Knob

Lake George

Sunshine Point

Map Key
- Road
- River or Creek
- Waterfall
- Lake
- Peak or Ridge
- Park Facility
- Fire Lookout
- Scale: *One mile*

NISQUALLY ENTRANCE

to Ashford

Oscar Brown Cabin

Westside Road (gravel), exits left at mile 1.0.

Westside Road

This now-truncated route once ran all the way to the North Pu-yallup; later it was closed at Klapatche Point, on the ridge above the river. During the 1980s and early 1990s, debris flows from the South Tahoma Glacier severely damaged the roadbed near Fish Creek, and today Westside Road is open to motor vehicles only along its first three miles. The section to the north, which offers access to the Lake George–Gobbler's Knob area and the Wonderland Trail, can still be used by foot, horse, and bicycle traffic. Motorists who make the abbreviated Westside excursion will find a canyon corridor filled with such diverse plantlife as alumroot, stonecrop, and bigleaf maple.

Nisqually-Paradise Road passes over Tahoma Creek, 1.2 miles, en-counters a section of forest heavy in western hemlock and western redcedar, and then crosses Kautz Creek, mile 3.4. The Kautz Creek Trail leaves from the left just past the bridge; a short boardwalk promptly branches from the trail, leading to an overlook of the creek.

Kautz Creek

The devastated channel of Kautz Creek testifies to the lingering effects of a giant mudflow that surged down the canyon in 1947. Here the flow washed out the bridge and covered the roadway with a mud and debris mix that included "boulders as big as automobiles." At the overlook is a close-up view of the destruction, including the stark white trunks of the many trees killed (but left standing) by the event. The silt-stuffed stream was named for Lieutenant August V. Kautz, who nearly succeeded in scaling Mount Rainier in 1857.

Soon the road reenters forest, winding past shadowy gatherings of devil's club. The Twin Firs Trail departs a parking pullout, mile 4.4, left. Another pullout, 6.1 miles, right, provides a long-range view of sharp-pointed Eagle Peak. At mile 6.4, right, is Longmire: the first turnoff, right, is for the main parking lot; the second turnoff, also right, immediately passes a spur to the Wonderland Trail, left, before passing through a complex of park administration and residence buildings. After curving uphill, this paved side road crosses the Nisqually River, runs past the Eagle Peak Trailhead (see p. 225), and then arrives at the Longmire Community Building a half mile from its start.

Longmire

Situated between the Nisqually River and a spring-fed meadow, Longmire has long been a center of park activity. The location takes its name from the family that developed a resort here in the 1880s.

Old Spot Finds the Spot

When James Longmire returned with the Bayley party from their 1883 climb of the mountain, he found that their horses, which he'd hobbled by the riverbank southwest of Eagle Peak, had disappeared. Some searching led him to a swampy meadow, where his horse, "Old Spot," was drinking from a spring. Longmire tasted the water and found it "charged with minerals."

"Old Spot" with Elcaine and Maude (?) Longmire

The discovery prompted the enterprising Longmire to file a mining claim on the property; he and his family soon developed the springs into a summer resort. Within a decade the site featured several cabins and a pair of bathhouses, along with a two-story, split cedar hotel. James's wife, Varinda, cooked on a stove composed of flat rocks and a piece of sheet iron, baking "the light breads and huckleberry pies for which the hostelry became famous." The building itself also made an impression on its guests, one of whom noted that it

> ...may be wanting in modern convenience, but it possesses a charm in being in keeping with the surroundings. Carved out of the cedars of the forest and painted with ochre from a mine near by, it is typical of pioneer life in the far west. (E. S. Ingraham, quoted in Molenaar, pp. 53-4)

The family improved the routes that connected the springs with both Ashford and Paradise, and their resort became a popular stopping place for travelers on their way to and from the mountain. In all, the Longmires made a living there for nearly 30 years, not a bad return on what started out merely as Old Spot's drinking spot.

The Tacoma Eastern Railroad, whose line had reached a terminus at Ashford in 1904, constructed a 36-room hotel at nearby Longmire just two years later. Soon known as the National Park

Inn, it was far fancier than the Longmires' aging, rough-hewn lodging house, but there was enough business to fill both establishments during the ensuing boom days of tourism. In 1908 the park service put up its first building at Longmire, a ranger's cabin; other structures soon followed.

Meanwhile, the Longmires had trouble with the government. Park officials were put off by the shabby appearance of the family's operations, and the General Land Office denied Varinda's claim to additional property. Her son Elcaine, who'd given up work on a claim of his own, died at the springs in 1915. The family leased out the hotel the following year, but kept ownership of their land until 1939, when the park finally bought them out.

In 1918 the Rainier National Park Company (RNPC), by then the park's main concessionaire, leased both the Longmires' hotel and Tacoma Eastern's inn. The RNPC dismantled and burned the old hotel two years later, at the same time moving the inn's recently built annex across the road. When the inn itself burned in 1926, the annex took over its name and, as such, operates to this day.

Two years after the loss of the original inn, Longmire had a new building to serve as its showpiece. Designed to house the park's headquarters, its lower story was composed of rounded, light gray

National Park Inn

Longmire Administration Building

stones that artfully decreased in size as the walls rose upward. Corners were crafted from huge vertical logs, several feet in diameter, and the second floor was finished with log half-rounds. Massive yet graceful, the structure still enhances its surroundings with an organic, eye-catching ease, proof that the hand of man, when well directed, can create in harmony with nature.

Today, with Rainier's main administrative operations removed to Tahoma Woods, the building houses staff offices and a ranger station. Southward, across a park service road, a cabin that served as an even earlier headquarters has long been home to Longmire's museum; within its walls are eye-catching exhibits, some dating back a half century or more, that display the careful printing and drawing of an era when pencil and hand accomplished what is now the province of computers.

Fronting Nisqually-Paradise Road is the National Park Inn, its long verandah lined with comfortable chairs, its shingled sides reflecting a rustic respectability undimmed by the decades. The facility offers 25 rooms, most with private bath, and a dining room and take-out food window (see p. 277).

Other noteworthy structures at Longmire include the gift shop, built in 1911 and first used as a club house for guests at the inn; the now-closed gas station — the Standard Oil Company's contribution to park architecture; the striking 1924 suspension bridge, which spans the Nisqually a short distance to the east; and, beyond the bridge, the 1927 Community Building that stands next to the now-closed Longmire Campground.

The Trail of the Shadows (see p. 223), begins on the left side of Nisqually-Paradise Road opposite the museum. From Longmire the auto tour starts uphill; the Wonderland Trail promptly crosses at a switchback, mile 6.8. A pullout, 8.5 miles, right, is the starting point of the Carter and Madcap Falls hike (see p. 228), which follows part of the Wonderland route. An intersection just beyond the pullout offers access to a large, well-shaded picnic area, right, and the Cougar Rock Campground, left.

Cougar Rock Campground

Set on a gently sloping benchland between Rampart Ridge and the Nisqually River, the campground offers a variety of forested settings in which to pitch a tent or set up an RV. The namesake rock, which sits at the base of the ridge, once served as an observation point for mountain lions; the far-sighted predators made up their day's menu while gazing down on deer grazing in the meadow below. Times change, and today most of the area's meals are those cooked on stoves in the camping area's 200 individual and five group sites. The facility's original fireplaces almost failed to last their first weekend. Alto Albright, in charge of the campground during its July Fourth opening, heard what he thought was the sound of firecrackers; going to investigate, he discovered the noise came from the river rocks used to line the fireplaces, which were shattering — the moisture-laden stones, upon being heated, first expanded and then exploded. Albright and the campers endured about a hundred blasts, but amazingly no one was injured by the unexpected explosiveness of Cougar Rock's rocks.

Pale gray granodiorite (white feldspar mixed with black hornblende and biotite) from the Tatoosh pluton is intermittently visible between Longmire and Christine Falls. The pluton was created about 12 million years ago when molten rock pushed through earlier formations and solidified; it serves as the bedrock for Mount Rainier and, as might be expected, forms much of the Tatoosh Range. The granodiorite's "salt and pepper" appearance makes it one of the most attractive rock types in the park.

Switchbacks take the road upward to the Van Trump Park–Comet Falls Trailhead (see p. 229), mile 10.5, left. Just ahead, the route passes above the frothy cascade of Christine Falls on a striking stone bridge. A pullout, right, is for the short path that leads to a vista of the falls.

Christine Falls

Christine Falls

The falls were named for P. B. Van Trump's daughter. When nine years old, little Christine Louise climbed two-thirds of the way up the peak; she hoped on her next attempt to reach the top. Plagued by a nervous disorder called Saint Vitus Dance, she never made it, but the falls that bear her name commemorate her unquenchable spirit.

A stark steel and concrete bridge carries the route across the Nisqually River, 11.7 miles.

Nisqually River

The bridge rises a hundred feet above the canyon bottom—high enough, it is hoped, to avoid the fate of two earlier, lower bridges that were ripped out by the rampaging river. First spanning the Nisqually here was a timbered truss built in 1910; pest damage caused its removal after only 15 years service. Then it was time for the river to take over. In 1932, a series of 50-mile-an-hour surges swept down a torrent of water and ice mixed with boulders 15 feet high, and away went the replacement bridge. A 1955 freshet, although slightly slower, again brought with it many room-sized rocks, sweeping sections of bridge #3 nine miles downstream to the park's Nisqually Entrance. Calamities such as these breed caution, so the 90-ton steel beams in the current structure's main pier were x-rayed prior to installation; found without flaw, they have withstood the water ever since.

Goatsbeard clambers up the roadbank, left, as the route ascends above the Nisqually. At mile 12.7 the auto tour takes the one-way scenic alternate, right, around panoramic Ricksecker Point. Overlooks provide views of the mountain, the Nisqually Glacier and its river canyon, and Eagle Peak.

Ricksecker Point

The point was named for Eugene Ricksecker, the engineer who surveyed the road to Paradise with such precision that much of his original course is still followed today. When working earlier for the Geological Survey, Ricksecker "explored and climbed the fastness of every mountain on the Pacific Coast, from Mount Baker in the north of Washington to Southern California." Later he helped develop the ship canal connecting Seattle's harbor with Lake Washington and, in 1902, supervised the dredging of Tacoma's harbor. Ricksecker began his survey of the Paradise road in 1904; he died in 1911, the year the first cars traveled the route's entire length. Motorists who drive the road today will likely agree with Asahel Curtis's comment on Ricksecker's work: "splendid."

For all its fine engineering, the upper stretches of the newly opened road were considered somewhat hazardous by park officials. So it was that soon after cars began to frequent the route, the following roadside sign was erected:

> Boys under 21 and women
> will not be permitted to drive automobiles
> between Nisqually Glacier Bridge
> and Paradise Valley.

*The auto tour (open to **all** licensed drivers) rounds the point and then passes a pullout, right, that showcases various mid-elevation conifers, including noble fir and western white pine. The loop rejoins the main road, 13.8 miles, passing through a regenerated forest once ravaged by fire.*

The Yellowjackets and the Yellow-cedars

The area east of Ricksecker Point was long known as the Silver Forest, where the pale spires of burnt Alaska yellow-cedar marked the site of a disastrous attempt by Ben Longmire to burn out a nest of yellowjackets. Fanned by high winds, the fire raced through acres of conifers before the flames subsided. The area's loss later proved to be the Rainier National Park Company's gain, for the forest remnants were salvaged for use in building the Paradise Inn. By then the weather had bleached the trees a beautiful silver gray, the decay-resistant cedar hardening and darkening with age. After the wood was worked, it finished to a rich satin yellow—a reminder, perhaps, of the timbers' colorful history.

At mile 14.7, motorists may hear a chorus of cherubic croakers at the marshy area known as Frog Heaven, right. Pinnacle Peak can be seen from a pullout, mile 15.2, right, as it rises from the center of the Tatoosh Range. Just ahead is the parking area, right, for the Narada Falls Trail (see p. 232) and the Narada-Paradise Trail.

Narada Falls

The presence of the Paradise River's premier cascade has long made this a favorite park stopping place. Ricksecker's original road crossed the river here, just above the falls, on the beautiful stone bridge that still serves pedestrians. A park ranger once occupied a small cabin nearby, maintaining a control station for the one-way traffic to and from Paradise; autos negotiated a set of switchbacks carved into the talus slope to the east. In the 1930s one of the park's six CCC camps filled the flat beyond the bridge.

Nisqually-Paradise Road twists and turns uphill past willow and various wildflowers, reaching a junction, mile 16.2, with Stevens Canyon Road, right (see p. 125). We go left, passing the lower turnoff to the Paradise Picnic Area, 17.6 miles, right, and then the upper turnoff at mile 18.0, right. Just ahead is the access road, left, for the visitor center parking lot, followed by the parking area, left, for the Paradise Ranger Station and the Paradise Inn.

Paradise

The upper reaches of the Paradise River were known to the local Indians as Saghalie Illahe — "land of peace." The current name was bestowed by the Longmire family when they visited the valley in 1885. Although the area had served as a camping spot for climbers and hikers since the Stevens-Van Trump ascent in 1870, it was 25 years before regular tourist lodging was offered. The most notable early facility was John L. Reese's "Camp of the Clouds," also known as Reese's Camp; it was located just below the Alta Vista point on the ridge north of the present-day visitor center. Reese maintained "a mountain hotel composed entirely of tents," supplemented by log cabins for cooking, eating, and lounging. It ran from 1897 to 1915; Reese then sold out to the Rainier National Park Company, which continued the operation until 1930. In later years, the square excavations for the camp's tent platforms pockmarked Alta Vista's south slope, but these were finally obliterated by the asphalt walkways that now ascend from the Paradise parking lot.

After its inception, the RNPC moved quickly to improve accommodations, taking less than a year to build the impressive Paradise Inn, which opened on July 1, 1917. Material for constructing the building proved close at hand — the square mile of dead but not decayed Alaska yellow-cedar that had burned over 30 years earlier east of Ricksecker Point. The trees, "left standing to cure in nature's own dry kiln," were also put to another use.

Hans Fraehnke's Hand-Made Friends

In September, 1949, an elderly man with wire-rimmed glasses and a walrus mustache could be found examining the furniture in the lobby of the Paradise Inn. He was Hans Fraehnke, a carpenter from Lübeck, Germany, who had learned his trade 70 years earlier under Europe's rigorous apprentice system, and his interest was both professional and personal. Fraehnke looked closely at the carefully crafted tables and chairs, the upright piano, and the huge grandfather's clock, all made of richly hued Alaska yellow-cedar. His attentiveness was not surprising, for Fraehnke was renewing an acquaintance with old friends—almost three decades earlier he had built all the pieces himself.

Every spring for seven years the conscientious craftsman trudged through the March snows to reach the inn, where he labored until the weather of November drove him out. In wintertime, Fraehnke made the sections of the clock at his shop in Fife, assembling them at the inn after they were moved there by truck. Tourists marveled at the furniture's beautiful workmanship, including a roll top on the piano made of tree branches, without knowing that Fraehnke accomplished it all with a left hand that had lost three and a half fingers in a work accident.

"I figured I couldn't make a living for a wife after that," Fraehnke said of his injury, "so I never got married." He lived a full life nonetheless, singing in Tacoma's Deutscher Sängerbund, writing poetry for the city's German-language newspaper, and, according to his neighbors, becoming a "splendid" cook. Although he lacked a family, Fraehnke nonetheless left a lasting legacy, as anyone who admires the inn's golden, gleaming furniture can attest.

Fraehnke's finest

The inn proved such a great attraction that in 1920 a large four-story annex was added to its eastern side. Despite the Depression, Paradise saw a slew of major modifications in 1931, with the construction of 275 frame housekeeping cabins, a lodge to service them, and, of all things, a nine-hole golf course. The latter was but one of many amusements offered during the decade: tourists could also take guided horseback rides on the Skyline Trail, up onto the Tatoosh ridgeline, or to other nearby locations; weather permitting, they could ride a ski tow to the top of Alta Vista. Indoors, the men

Lobby, Paradise Inn

might visit the inn's barber shop, where they could get a shave or haircut, have their hair bobbed or singed, have their beard trimmed, be given a shampoo or one of three different massages, and receive a sunburn treatment; at the inn's beauty shop, madame found an even wider range of services, from a marcel and bob curl to an Egyptian rinse.

When it came time to eat, Chef Harry Pappajohn was always ready with a kitchen full of food. Pappajohn, who started as a cook's helper when the inn opened in 1917, came to oversee the entire restaurant operation. By 1959, he estimated that he'd fed more than a million and a half hungry visitors, including millionaire John D. Rockefeller, who was impressed enough to leave a $400 tip.

When the RNPC ended its tenure as concessionaire in the 1950s, the park purchased the company's buildings; many of those at Paradise, including the lodge, were removed. For a time it seemed the inn would meet the same fate, but an upheaval of public protest saved it. During 1980-81 the inn received a much-needed overhaul; in the meantime it had gained a new neighbor on Theosophy Ridge, the flying-saucerlike Henry M. Jackson Memorial Visitor Center that appeared to have landed there while searching for the Space Needle. The structure, it turned out, was indeed somewhat out of place, having originally been designed for a park facility in Hawaii. Aside from giving tourists the impression they've arrived on Mars instead of at Paradise, much of the building is remarkably functional, moving sight-seers up spiral ramps to mid-level exhibits and a top floor observation room that offers a close-up of Mount Rainier and longer range views of the Tatoosh Range and other peaks. A bookstore, information desk, scale model of the mountain, restrooms, gift shop, and snack bar occupy the main floor, while public showers are in the basement.

East of the visitor center is the rustic stone ranger station that dates from 1921, and beyond it, still flourishing, is the inn. The building's vast lobby rises three stories to an open-beam ceiling, its ground floor anchored at either end by a great stone fireplace and the intervening space still filled with Hans Fraehnke's finely crafted furniture. The dining room, although no longer supervised by Pop Pappajohn, features an attractive setting with its own complement of rustic wood chairs and tables. A cocktail lounge, gift shop, and snack bar all lie off the lobby, while rooms of various shapes and sizes are upstairs and in the adjacent annex (see p. 278).

Departing from the visitor center parking lot are the Nisqually Vista hike (see p. 234), and the Alta Vista–Deadhorse Creek hike (see p. 235); the latter connects with the Moraine Trail. Leaving the parking area near the ranger station is the Skyline Trail (see p. 237), which connects with the Golden Gate and Paradise Glacier trails. The Lakes Trail leaves the road, mile 18.5, right, beyond the east end of the parking lot.

From the parking area the auto tour proceeds down the one-way exit road, passing the rock-framed outlet for Myrtle Falls, mile 18.9, left, and

Paradise Ranger Station

entering the top of a meadowy valley. Just after crossing the Paradise River, 19.1 miles, the route reaches the Fourth Crossing Trail, left; in summer, wildflowers fill the surrounding slopes. At mile 20.3 the Lakes Loop crosses the road. The auto tour then ends at Stevens Canyon Road, 20.7 miles (see p. 125). A right turn here connects in 0.2 mile with the two-way section of Nisqually-Paradise Road.

Stevens Canyon Road

Delayed by World War II, Stevens Canyon Road took 25 years to build; its completion in 1957 at last offered an in-park link between Paradise and Sunrise. Spectacular scenery marks the entire route, from the postcard-perfect Reflection Lakes to the awesome declivity of Stevens Canyon, to the deep defile of Box Canyon. Here, as elsewhere in the park, Mother Nature has writ large, and, thanks to Stevens Canyon Road, the writing is readily apparent.

The auto tour begins at a junction with Nisqually-Paradise Road (see p. 108), promptly crossing the Paradise River and the Narada-Paradise Trail. At 0.2 mile our route passes the lower end of the one-way road from Paradise, left. Stevens Canyon Road then runs below the end of Mazama Ridge, left; downhill to the right are the famed scree-slope switchbacks of Ricksecker's original road, which zigzagged their way up from Narada Falls. A pullout, mile 0.5, right, marks Inspiration Point.

Inspiration Point

For years the park road from the Nisqually Entrance ended here, with only a trail continuing on to Ohanapecosh and the East Side. An ill-conceived "Around-the-Mountain" road was considered as a connecting link; its course would have taken it high on the side of Stevens Ridge and past the snout of the Cowlitz Glacier, but in so doing the route would have run through fragile subalpine country and remained snowbound almost the entire year. In 1932, the park sided with preservationists and approved a lower route down Stevens Canyon, over Backbone Ridge, and on to the Ohanapecosh. During the next decade some $2,000,000 was spent on construction, but World War II interrupted work with the project far from finished. Still stalled in 1949, the Seattle *Times* labeled the route "Rainier's Forgotten Road." The following year finally saw renewed activity, but it was not until September 1957 that the highway at last opened.

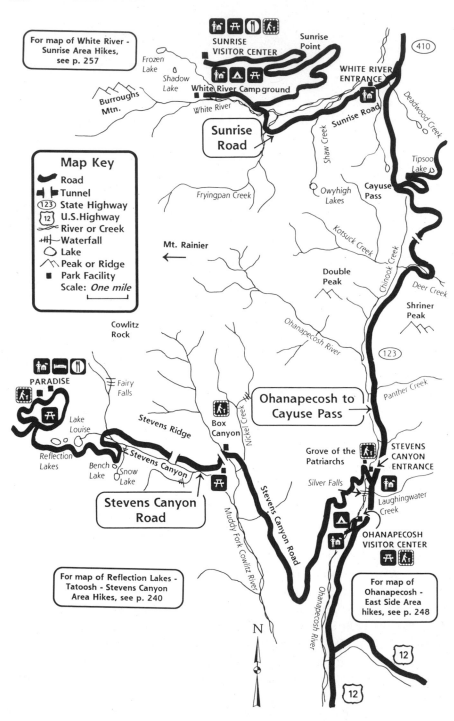

For map of White River - Sunrise Area Hikes, see p. 257

SUNRISE VISITOR CENTER

Sunrise Point

410

WHITE RIVER ENTRANCE

Frozen Lake

Shadow Lake

White River Campground

Burroughs Mtn.

White River

Sunrise Road

Deadwood Creek

Shaw Creek

Sunrise Road

Tipsoo Lake

Owyhigh Lakes

Cayuse Pass

Map Key

〰 Road
🯅 Tunnel
(123) State Highway
(12) U.S. Highway
〜 River or Creek
╫╫ Waterfall
◯ Lake
⋀ Peak or Ridge
■ Park Facility
Scale: *One mile*

Fryingpan Creek

Kotsuck Creek

Mt. Rainier ←

Double Peak

Ohanapecosh River

Chinook Creek

Deer Creek

Shriner Peak

123

Cowlitz Rock

PARADISE

Fairy Falls

Lake Louise

Stevens Ridge

Box Canyon

Ohanapecosh to Cayuse Pass

Panther Creek

Reflection Lakes

Stevens Canyon

Bench Lake

Snow Lake

Grove of the Patriarchs

STEVENS CANYON ENTRANCE

STEVENS CANYON ENTRANCE

Nickel Creek

Silver Falls

Laughingwater Creek

Stevens Canyon Road

Muddy Fork Cowlitz River

Stevens Canyon Road

OHANAPECOSH VISITOR CENTER

For map of Reflection Lakes - Tatoosh - Stevens Canyon Area Hikes, see p. 240

For map of Ohanapecosh - East Side Area hikes, see p. 248

N

Ohanapecosh River

12

12

Soon a roadcut, left, exposes orange-yellow rocks and clay that some 6,000 years ago slid down the side of Mount Rainier from near its summit. On the right, mile 1.1, is a view of Pinnacle Peak; the Wonderland Trail crosses the road just ahead. Big Reflection Lake, left, then comes into view. A large parking area, mile 1.4, left, offers the trailhead for the Reflection Lakes - Mazama Ridge hike (see p. 240) and connections with both the Wonderland and Lakes trails.

Reflection Lakes

Sightseers here witness perhaps the quintessential view of Mount Rainier — the peak rises above conifer-crenelated Mazama Ridge and the icy, rocky slopes of Paradise, while below, the lakes' mirrorlike surfaces each create an inverted image of the mountain, shimmering ever so slightly beneath the afternoon breeze. Once the scene was less striking, confounded by a rampant commercialism that brought a dozen rental boats and a small shoreside store. Also on hand was the store operator, who one summer added an auditory ambiance to the surroundings.

The Resonant Resident of Reflection Lake

Most people come to Mount Rainier for rest and relaxation, but for George Loidhamer, the summer he spent there was probably the busiest of his life. It was 1938, the Depression dragged on, and George, not yet twenty, was happy for any work he could get.

He got lots of it. Entrusted with the concession at Big Reflection Lake, George was on duty every day for the entire summer, and his extensive job description included some unusual tasks.

Selling beer and soda pop and renting out the two-person rowboats were all pretty straightforward activities, but accommodating the needs of inept fishermen was more complex. Certain tourists, who tended to be from the East, seemed unable to land any fish; George, however, devised a way to assist them. Early in the morning he would catch a few trout at the lake, bring them back to the store cabin, and put them in the stream-fed tub where he chilled his drinks. When a disconsolate angler complained about his lack of luck, Loidhamer instructed him to reach into the tub and grab what was swimming there. Clutching two or three fish, the ecstatic Easterner was soon bound for the Paradise Inn, where he'd ask Chef Harry Pappajohn to fry up his "catch."

Much of George's time was spent in his spartan, two-room cabin, either out front in the store or in back utilizing the bed or the cookstove. He did, however, manage two entertainments. On Monday nights he would walk around Inspiration Point and then up to the Paradise Inn for the weekly workers' party, leaving at 11 P.M. to return to the lake. Other times, George would climb the tree next to the cabin and listen in on the park telephone that was attached there. Soon, however, he would answer his own call—the need for sleep—since morning meant the early fish catch and then serving the hundred or so visitors who would come by the store.

There was also one other assignment. Every day the horse guides brought a party down from Paradise, and George, whose family came from Austria, was slated to provide an appropriately alpinesque performance. As the riders approached, he'd "let out a yodel that would echo through the hills." Not unexpectedly, a certain clientele was especially approving—"the Easterners loved it."

Across the road from the Reflection Lakes parking area is the Pinnacle Peak Trailhead (see p. 243), which leads to a panoramic ridge saddle in the middle of the Tatoosh Range.

The Tatoosh Range

A jagged ridgeline of some thirteen pointed peaks that defines the southern side of the park, the Tatoosh (ta-TOOSH—Chinook jargon for "breast") has long enticed climbers who wanted a steeper, rockier challenge than Rainier's more gently sloped snow and ice. The range's somber gray spires have proved more than equal to the task.

Traversing the Thirteen-Peaked Tatoosh

The first climbers to come to the Tatoosh didn't want to be there at all. In 1870 Hazard Stevens and P. B. Van Trump were led across

Scaling the face
of Pinnacle Peak

the range by their guide, Sluiskin, on their way to ascend Mount Rainier. Stevens had suggested going up the Nisqually River valley, which looked easier, but Sluiskin insisted on the Tatoosh traverse, perhaps hoping the extra time required for the longer route would increase his pay.

Within a few years, people needed no prodding to tramp into the Tatoosh. The Mazamas climbing club warmed up for its 1897 ascent of Rainier by practicing on Pinnacle Peak, prompting one of their party, Edward Parsons, to wax eloquent on the ridgeline's allure: "the sawtoothed Tatoosh range stood in serried outline with fire-scarred sides, timber patches, rocky flanks, and beauty spots of flowery meadow between."

Eight years later, a party from the Sierra Club, determining that Pinnacle Peak "did not deserve the honor accorded it of being the highest point of its chain," decided to climb the challenger, a heretofore unnamed, horn-shaped rock mass to the southeast that they promptly christened Unicorn Peak. A frontal assault of the horn itself defeated the attempts of all but the one member of their group, "who combined a longer stretch of arm with more than usual strength and skill." Only later did the Sierrans find a much easier way to the top.

The lure of the Unicorn later led to tragic results. In 1924, Paul Moser, a park guide from Switzerland, and fellow guide Joseph Griggs Jr., of Tacoma, attempted an unscaled route up a thousand-foot perpendicular rockface. Only 30 feet from the top, Moser found his ascent blocked; worse yet, he was unable to retrace his steps. As Griggs attempted to help him down, Moser lost his balance, let go of Griggs's hand, "and dropped like a plummet." He was killed instantly on the rocks near Snow Lake far below.

In 1931 a trio of Tacoma Eagle Scouts created what might be the ultimate test of the Tatoosh. Starting with Eagle Peak in the west, Donald H. Cooper, Verrol Swartz, and Kenneth Powers proceeded east along the entire ridgeline, polishing off all thirteen summits in three days. At Tatoosh Peak they found a register with only 15 names in it; the register on top of the Unicorn held only a dozen. A thirteenth name, Paul Moser's, was missing, but on that summer day seven years after his death, three triumphant boy scouts had found a way to commemorate his daring and determined spirit.

Immediately east of Little Reflection Lake, 1.7 miles, the Wonderland/ Lakes trail departs to the left. The road now drops into Stevens Canyon, crossing Sunbeam Creek and then passing above Louise Lake, 2.4 miles, left. Lining the road are scarlet paintbrush and pearly everlasting.

Stevens Canyon

From the saddle that cradles the Reflection Lakes, the terrain drops eastward into gaping Stevens Canyon, whose void separates the towering Tatoosh Range and massive, wall-like Stevens Ridge. Much of the canyon is scarred by The Burn, the result of huge fires that ravaged the Cowlitz River watershed in 1856 and 1886.

Upper Stevens Canyon

On the right, mile 2.9, is the trailhead for the Bench and Snow Lakes hike (see p. 244); the roadside is seasonally colored by goatsbeard and various penstemons. A hairpin turn, mile 3.6, then takes the route back towards the mountain. After crossing the Wonderland Trail, 4.3 miles, the road bends east at Stevens Creek and begins a long run across the rocky face of Stevens Ridge, offering a view, mile 5.4, right, of the Unicorn and below it, forest-framed Martha Falls. Fireweed and oceanspray now brighten the way.

A tunnel, 7.0 miles, is bracketed by roadbanks containing welded tuff, a white or light gray rock speckled with flecks of darker pumice; the tuff is indeed tough, for it is the long lasting remains of lava erupted some 25 to 30 million years ago. The Box Canyon picnic area appears at mile 8.2, right, followed shortly by an access spur for the Wonderland Trail, also right. The road enters another tunnel, exits at a crossing of the Muddy Fork Cowlitz, and then immediately arrives at the Box Canyon parking area and viewpoint, right. Across the road is the Box Canyon Trail (see p. 246) and a connection with the Wonderland Trail.

Box Canyon

Plunging 180 feet below the road bridge is the dark, rock-sided gorge of the Muddy Fork Cowlitz, whose name derives from its debris-laden cargo of glacial melt. Another branch of the river, the Clear Fork, carries its limpid water down from the Goat Rocks near White Pass; a third stem, once called the Main Fork, has since taken the name of its hot springs and is now known as the Ohanapecosh.

The route turns southeast, running across the forested hillside above the canyon of the Muddy Fork. Roadcuts then expose the reddish laterite soils of the Ohanapecosh Formation. The rock is some 40 million years old and its bed at least 10,000 feet thick.

Vista point west
of Backbone Ridge

A vista point (with telescope), 13.3 miles, right, offers a last view of Mount Rainier. The route then cuts through Backbone Ridge; here the light gray rock of the Stevens Ridge Formation is replaced by the gray-green coloration of the Ohanapecosh Formation. Now the road begins a long, switchbacking descent into the valley of the Ohanapecosh. Vast tracts of conifers cover the slopes, providing a sense of what much of western Washington was like in its pre-logging days. Alder and bigleaf maple add their leafy foliage to the roadside. The Olallie Creek Trail crossing, mile 18.5, is soon followed by cascading Falls Creek, left. The Eastside Trail crosses at 19.0 miles, just before the parking area, left, for the Grove of the Patriarchs Trail (see p. 251). South of the road, the Eastside Trail forms part of the Silver Falls loop hike (see p. 248).

Grove of the Patriarchs

One of the park's most popular pathways leads from Stevens Canyon Road to an island-bound collection of colossal conifers called the Grove of the Patriarchs. Isolated from the surrounding forest by the Ohanapecosh River, the trees owe their longevity to the protection from fire the river thus affords. At Silver Falls, a half mile south of the Grove, the previously placid Ohanapecosh makes a spectacular, spray-filled drop.

The road then crosses the Ohanapecosh bridge and arrives at the Stevens Canyon Entrance Station, where westbound travelers must pay their park use fee. The auto tour ends just ahead, mile 19.3, at a junction with State Highway 123, known in the park as East Side Road (see p. 134).

Ohanapecosh to Cayuse Pass

The canyons of the Ohanapecosh River and Chinook Creek form the corridor for State Highway 123 (East Side Road), which connects U.S. Highway 12 in the south with State Highway 410 (the Mather Memorial Parkway) at Cayuse Pass in the north. Along the way are the Ohanapecosh Campground and Visitor Center, Silver Falls, Stevens Canyon Road and the nearby Grove of the Patriarchs, and the abundant sylvan streamcourse scenery. In fall the roadside comes alive with color—blushing huckleberry bushes, bright red mountain-ash berries, and the golds and scarlets of vine maples. More subtle is the gray-green volcanic rock from the ancient mudflows of the Ohanapecosh Formation, visible along various parts of the route, that adds a year-round tinting. (for map, see p. 126)

State Highway 123 begins at a junction with U.S. Highway 12, entering the park at 2.5 miles and then reaching the turnoff, mile 3.6, left, to the Ohanapecosh Campground and Visitor Center. The Silver Falls Trail (see p. 248) starts in the campground's "B" Loop, while the Hot Springs Trail begins behind the visitor center. Across from the center is a picnic area.

Ohanapecosh

Here an expansive, shaded camping area of 205 sites (none for groups) straddles the stone-filled Ohanapecosh River. The visitor center at the campground entrance features a striking mural by noted artist-naturalist (and illustrator for this book) Larry Eifert.

According to local lore, the term "Ohanapecosh" has several meanings, including "looking down on something," "oh look!," and "magnificent!" Perhaps rendered as "deep blue pool," it was applied by the Taidnapam Indians to a hole located on the Main Fork Cowlitz River a short distance above its confluence with the Clear Fork. After "Ohanapecosh" became the popular name for the hot springs located above the Main Fork's east bank, the river came to be called for the springs.

Restroom, Ohanapecosh
Campground "B" Loop

The first whites to locate the springs were Packwood pioneer
John Snyder and "Water Right" Green, who passed through the
area in 1906 while on one of their frequent scouting trips. Green unsuccessfully attempted to lease the spot from the government; in
the process he developed the site for public use, putting in a trail,
building a cabin, and digging a small bath hole. The springs soon
gained a salutary reputation for providing everything from general
relaxation to a cure for rheumatism.

Starting in 1912, Eva O'Neill came up from Packwood each summer to run "Ohanapecosh Camp," which consisted of several tents situated just above the six springs. Travelers from Tacoma commented favorably on the food: "There was but one opinion regarding Mrs. O'Neill's dinner. It was perfect."

As O'Neill was establishing her camp, access to the springs was improved by the completion of a 16-mile park trail that ran from Reflection Lakes, down Stevens Canyon, over Backbone Ridge, and on to the Ohanapecosh River. In 1921 Morton postmaster N. D. Tower took over operation of the springs; three years later, in need of funds to develop the site, he joined forces with a dynamic doctor.

Busy Doctor Bridge

In April 1934 *Time* magazine informed its readers that Dr. Albert Wellington Bridge, 54, of Tacoma, "had just signed a new, 20-year-lease on Ohanapecosh Hot Springs in Mount Rainier National Park." Hardly news of national import, perhaps, but it amplified the magazine's intriguing sketch of the Doctor.

Bridge had come to *Time's* attention because "the health of some 10,000 lumbermen and miners...are under his care by contract." In a year when Socialist Upton Sinclair was running for governor of California and Franklin Delano Roosevelt was steering the federal government toward increased supervision of private enterprise, the doctor's "socialized medicine" was a timely topic for the magazine.

Bridge had traveled a long road to reach his current status. The orphaned son of Vermont farmers, he worked at a sawmill after finishing high school, putting in 16-hour days for something less than 2½¢ an hour. Deciding there were better ways to make a living, Bridge enrolled in medical school. He went west following graduation and in 1909 purchased an "industrial contract practice" in Eatonville. The young doctor, who rode into town on a bicycle, soon flourished, becoming mayor, volunteer fireman, and all-around civic booster. To raise money for a World War I Red Cross drive, he stepped into an Eatonville boxing ring; Bridge lost the fight and got a black eye to boot, but he was at least able to receive prompt medical attention.

Doc Bridge

Within 15 years Bridge was wealthy; he expanded his contract practice to Tacoma and, as a sideline, went into partnership with N. D. Tower at Ohanapecosh Hot Springs, building a lodge and bathhouse. Tower left after two years but Bridge continued to make improvements, paying 10¢ a foot to have the trail to the springs widened into a road, moving in a portable sawmill to cut timbers and lumber, and then using the wood to build cabins and other structures.

Visitors to the resort could take the waters, which bubbled forth at anything from 110 to 124 degrees, while seated in one of five porcelain tubs; a soaking was "found valuable in the treatment of rheumatism, neuritis, and skin diseases." Fishing, mountain climbing, and other outdoor activities were followed by meals at the lodge, whose "table fare is especially planned to satisfy the appetites stirred by clean, bracing mountain air." Retiring for the evening, guests found their cabins complete with stoves and firewood. Making travel easier was the conversion of Bridge's rough road into a state highway, which by 1933 reached to within a half mile of the doctor's resort.

Meanwhile Bridge was busy on the other side of the mountain, establishing a string of 15 branch medical clinics in southwestern Washington. At tiny Mineral, southwest of the park, he maintained an emergency ward with a nurse in charge, while in nearby Morton he built a $4,500 hospital. Full-scale clinics had their own

Bathhouse, 1940

physician's house, office, drugstore, ambulance, and complete staffs. Bridge came to employ a widely dispersed workforce of some 65 doctors, nurses, office assistants, and business managers.

Industrial contract insurance originated in isolated lumber camps and mining towns where the injury rate was high but medical services scarce. Contracting employers deducted a small fee (which averaged about $1.00 per month in Washington at the time) from their workers' paychecks, and in return employees and their families were guaranteed limited medical and surgical care. During the 1930s more than a half million workers in 37 states were thus covered, and Bridge, according to *Time*, was the "undisputed leader in Washington contract practice." Although the magazine also labeled him a "medical tycoon," Bridge was known locally as an able surgeon and honest businessman.

The hot springs were hardly a money-maker like his contract practices, but Bridge kept plugging away at the Ohanapecosh property, adding more cabins, and, in 1942, doubling the size of the bathhouse. One plan he did not bring to completion was the construction of a swimming pool, the excavation for which still forms a depression next to the Hot Springs Trail.

In 1947 ill health compelled Bridge to sell the hot springs operation to his manager, Martin Killian. When the doctor died two years later, he willed $400,000 for construction of a children's hospital in Tacoma, to be named for his mother, Mary Bridge.

For someone who had first worked for about 40¢ a day, it amounted to quite a legacy.

It was necessary for Bridge to sign his 1934 agreement with the government because a boundary change three years earlier had put the hot springs within the park. Previously the line had run just north of the springs, where a patrol cabin sat by the trailside at the park entrance. The cabin served rangers until its removal in 1965, but the focus of park activity had earlier shifted to south of the springs, where the Civilian Conservation Corps set up a camp in 1933 and began making improvements. The older section of the campground, east of the river, dates from this time; gone, however, is "Forest House," a museum spliced together from a pair of CCC buildings. It was replaced by the current visitor center in 1963.

The hot springs facilities deteriorated after Bridge departed. Guests complained frequently, and the park service prodded Killian, unsuccessfully, to make improvements. After several years of haggling, Killian finally gave up control of the concession. By 1967 all of Doctor Bridge's buildings were gone, replaced by the regenerating vegetation.

Ohanapecosh was linked to Cayuse Pass in 1940 when, after some six years' work, the 14-mile East Side Road was finished. The new route cost a then-whopping $100,000 per mile and featured a 507-foot tunnel and three bridges, each constructed from a different material: stone, concrete, and one "of mammoth logs, fallen coniferous giants" at Panther Creek. Completion came none too soon; within two years World War II had interrupted park work projects, and the half-built Stevens Canyon Road had to wait 15 years to be finished.

After crossing Laughingwater Creek, mile 5.0, the highway reaches a parking area, 5.2 miles, left; from here a short spur trail drops to connect with the Silver Falls Trail (see p. 248). Across the road and a short distance ahead is the Three Lakes Trailhead.

At a junction, mile 5.4, Stevens Canyon Road (see p. 125) forks left, immediately arriving at the Stevens Canyon Entrance Station. Our route continues to the right, following the valley of the Ohanapecosh until mile 8.9, where the Shriner Peak Trail departs to the right. Here the river, left, bends northwest, pointing toward its headwaters in Ohanapecosh Park; the stream the highway now runs above is a tributary of the Ohanapecosh, Chinook Creek. We soon begin climbing, the roadside on our right suddenly bedecked with goatsbeard and fireweed. The Owyhigh Lakes Trail, 11.5 miles, left, forms the first section of the Deer and Chinook Creeks hike (see p. 253). After curving east to bridge Deer Creek, the highway passes through the route's solitary tunnel, crosses the Chinook Creek Trail at mile 16.0, and then ends at State Highway 410, 16.5 miles, at Cayuse Pass (see p. 181).

Chinook Creek drainage
from south of Cayuse Pass

Sunrise Road

Mount Rainier's striking northeast side is approached via Sunrise Road, which runs part way up the wide White River Valley before climbing high onto scenic Sunrise Ridge. Conifer-covered mountainslopes, a rock-filled riverbed, and spacious ridgeside meadows complement magnificent views of the glacier-girdled mountain and numerous nearby peaks. Tourists already familiar with Rainier's heavily visited south side will discover at Sunrise a second Paradise. (for map, see p. 126)

Sunrise Road departs from a junction with State Highway 410, aka the Mather Memorial Parkway (see p. 181), running southwest through thick forest before arriving at the White River Entrance Station, 1.4 miles.

White River Entrance Station

The station was built in 1929, two years before the road past it was opened to Sunrise Park. Construction of the thoroughfare did not always proceed smoothly — one Friday night the contractor, apparently worried about losing his crew to a weekend fling, dynamited the uncompleted road shut, stranding his workers uphill with no way out. No way, that is, until ingenuity triumphed over interdiction: "There was a little fisticuffs going on," recalled a park guard nonchalantly, "and we lowered two or three of the cars over one of the switchbacks with 200 or 300 feet of rope." Some 15 or 20 workers thus escaped, presumably to then enjoy the fleshpots of Enumclaw.

At 3.6 miles the Owyhigh Lakes Trail (see p. 257) ascends to the left. Just past Fryingpan Creek, mile 4.3, is the trailhead, left, for the Summerland hike (see p. 259). The creek drains from the Fryingpan Glacier; how the two features derived their names is the subject of some controversy — either some campers lost their fryingpan in the creek, or Professor I. C. Russell named the glacier for its skillet-like shape, or (best of all) it was one of Ben Longmire's dazzling designations.

White River Entrance Station

Tell Me, Ben,
What Were Their Names?

Fairy Falls, Mystic Lake, Devil's Dream Creek—the words trip off the tongue, evoking images far away and fantastic. They, like many others given to sites around the mountain, were the product of Ben Longmire, whose use of fanciful nomenclature kept pace with his wide-ranging tramps through the park. While out hiking, guiding, or blazing new trails, Ben frequently happened upon a spot ripe for naming; after a brief wait until the muses spoke, he would transcribe their utterings onto a cedar shake (which he'd just split from a nearby log) and post the pronouncement on a prominent tree. The signs were still conveniently close at hand when the

U.S. Geological Survey came through a few years later, charting the mountain, and the crews dutifully transferred Longmire's labels to their new map.

Some of his creations were simple and obvious, like Martha Falls, which commemorated his late mother; so too, was the set called the "girl" waterfalls, a quartet of Cowlitz Park cascades—Marie, Mary Belle, Trixie, and Margaret—named for park superintendent Edward S. Hall's four daughters. In many cases, however, Ben's bestowals required a bit of explaining:

Fisher's Hornpipe Creek—"because it sang a regular 'Fisher's Hornpipe' (a dance tune) to us at our camp."

Devil's Dream Creek—"it is crooked as a devil's dream."

Then there were the true masterpieces, when Ben's genius nearly exceeded itself. One such was Mount Ararat: "I named it because I found there some long slabs of wood that had turned to stone and I thought they might have been part of old Noah's boat. I also found a stump with a ring around it as if his rope might have been tied there."

Lengthy phrases and elaborate images thus became Ben's trademark. His appellations are thus often easy to identify, for if the name is long enough, it's probably Longmire's.

The Wonderland Trail meets Sunrise Road, mile 5.2, left. After crossing the White River, the auto tour reaches the access road, 5.4 miles, left, for the White River Campground.

White River Campground

A paved, one-lane road follows the White River upstream 1.1 miles to the campground. The thickly forested site (which features some ten different species of conifers) occupies a benchland between the river and the steep ridgeslope that descends from Sunrise. Two paths leave the area: the switchback-filled Wonderland Trail departs from between site C–21 and the aging, abandoned White River Patrol Cabin, while the Glacier Basin Trail exits from between sites D–16 and D–18 at the upper end of the campground.

The Mount Rainier Mining Company provided the first access into the upper White River drainage in 1911, when it built a trail to reach its claims in Glacier Basin. Within three years the route had been improved to a wagon road that extended some 12 miles south from the original White River Ranger Station. In 1920, with the highway from Enumclaw approaching from the north, the park took over the lower three miles of the mine road. A 160-car campground on the White River, close to the snout of the Emmons Glacier, followed; it was embellished in 1927 by the rustic patrol cabin found at the upper end of the "C" Loop.

The Mountain's Mining Miseries

On November 5, 1914, park ranger Thomas O'Farrell, leading a lone packhorse, rode out of Enumclaw in a driving rain. He was bound for an important assignment in Glacier Basin, and it would take more than an autumn storm to stop him.

O'Farrell had been driven by a singular sense of purpose since 1908, when he started as a ranger at the Carbon River entrance. Until that year mining claims were allowed inside the park, and speculators had filed frequently in O'Farrell's district as well as at other locations around the mountain. The ranger, who had seen his share of shaft-scarred hillsides along the lower Carbon, was soon waging a one-man war against the park claims, compiling evidence that the sites either lacked mineral value or were not properly maintained. By 1924, when he left the park service, O'Farrell had eliminated some 90 of Rainier's 98 claims, but the ones he was bound for on this November day would elude him.

The sites O'Farrell sought belonged to the Mount Rainier Mining Company. Incorporated in 1905, it held land originally claimed by its vice-president and general manager, Peter Storbo, who'd found copper and a little silver on the parcels in 1897-98. The new venture did not have an auspicious start: during the second winter of operation, an avalanche swept down Mount Ruth and into the basin; two workers were buried by the debris and never found, while a boy, arguably luckier, was carried out in a log coffin.

A sawmill and several other buildings went up in 1909, but within two years activity decreased so dramatically that the Land Office was able to cancel all but nine of the company's forty-two

Storbo's "Hotel"

claims. In 1914, however, work started on a rooming house that became known as the "Storbo Hotel." By then O'Farrell was convinced that the building's namesake was bilking midwestern investors, offering them stock in a venture that would never turn a profit. The chill November air no doubt dropped a few degrees lower when Storbo met O'Farrell near the park boundary and accompanied him back up the basin.

Storbo subsequently improved the mine road, using it for transporting mill machinery to the claims. The park duly granted the company a series of special use permits; as Storbo prospered, O'Farrell seethed. In 1924, the Mount Rainier Mining Company received patents on eight of its Glacier Basin claims. O'Farrell quit his job the same year.

Events soon caught up with Peter Storbo. Complaints from the swindled stockholders led to the prosecution of Storbo and an associate for fraudulent use of the mails. Found guilty in 1930, the men were each fined $1,000 and sentenced to 18-month terms in the McNeil Island penitentiary. Their company was subsequently disenfranchised for failure to pay corporate taxes and was then purchased at a sheriff's sale for only $500. Later some stockholders in the old company, led by Ole and Thor Oakland, bought the claims and reincorporated. By the early 1950s the new organization was trying to revive the never-successful Storbo mines.

They didn't have much luck. The camp was in disarray, with the old Storbo Hotel flattened by the winter snows, other buildings similarly destroyed, and the upper section of road reduced to no more than a trail. By 1952 the mines were operating on a limited basis, but there was little about them to inspire confidence. Park ranger Bill Butler, visiting the site, found that an army-surplus weapons carrier served as the corporate vehicle, bringing workers to Snowflake Tunnel #2, which, unfortunately, was filled with water at the 240-foot level. The crew, Butler noted, consisted of the two Oakland brothers, "another old fellow," and an Eskimo.

Once again, Glacier Basin refused to give up its glitter in any profitable amount. The park attempted to purchase the properties, but could not agree with the owners on a price. All mining ceased in 1957; the buildings, such as they were, rotted peacefully away for a few years before their remains were nocturnally incinerated by anonymous "anti-miner volunteers" in the 1960s.

It had come fifty years later than he'd hoped, but Thomas O'Farrell would surely have smiled to see the flames licking at the lumber pile that was once Peter Storbo's mining camp.

Leaving the campground turnoff, Sunrise Road rises up the hillside, crossing Yakima Creek at mile 7.8. The roadbank, left, exposes a collection of dark gray andesite columns, resistant rock that flowed as lava from Mount Rainier several hundred thousand years ago. The route then switchbacks past a wealth of wildflowers before reaching rock-wall-rimmed Sunrise Point, 13.0 miles. Here the road makes a hairpin turn around a large parking area; at the apex of the turn is the Palisades Lake Trailhead, right. Vast views extend in several directions from the point.

Our route passes the Sourdough Ridge Trailhead, right, at the west end of the parking area. Rusty brown pumice, from Mount Rainier's last major eruption (some 2,000 years ago), is visible at the ensuing roadcuts. The auto tour enters the great sloping meadow of Sunrise Park, mile 14.4, passing acres of wildflower-graced grassland before ending at the Sunrise parking lot, 15.7 miles.

Sunrise

The scenic ridgeside meadow area was previously known as Yakima Park, but the name was changed to avoid confusion with

Sunrise Lake

the city of Yakima, which lies over the Cascades to the east. Even earlier, the locale had yet another name; this one referred to *a* Yakima—one of the tribe's most noted warriors.

The "Place of the Chief"

It was called Me-yah-ah Pah, the "Place of the Chief," and it was a summering ground that befit the Yakimas' second most powerful leader. Each year his band traveled from their winter home in the Wenas Valley, which lay east beyond the Naches River, to visit this great grassy hillside that swept down from a shoulder of the mighty peak. There, amid the flowers and the berries, they would graze their ponies and hunt and harvest during the warm months when the snows moved farther up the mountain. It was a place, too, for games and other amusements, where the young men raced horses, staged sham battles, and danced by day, while courting Yakima maidens at night. It was, for many summers, Owhi's place.

Then, in the year the whites called 1855, trouble came to the Yakimas. The hard-talking little man called Captain Stevens, who was governor of Washington Territory, summoned Owhi and the other eastside chiefs to a great council and told them they must sign a piece of paper that gave up most of their lands to the whites. You must go, Captain Stevens said, "and select a certain place for a reservation and you must be farmers....You must choose places in which to live, put fences around them, plow, and reap crops."

The chiefs listened and then considered the Captain's words overnight. The next day many of them spoke. Owhi told Stevens, "What you say is good, but I do not see how we are going to farm. How are we going to plow? We have nothing to plow with, and I do not see how we are going to do it. You must go back and get us things to work with. If you do that, perhaps we can farm."

To which Stevens replied, "I will do that."

"Good!" answered Owhi, "That is all I have to say."

When the council ended, Owhi went to Captain Stevens and shook his hand, telling him, "I will do as you say, and I am going home now."

Several of the Yakimas were angry with Owhi for making the agreement, calling him a coward. Soon they all learned that the little Captain's word was bad, for he sent none of the plows he'd promised, and had instead taken out newspaper ads urging the whites to come and settle on the Indian lands.

Some whites came soon enough, although they were miners, not settlers, bound for the gold strike over near Fort Colville. Five of them did not leave the Yakimas' country—shot, some people said, by Owhi's own son, Qualchan, with a set of pistols the Yakimas' head chief, Kamiakin, had given him. The Indian agent,

Bolon, was also killed, and that brought the white soldiers to seek revenge. Kamiakin was ready for them, though, and he sent Major Haller and his men streaming back to The Dalles in defeat.

But then more bluecoats came north that fall, all the way into Owhi's home territory at Two Buttes, which the whites called Union Gap. As the soldiers swarmed into the valley, the chief and his warriors escaped up the Naches River; although they taunted the troopers that followed them, their going was still nothing more than a retreat.

Owhi of the Yakimas

Winter stopped the fighting in Yakima country, but from over the mountains came a messenger from Leschi, who was leading the tribes of the Sound in their own war against the whites. He was planning an attack on the settlers' small village of Seattle and sent to Owhi for help. Soon Qualchan and a hundred warriors set off through the snow; four days later they reached Leschi's camp at Lake Washington. Despite their support, the attack on Seattle did not succeed.

In the spring of 1856, many more soldiers, including volunteers from the coast, came onto Yakima land. The Indians could not stand up to such numbers and the fighting slackened as the two sides settled into a sort of truce. September came, and little Captain Stevens ordered the chiefs to a new council, demanding that they offer him their unconditional surrender, but Qualchan, Owhi, and Kamiakin refused to attend.

There was peace all through 1857, when the soldiers kept white settlers out of Indian country; the next year, however, some miners crossed through from Walla Walla and were attacked. Colonel Steptoe marched his men north, but the Yakimas and their allies whipped him and his troops.

It was bad going for the Indians after that. Colonel Wright came out of the south, crying for blood, and for a month he and his soldiers found all they wanted, killing Indians whether they were hostile or not, destroying grain and hay, shooting the cattle and even the horses—eight hundred of them—so that the warriors had nothing to ride and their families nothing to eat. As summer came to an end, so did the alliance of tribes; first the Spokanes surrendered and then the Coeur d'Alenes. Soon even the Nez Perces had given up the fight.

Now it was the day called September 22, about the time when summer slips into fall. Near dusk, one of Colonel Wright's officers, Captain Keyes, saw a figure riding towards their headquarters: "I observed an old man of medium stature and robust frame, dressed like an American, approaching our camp on horseback," Keyes reported. "The old man's name was Owhi...and he came in to make peace."

Colonel Wright remembered Owhi from three years earlier, when they'd met at Two Buttes. The chief had told the Colonel he would bring his people in, but they had fled across the Naches River instead. Now the Colonel's heart was against Owhi; he ordered the chief to send for his son Qualchan and then had the old man put in irons.

Before Qualchan received his father's message he came of his own accord to Wright's camp. The Colonel wanted to punish Qualchan for the deaths of the miners three years earlier; Wright gave an order and within fifteen minutes, the young warrior was hanging from a nearby tree, dead. Only later was it learned that Qualchan was innocent.

Owhi remained Colonel Wright's prisoner. Captain Keyes came to know the chief:

> I often visited him, and it interested me to mark the effect of time (he was seventy years old), bereavement and captivity upon a savage prince, who, in his prime, must have possessed extraordinary physical and mental vigor. I never saw him smile, and frequently deep sadness would mantle his countenance and impart to it an air of dignity. Without doubt he felt sharp pangs, for he

had lost all his power, had witnessed the ignominious death of his son, who excelled all his tribe in strength and savage prowess, and now, bereft of hope, he seemed resigned to whatever might be in store for him. (Keyes, p. 280)

Colonel Wright's troops took up the march on October 3. Owhi, in chains but mounted on his own horse, traveled with them. At a river crossing he lashed his guard across the face and tried to escape; he was pursued by the soldiers and shot. The Yakima was a tough old warrior, but four bullets in his body were too much for even him, and there, near the Tucannon River, Owhi's spirit left the earth. He died far east of the land of his people, farther still from the Place of the Chief.

Blockhouse, Sunrise

Sunrise Lodge

The summer migrations of Owhi's band were followed in later times by those of sheepherders and their flocks; they came from the same Yakima-area valleys as had the chief and his people. The canyon south of Me-yah-ah Pah eventually saw visitors of its own, first as miners and mountain enthusiasts used Storbo's mine road, and then, starting in 1923, as vacationers frequented the newly established White River Campground. But Owhi's place, which had become known as Yakima Park, largely remained vacant.

Then, in the summer of 1931, during the depths of the Depression, both the park service and the Rainier National Park Company opened facilities at Yakima Park, whose name was now changed to "Sunrise." Each organization was plagued by budget shortfalls, but the park service, initiating the first development completely planned by its new Landscape Office, managed to create a striking multi-purpose center; designed to resemble a frontier blockhouse, the building provided an ironic reminder that the spot was once war chief Owhi's summer haunt.

The RNPC also started with a grandiose design, but the building that eventually developed lacked the character of the park's fortresslike facility. Only a single wing of the concessionaire's proposed hotel was ever completed; what came to be called Sunrise Lodge never offered tourist accommodations but rather provided only a public dining room, gift shop, and employee housing. The stark structure still stands in shambolic, shingle-covered majesty, a monument to its unfulfilled potential.

Three other landmarks also date from the early 1930s: a vertical-log palisade that encloses the yard behind the visitor center and two small, stone-and-log buildings that flank the lodge—the restroom on the west side and the now-abandoned gas station to the east. In the 1940s a second blockhouse and the visitor center were added to the park's facilities.

A collection of some 215 housekeeping cabins for a time covered the meadow in back of the lodge, providing sleeping accommodations that the uncompleted hostelry could not offer. After World War II the buildings were sold off, with many of them going to farmers east of the Cascades. The cabins' location is marked today by a series of shallow scars visible from the Sourdough Loop Trail.

Leaving the Sunrise parking area are several hiking routes: the Sunrise Rim Trail (see p. 261) and Emmons Vista/Silver Forest Trail start from the southern side of the lot, while the Sourdough Ridge Nature Trail and a pet exercise loop depart to the north. The nature trail not only leads to the Sourdough Ridge–Dege Peak Trail and the Huckleberry Creek Trail, but also forms the first part of the Frozen Lake - Berkeley Park hike (see p. 262). At the west end of the parking lot is the Sunrise Visitor Center, and behind it, the Sunrise Picnic Area. The Sunrise Lodge, on the north side of the lot, offers summertime food service and a gift shop.

Morton to Elbe

The Cowlitz and Nisqually drainages are linked by State Highway 7, which runs through a rural landscape long mined and logged. Here the ghost of once-bustling Lindberg slumbers in peaceful perpetuity, while (via a short side road) little Mineral Lake still draws scenery seekers like an emerald magnet. In addition to such attractions, this history-filled highway also offers the shortest southern approach to the park.

Beginning at the junction with U.S. Highway 12 (see p. 162) on the southern outskirts of Morton, the auto tour follows State Highway 7 north through town, passing businesses that cater to both tourists and timbermen. Morton provides a full range of services, including grocery stores, gas stations, dining, lodging, and public showers.

Morton

Had Morton gotten its start either a few years earlier or later, it might have been called Hendricks, Stevenson, or Hobart after the then-sitting Vice President, but Levi P. Morton held the office when the town applied for a post office in 1891, and his name was chosen when it was found that the first selection, McKinley, was already taken. No one was more disappointed with the choice than Mrs. A. H. Boomhauer, who, as the first white woman in the valley, saw herself as a compromise candidate for the honor.

But Boomhauer it was not to be, and so it was Mortonians, not Boomhauerites, who set about building up their newly named town. By 1901 their work amounted to no more than a log schoolhouse, split-cedar community hall, and small general store–post office, but a decade later the Tacoma Eastern Railroad made Morton its southern terminus and the town finally took off. The railroad brought an unexpected bonus with it—a vein of cinnabar discovered in the cut for the line's right-of-way. The nearby hills also contained coal, and the area was blanketed by a heavy growth

154

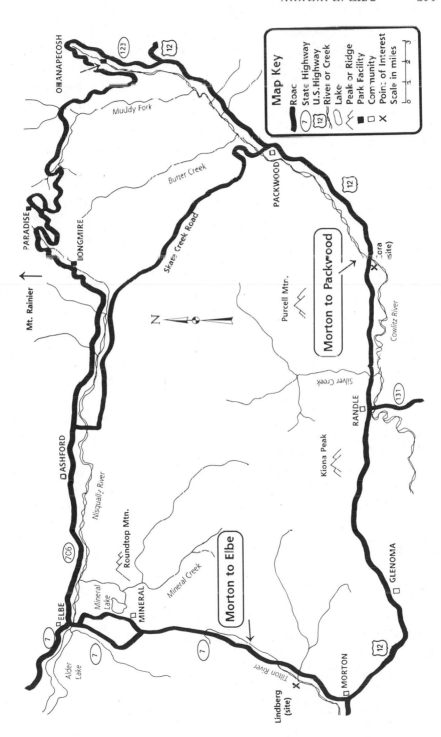

Map Key

Road
State Highway
U.S. Highway
River or Creek
Lake
Peak or Ridge
Park Facility
Community
Point of Interest
Scale in miles

OHANAPECOSH
123
12
Muddy Fork
Butter Creek
PACKWOOD
12
PARADISE
LONGMIRE
Skate Creek Road
Mt. Rainier
N
Morton to Packwood
Purcell Mtn.
ora (site)
Cowlitz River
Silver Creek
RANDLE
131
Kiona Peak
ASHFORD
Nisqually River
Roundtop Mtn.
Morton to Elbe
GLENOMA
706
Mineral Lake
MINERAL
Mineral Creek
ELBE
7
Alder Lake
7
7
Tilton River
12
MORTON
Lindberg (site)

of timber to boot; thus endowed, Morton by the early 1920s claimed three large mills, several smaller ones, a busy mining industry, and status as the shipping point for the region's dairy and potato farms.

Then, in July 1924, disaster struck. A huge blaze swept through town, defying the efforts of over 300 firefighters, and destroyed all but a few of Morton's buildings. A relief train rushed up food and supplies from Tacoma, the residents set about rebuilding, and the community was back in business by October. Within two years Morton boasted some 14 brand-new, fire-proof structures.

High prices for mercury during the 1920s accelerated the mining of its parent material, cinnabar; by 1930 Morton was the largest producer of the red-streaked mineral in the United States. Four coal mines were also operating, and the timber supply seemed good for at least another 25 years. Even more impressive than its cinnabar production was Morton's output of railroad ties, which ranked not only first in the nation but in the entire world, with a hundred rail-car loads shipped out daily on the Tacoma Eastern.

Adding to Morton's reputation as a big-time town was the Logger's Jubilee, an annual event started in the late 1930s. Featuring many of the top timbermen in the Northwest, by 1960 the Jubilee attracted some 2,000 spectators to watch competitions in ax throwing, cable splicing, log rolling, and nine other events. That year a father and son team from Toutle Lake, Paul and Max Searles, won their fourth consecutive championship in the hand falling contest by rapidly chopping, sawing, and wedging their way through a thick section of timber; at 53, father Paul once again proved that youthfulness was no substitute for experience. It's a claim that Morton itself, so proudly rooted in its past, can also make.

North of Morton the highway follows the Tilton River, passing at mile 2.9 the remains of a multi-named lumber and mining town.

Lindberg/Millberg/Coal Canyon

The community was first named for Gustaf Lindberg, whose lumber company owned it; in his capacity as an official of the Scandinavian-American Bank of Tacoma, Lindberg was convicted of fraud in the 1920s after the bank failed. A new mill owner, appropriately named Miller, took over, so the place became *Mill*berg.

Paul and Max Searles,
champion choppers

Later the Everett Fisher Company mined coal here, during which time the locale was duly called Coal Canyon. Both the lumber and mining enterprises faded, so that by the 1940s most of the workers' shanties were abandoned and the mill lay in ruins. Today a row of brick cottages repose by the roadside, recalling what was once a town of some 200 people.

The area's lengthy logging history is chronicled by the clearcut-checkered countryside through which the highway now passes. Just beyond the site of Carlson, a one-time sawmill town, is a junction; here Mineral Road branches from the highway, mile 11.9, right. This paved side route leads to the tiny town of Mineral, which perches beside a lake of the same name.

Mineral

First called Round Top for the mountain to the east, the community by 1892 had changed its name, acquired a post office, and established a half dozen businesses serving the galena, silver, and lead mines located up nearby Mineral Creek. These early operations never amounted to much, but a vein of red realgar, from which arsenic is extracted, was discovered in 1900 and worked for over 20 years. The area became better known for its large trees, one of which helped provide a striking study in contrasts: an enormous 16-foot-diameter Douglas-fir stood next to the first Mineral post office, which itself measured a minuscule eight feet by eight feet. So tiny was the structure that postmaster Lester I. Walrath published a postcard of the building, labeling it "Smallest Post Office in U.S."

Perhaps believing the town was belittled by its pint-sized P. O., one Mineral resident penned a bit of bravado for the Elbe *Union* in 1896:

> Though Mineral is standing silent
> She is waiting for her boom
> For she will be firm and solid
> When others go down the flume
>
> . . . .
> Mineral, in her world of wealth
> Will surely come to fame
> When Elbe and Eatonville
> Will barely hold their name.

During the 1920s it was Mineral that seemed to be barely holding; a fire destroyed her lakeshore lumber mill, the arsenic mine shut down, and the "artistically constructed" Mineral Lake Inn closed for several years. However, other nearby mills and mines remained active, the inn eventually returned to business, and the town managed to maintain itself. The West Fork Logging Company made Mineral headquarters for its 23,000-acre operation, which did not always run smoothly; a labor strike by the company's employees culminated in a bitter anti-worker demonstration that saw a man shot on Mineral's main street. Several years after the incident, West Fork Logging drew praise for its practice of selective timber harvesting and for the "attractive brick and tile

Minuscule Mineral Post Office

buildings maintained by the company…[that] contrast with the flimsy impermanence of most lumber towns." (*Washington: A Guide to the Evergreen State*, p. 534)

Despite its sturdy structures, West Fork Logging followed the town's other timber companies into oblivion; a steam donkey on the south shore of the lake serves as Mineral's sole monument to its long-lost lumbering enterprises.

Mineral offers a grocery store, dining, and lodging. Side trip excursionists can leave town by Mineral Hill Road, which skirts the west shore of the lake, passing the recently restored Mineral Lake Lodge before meeting Highway 7 just south of the Nisqually River.

Those travelers who omit the Mineral side trip will continue north on the highway from Carlson; in the midst of a logged over landscape is a junction with the other end of Mineral Road, mile 13.3, right. Pleasant Valley Road then departs the highway, 14.8 miles, left, on its way to the south shore of Alder Lake. A century ago, the valley attracted a family of hard working (and hard walking) settlers.

Homesteading with Ole Holm

It was a slow trip that Ole Holm and his family made from Tacoma to their new homestead, far up the Nisqually, at Pleasant Valley. Not that they weren't determined travelers, but Ole kept holding them up. He'd be carrying along half of their cast iron stove, and then he'd set it down by the road and vanish; a while later, he'd reappear with the rest of the stove, which he placed next to the first half. Another delay while Ole went back to their last resting place and returned with their sewing machine, and then the group set off again.

Having endured that first heavily laden hike, it was nothing for Ole to later stroll into Tacoma (making the 47-mile trip in a mere 16 hours), visit the Northwest Grocery Company, and then return the following day with 50 to 70 pounds of supplies. On one such journey Ole did, however, encounter a bit of difficulty. He arrived at Elbe with a 55-pound pack of Tacoma goods on his back, no-ticed a snowstorm was brewing, and prudently picked up an extra 49-pound sack of flour at Adam Sachs's store. All went well until he started across the Nisqually on a single-log bridge. At the half-way point Ole slipped, dropping the Sachs sack into the river. Only by catching hold of a conveniently placed tree limb did he manage to save himself and the rest of his load.

Like many of the region's pre-1900 homesteaders, the Holms were poor. Ole saved money by taking his long walks to Tacoma; supplies were cheaper there than at the local stores, and some-times he'd stay in the city for mill work, initially making a dollar for a 12-hour day. His son Edward went down to the Ohop Valley and hoed potatoes, collecting enough cash to first buy a rifle and then a shotgun. After that the family feasted on deer, pheasants, and rabbits.

Ole began delivering milk to Elbe once the road across the Nisqually went in, charging 5¢ a quart. Later he sold milk to the mines above Mineral and took over a hundred pounds of butter to

Elbe each week. By 1906 the Holms were flush enough to build a new home. They made sure it had a large front room, and there they held dances and other gatherings for their Nisqually neighborhood. With his wife, Ole would waltz the night away, his feet—trained on those 94-mile round trips to Tacoma—never tiring.

Highway 7 continues north from Pleasant Valley Road, passing the turnoff for Mineral Hill Road, mile 16.5, right, before crossing the Nisqually River and arriving on the outskirts of Elbe, 17.0 miles. A right turn at the junction leads along State Highway 706 to the park's Nisqually Entrance (see p. 108).

Morton to Packwood

The remote Upper Cowlitz region, long known locally as the "Big Bottom," early on proved a highly hospitable section of the lower Cascades. The Taidnapam Indians lived along the river and its tributaries until decimated by disease; they were followed by waves of emigrants, chiefly from the southern Appalachians, who found the fertile valley lent itself to farming. Logging and tourism came later, and today the region reposes in slow-paced relaxation, its slumber seasonally punctuated by passing lumber trucks and travel trailers. Park visitors from the south may thus find the Upper Cowlitz-Ohanapecosh approach an alluring alternative to the more crowded Ashford-Nisqually entrance. (for map, see p. 155)

Starting on the south side of Morton at a junction with Washington State Highway 7 (see p. 154), the auto tour proceeds eastward on U.S. Highway 12 toward Packwood. At mile 3.0 the route passes a ridgeslope, left, where the eagle-eyed may discern the remnants of the Morton Cinnabar Mine. The road then crosses Fern Gap, 3.9 miles, and runs above the end of Riffe (RIF) Lake, a reservoir that bears the name of the farming community it inundated. Valley-enclosed pasturelands announce the appearance of Glenoma, mile 7.2.

Glenoma (glen-OH-mah)

At different times a turn-of-the-century post office near here bore the uninspired names of Vern and Verndale. Poetic settler Beverly W. Coiner then coined "Glenoma," which has served the community ever since. Logging cut a wide swath through the area but poor soil made farming marginal; in the 1940s the town consisted of "a cluster of houses, brick and frame, gray school buildings, and a State Highway Department depot." At the time, the area east of Glenoma featured a string of small railroad-tie cutting operations, each with "pyramids of yellow sawdust or piles of freshly cut ties...[where] huge sawdust piles, turned the color of copper with age, indicate locations that have been worked out or abandoned." (*Washington: A Guide to the Evergreen State*, p. 534)

Soon the highway descends into the Upper Cowlitz valley. Randle, mile 17.6, offers gas, groceries, dining, lodging, and shops. Here State Highway 131 branches right, providing access to Mount St. Helens.

Randle

Located in the heart of the Upper Cowlitz, the small community of Randle has long served as a center for the area settled by emigrants from the Appalachian Mountains.

From Big Sandy to Big Bottom

On the night of August 9, 1882, near the Kentucky–West Virginia border, three brothers—Tolbert, Phamer, and Randolph McCoy—were taken to a bluff above the Tug River, tied to some pawpaw bushes, and shot. They had themselves recently killed Ellison Hatfield, and now the victim's family had its revenge.

The four deaths were but the bloodiest incident in a long string of killings that made the names of two families, the Hatfields and the McCoys, synonymous with the word feud, and which hastened the departure of many area residents to places of greater peace and prosperity.

Even without the Hatfield-McCoy trouble, Appalachian hillfolk had plenty of reasons to emigrate: the mountain ridges that ran through West Virginia, Virginia, Kentucky, Tennessee, and North Carolina were peopled to full capacity; moreover, good farming bottomland was long gone, and timbermen and miners had swept across the hillsides, stripping the cover of trees and earth. One Kentuckian who left a few years later was recorded (in the vernacular) as he explained why he'd moved on:

> Folks way back thar didn't 'pear civilized. They were fergittin' the Lord and sinnin' one way or other—liquor makin', drinkin', and shootin' seemed to get worse as they got hold a little money. The land was gettin' corned out and settled up. 'Twas gettin' so a man couldn't rustle a livin' any more...(Clevinger, 1938, p. 125)

Like many others who departed, the speaker of this piece knew just where to go: west to Washington, to a welcoming bit of greenery called the "Big Bottom,"—the Upper Cowlitz River Valley.

The first southern highlanders to arrive there were Rufus Siler and his sister, Louisa, who came from Franklin, North Carolina, in 1884, bringing with them 60 head of cattle they'd picked up in Chehalis. Siler wanted a post office at his new homestead, close by the Cowlitz, and he soon enlisted the support of someone with influence—his home state senator, Zebulon B. Vance. Within a few months the office, with Siler as postmaster, was in operation; it was named, not surprisingly, Vance.

More emigrants soon followed, drawn by descriptions of an area similar to the Appalachians, with low-elevation valley farmlands and timbered slopes rising above them. Only later did the newcomers learn that western Washington's long wet season and dry, cool summers ruined their most cherished crop, making the Upper Cowlitz "poor corn country."

Finding the Big Bottom too cold for corn, the recent arrivals soon adapted, growing potatoes and other root vegetables, and taking up dairying, logging, and trapping. James L. Randle, part of an influx from Loudon County, Tennessee, helped introduce beef cattle, swine, sheep, and turkeys into the area.

By 1900, the trickle of Southerners coming to the Big Bottom had increased to a near flood. Many began their journey by flat-bottomed boat, floating down the Big Sandy and other mountain streams to the Tennessee River, continuing on to the Ohio, and then taking a river boat up the Mississippi and Missouri to Omaha, Nebraska, whence the railroad transported them west. Once on the train, the mountaineers often made quite a sight: one family from Pike County, Tennessee, brought along a brace of black and tan coon hounds, watched over by several menfolk carrying rifles; not to be outdone, other emigrants displayed pistols and long knives while tilting back jugs of mountain moonshine.

The rush of refugees eased after 1917, but Appalachianites still made their way to the Upper Cowlitz during the Twenties and Thirties. By then some had spilled over into the nearby upper Nisqually drainage, so that by 1940 a staggering seventy percent of the region's residents traced their roots back to Blue Ridge and Cumberland country.

Their highland heritage was readily apparent, from the lilting speech heard around Glenoma, to the ballad singing of Virginian James Compton down on the Cowlitz at Riffe, to the old-fashioned spinning wheels that John Slagle turned out at Randle. There was even a scattering of McCoys that had relocated in the Big Bottom, but— fortunately for the valley's peace—there were no Hatfields.

Siler's Vance post office was located southeast of present-day Randle, just across the Cowlitz River. A subsequent postmaster, Joseph T. Chilcoat, couldn't read, which made sorting the mail difficult. Chilcoat's solution was simplicity itself: he merely dumped the postal pouch on the floor and let the patrons pick their own letters out. In 1899 James L. Randle served as postmaster at Vance; not only literate but ambitious, he moved across the river and established a new post office, which he named for himself. Three years later the Randle Logging Company started up, and for decades it anchored the town's activity. Situated on the surrounding bottomland were ranches for such "walking crops," as pigs, cattle, and turkeys, all of which were driven along the roads to Chehalis, Kelso, and various communities on the Sound. At Spanaway and Tacoma,

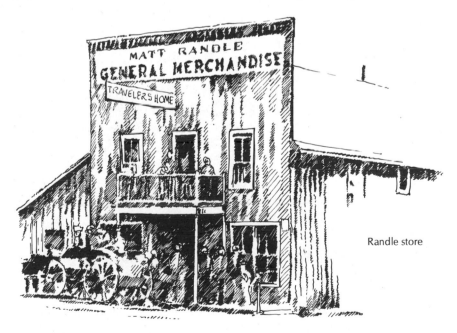

Randle store

residents periodically witnessed impromptu "poultry parades" that featured flocks of up to 500 turkeys streaming down the thoroughfare on their way to market; the gobblers had walked all the way from the Upper Cowlitz, foraging on grasshoppers and berries, while roosting in trees during their nightly stops.

The region's economy was not limited to the sale of lumber and livestock, and by the 1940s Randle possessed a cheese plant to process its other chief commodity, dairy goods. Another local activity was the harvesting of cascara bark, which at the time served as the active ingredient in laxatives. The bark sold for anywhere from 3¢ to 10¢ a pound, but this provided a good wage at the time, since harvesters could gather 40 to 50 pounds in an hour. Today Randle derives part of its income from its status as gateway to two federally protected peaks: Mount Rainier National Park and Mount St. Helens National Monument.

Highway 12 continues through the broad valley of the Upper Cowlitz, crossing the river, mile 25.5, at the site of Cora.

Cowlitz River – Cora

Levi Davis and his three sons homesteaded here in 1883, and seven years later Davis became the first postmaster at the now-vanished river crossing community of Cora. Motorists of today will have difficulty envisioning early-day travel conditions, when wagoners from the east end of the valley forded at this spot on their two-week roundtrips to Chehalis. During high water, the journey took somewhat longer, for each wagon had to be dismantled, transported (along with its cargo) piece-by-piece across the river in dugout canoes, and then reassembled; the horses swam the torrent. By 1905 crossing conditions had improved, thanks to the addition of a ferry operated by one of the valley's last remaining Taidnapam Indians, Baptiste "Bat" Kiona. A bridge replaced the ferry in 1916 and served until 1943, when it collapsed under the weight of a loaded log truck; the bridge was subsequently rebuilt, but this time it was made of concrete.

Locals delight in telling of a pair of early settlers, brothers William and Joe Von Oy, who had transportation troubles of their own. On a trip back from Chehalis, one of their horses died. William, smaller and more assertive than his brother, decided that Joe

Packwood Hotel

would have to become the dead horse's replacement. Joe was accordingly put in harness and hitched up; William helped the new "team" by pushing the wagon from behind. While passing a local homestead, Joe was observed poking the remaining horse, Mike, in the ribs while shouting, "Come on, Mike! Do your part!" Joe did so well at his new job that come spring planting, he was allowed to join Mike in pulling the plow.

At mile 32.8 the route enters Packwood, the largest community in the Upper Cowlitz. Available here are showers, gas, groceries, meals, and lodging.

Packwood

In 1890 a post office called Sulphur Springs was established near the mouth of Johnson Creek; the facility moved around the area, landing at the house of whomever was the current postmaster, until 1910, when it was permanently located at the up-and-coming community of Lewis. By then the town, which started with some merchandise being sold in the home of Henry Hager, had high hopes. Originally optimistic that one of the railroads would put a line through the valley, Lewis had recently shifted its focus—now its future rode on a hydroelectric facility, to be built by the Valley Development Company, that would utilize the water from nearby Packwood Lake. The workers of the VD Company (as it was later derisively called) were already busy on the project. All too soon, however, activity halted and the VD's equipment was sent to Portland to be sold. A scar on the hillside east of town remained to mark the company's tramway route to the lake.

Despite the VD Company's demise, Lewis prospered. A sawmill opened in 1911, the same year that postmaster Walter Combs built the "rough" hotel that serves as a still-operating town landmark. The building also housed the phone switch for the Forest Service, whose ranger station was located north of town, just across the Cowlitz. The establishment of the Pacific Forest Reserve in 1891 had closed off all of the valley's uninhabited land to homesteading, and only in 1914 was the Upper Cowlitz again opened to settlement, setting off an Oklahoma-style land rush that brought a new surge of immigrants.

The Forest Service provided a seasonal source of jobs for locals; the opportunities were augmented by the construction of some 25 fire lookout stations between 1917 and 1930. An annual event in Lewis was the springtime "farewell" dance for the lookouts, foresters, and game wardens just prior to their departure for the woods. At such times, "to the music of a four-piece orchestra of piano, fiddle, bass viol, and drum, punctured with laughter, yells, 'stomping' of feet, and an occasional shot from the pistol of an over-exuberant hillman, the crowd dances until dawn." (*Washington: A Guide to the Evergreen State*, p. 536)

To avoid confusion with Fort Lewis, the town became Packwood in 1930. The new name honored Billy Packwood, who explored the Upper Cowlitz in 1854 with James Longmire, and who later maintained a local coal mine for some 28 years.

The town received a boost in 1935 when the Kerr Brothers Mill went into production. The mill's electric plant also served the community; a two-blink warning each night at 9 P.M. alerted residents that the power was about to go off. Later transformed into the Packwood Lumber Company, the mill has been a town mainstay.

A Taidnapam Thank You

When Jim Yoke posed beside Packwood's imitation elk in about 1940, he was over a hundred years old. His life had more than spanned the time of whites in the valley; as a youngster he had seen the first of them, James Longmire and Billy Packwood, when they came up Skate Creek in 1854. Jim was so excited by the sighting that he dropped his just-caught fish back into the stream.

Yoke stayed in the area with his Yakima wife, Anna, after most of his people had left. The couple became a part of the new community, and when the first election precinct in the Big Bottom was established in 1896, Jim was the only Indian among the 17 registered voters. Many years later, during the Depression, Yoke, by then over 90, left salmon and venison outside the houses of hungry white families. Nonetheless, some people in Packwood ignored such good deeds and refused to accept the Yokes.

Packwood scene:
Jim Yoke and friend

One who did befriend them, however, was Martha Panco. She once baked Anna a birthday cake, the Yakima woman's first ever. The following Thanksgiving, Martha received a parcel in the mail from down the valley at Randle. Inside was a dressed turkey, sent by Anna's relatives.

The Yokes, who'd waited so long to say "you're welcome," at last had a chance to say "thank you" instead.

After leaving Packwood, Highway 12 continues up the valley of the Cowlitz, entering the Gifford Pinchot National Forest and then passing the Forest Service's lovely La Wis Wis Campground, 40.8 miles, left. The auto tour ends at the junction of Highway 12 with State Highway 123 at mile 41.5, left. Highway 123 soon enters the park (see p. 134), while Highway 12 continues east, over White Pass and past Rimrock Lake, on its way to Naches and Yakima (see p. 171).

Tieton River to White Pass

This southeasterly approach to Mount Rainier follows U.S. Highway 12 up the valley of the Tieton River, past Rimrock Lake, over White Pass, and down into the Cowlitz drainage. Before reaching a junction with the park turnoff, the route encounters spectacular scenery — biologic, hydrologic, and geologic — that amply acclimates motorists to the forthcoming wonders of the park.

Four miles north of Naches, Highway 12 turns left at a junction with State Highway 410 (see p. 176) and follows the Tieton River upstream.

Lower Tieton River Valley

The broad lower reaches of the Tieton Valley (TIE-uh-tahn, probably a corrupted reference to the Taidnapam tribe of the Upper Cowlitz) are framed by the basaltic cliffs of the western Columbia Plateau; the dark rock masses brood over the landscape, their dominance unchallenged until a single light line cuts across the southern canyonside — the flume for the Yakima-Tieton Main Canal that carries water from Rimrock Lake. On the valley floor, a summer-green ribbon of cottonwood follows the river west.

Rimrock Retreat, mile 12.6, offers a store, cafe, gasoline, and lodging. The highway then passes a bevy of summertime blossoms — oceanspray, blue elderberry, and, most noticeably, mock-orange. Rimrock, 19.8 miles, has a store; a tunnel promptly takes the road past Tieton Dam, exiting above the north shore of Rimrock Lake, mile 20.6, left.

Rimrock Lake - Tieton Dam

The lake's earthen dam was started in 1917, languished in partial completion both during and after World War I, and was finally finished in 1925. Reaching a height of some 220 feet, with its foundation dropping another hundred feet below the canyon bottom, the dam was for a time the largest of its type in the world. Its construction relied on *very* heavy equipment: a 100-ton electric shovel

171

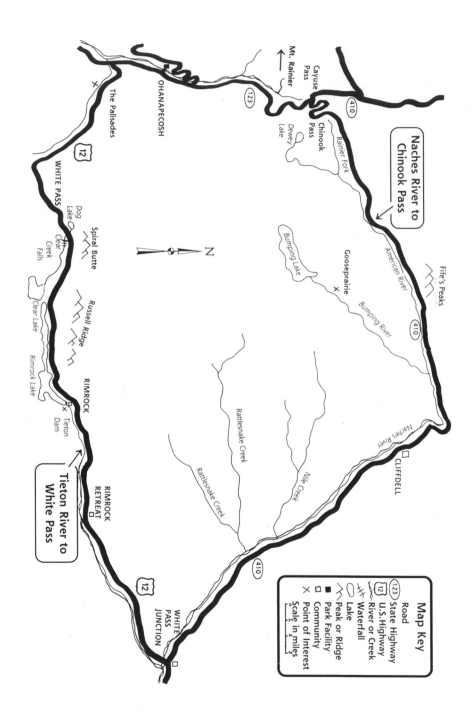

Naches River to
Chinook Pass

Tieton River to
White Pass

Map Key

⑫	Road
⑫	State Highway
⑫	U.S. Highway
	River or Creek
	Waterfall
	Lake
	Peak or Ridge
▪	Park Facility
□	Community
✕	Point of Interest

Scale in miles
0 ⅓ ⅔ 1

dug the fill material for the upper side of the dam, while a smaller, compressed-air shovel excavated filler for the lower side; the fill was loaded into railcars that were then hauled to the dam by a 14-ton locomotive. Just getting the steam engine up the river valley was an engineering feat in itself, requiring a regiment of mules to pull the bulky behemoth on sleds the 26 miles from Naches. Tieton Dam created the third and last storage reservoir in the area; a pair of previous dams had impounded the Bumping River, to the north, and Clear Creek, which ran down the canyon northwest of Rimrock Lake. Together, the three sites provide water for 30,000 acres of otherwise-arid Yakima basin bottomland.

After passing a view of the craggy Goat Rocks, 24.7 miles, left, Highway 12 departs the Rimrock shore near the west end of the lake. Soon the road picks up the canyon of Clear Creek; a section of ancient rock, volcanic sediment from the Russell Ranch formation about 140 million years old, is followed by hardened dacite that spilled down from Spiral Butte a mere 20,000 years or so ago. The dramatic cinder cone, which rises above the right side of the road, derives its name from the spiraling flows of lava that twisted down its northern and eastern sides. Opposite the butte at mile 32.2, left, is the turnout for Clear Creek Falls.

Clear Creek Falls

The pullout allows motorists to debark their autos and hike a few feet to an overlook of lovely Upper Clear Creek Falls, a broad, spreading horsetail of water; Clear Creek Falls, even lovelier with its crystalline 300-foot drop, is worth an additional walk of some hundred yards along the canyon rim to the left. Both cataracts plunge through a chute composed of thin andesite plates, formed from lava erupted by Deer Lake Mountain to the west. Later, just upstream from the falls, Spiral Butte's dacite poured down on top of the Deer Lake Mountain flow, impounding the waters of Clear Creek and forming Dog Lake.

The highway promptly passes Dog Lake, mile 32.4, right, and then runs beneath pale, pink-tinted cliffs composed of Deer Lake Mountain andesite. At 34.8 miles the road reaches White Pass, where a ski resort offers a store, gas, food, and lodging. West of the pass, the highway descends the canyons of first Milridge Creek and then the Clear Fork Cowlitz River; roadcuts display cross-sections of dark gray sandstone, marine sediment

from the Russell Ranch formation that is often covered by Cascade volca-
nic rock. A one-way side road, mile 45.0, left, loops past a vista point for
The Palisades before rejoining the highway.

The Palisades

The one-way access road leads a short distance to an overlook of
The Palisades. On the far side of the canyon, a 486-foot-high wall of

Lower Clear
Creek Falls

The Palisades

red and gray dacite columns rises from the canyon of the Clear Fork Cowlitz River; brightening the conifer-crowned rock mass is a tinting of greenish lichen. Some 20,000 to 110,000 years ago (estimates vary), the rapidly cooling lava of the Clear Fork flow fractured into the forms visible on the far-reaching cliff face—perfect pillars for this tree-rimmed temple of Vulcan.

West of the overlook, the highway continues its steep descent to mile 47.4, where it reaches a junction, right, with State Highway 123 (East Side Road), which presently enters the park (see p. 134). To the left, U.S. 12 runs down the Cowlitz River basin, in seven miles arriving at the town of Packwood (see p. 162).

Naches River to Chinook Pass

One of two eastern approaches to Mount Rainier, State Highway 410 follows the canyons of four rivers — the Naches, Bumping, American, and Rainier Fork — en route to the park entrance at scenic Chinook Pass. A series of striking rock formations and the conifers of the Wenatchee National Forest add interest along the way. (for map, see p. 172)

At White Pass Junction, some four miles north of the town of Naches, State Highway 410 branches right from U.S. Highway 12 (see p. 171), proceeding up the valley of the Naches River (na-CHEEZ, an Indian term for "plenty of water" or "turbulent water"). Outcroppings of dark basalt project from the hillslopes, their forms strange and fantastic, marking the western edge of the Columbia Plateau's ancient lava flows.

Horses and cattle graze the cottonwood-fringed grasslands of the upper Naches bottomland, an area known locally as the Nile Valley. The highway passes the hamlets of Eagle Rock, 8.1 miles (gas and store); Squaw Rock, mile 14.6 (gas, store, and cafe); and Gold Creek, mile 18.1 (store). Conifers replace the cottonwood near Cliffdell, 20.5 miles.

Cliffdell

Nestled between the Naches River and the steep canyonside is the roadside community of Cliffdell, described in the 1940s as "an exclusive resort town owned by Yakima Valley residents." Today, travelers will find a gas station, grocery store, restaurant, and lodge — the last such facilities along the route. The town was named not for the nearby topography but for two friends of local homesteader and developer Russell Davison, *Cliff*ord and *Della* Schott.

Starting at mile 22.4, a series of spectacular basalt cliffs rises above the roadside, right; the hardened lava has formed into numerous tightly packed columns, as if extruded through a giant pasta maker. The highway bends west to cross the Little Naches, 24.7 miles, and then follows the Bumping River.

176

Fife's Peaks

Naches Pass

The pass at the head of the Little Naches River long served as a corridor for crossing the Cascades. Indians from several tribes used the route, as did traders from the Hudson's Bay Company; in 1840 the Yakima chief Owhi brought a herd of cattle over the divide after trading horses for them at Fort Nisqually. Government surveyors scouted the area the following year, and then Captain (later Civil War general) George McClellan studied the gap in 1853 for a proposed rail line. Spurred on by rumors of a road over the pass, the James Longmire party of 36 wagons left the Oregon Trail later that year and headed for the Naches. Fording the river some 68 times, they reached the pass in October, where they found a fall covering of snow but no road. The undaunted emigrants forged ahead, lowering their wagons down the steep western slope by rope (they lost only one wagon in the process). Their teams, without regular feed for seven days, subsisted on vine maple leaves during the descent of the Greenwater and White river canyons. Eventually the long-suffering Longmire contingent reached the

Chinook Pass
Entrance Arch

Puget lowlands, where many of the trail-tested settlers soon prospered. To this day, the pass remains roadless.

At mile 28.3 is the turnoff, left, for American River, Gooseprairie, and Bumping Lake. Now the highway picks up the American River, passing through meadow-dappled forest; roadcuts expose rubbly till that marks the course of the canyon's long-vanished glacier. The paved parking area for the Crow Lake Trail, mile 35.3, right, offers a vista up Miner's Creek of the looming landform known as Fife's Peaks.

Fife's Peaks

Rising above the dark, conifer-spired forest are the jagged Fife's Peaks, which thrust themselves almost threateningly into the firmament. Some 20 to 30 million years ago, the Fife's Peak volcano added its eruptive accretions to the rockwork of the Cascades; although much of the volcano has eroded away, its remnant lava is still found at such diverse sites as the Tieton River basin, to the south, and in the area below Mowich Lake, on the northwestern side of Mount Rainier.

Tom Fife and his father John homesteaded at isolated Gooseprairie in 1886. When John died four years later, his son made a coffin and dug a grave; finding he needed help to carry the body of his 250-pound father *and* the casket, Tom hiked 23 miles and brought back a pair of "neighbors" to help with the job. The Boy Scout camp that later occupied Gooseprairie was a gift from Tom. Youngsters who went to Camp Fife fondly recall "Uncle Tom's Cabin," the tiny, 7-by-9-foot structure that had been their benefactor's home.

Leaving the lowlands, the highway climbs above the deep canyon of the Rainier Fork American River, left; in summertime penstemons purple the roadside. At mile 47.8 the route reaches the Cascade crest at Chinook Pass (for the Enumclaw to Chinook Pass auto tour, see p. 181). Here the wide-topped Mount Rainier National Park entrance arch carries the Naches Peak Trail (see p. 254) over the road. To the left, the path bends around the northern side of Naches Peak, soon to enter the William O. Douglas Wilderness Area.

The Cascadian on the Court

On a crisp fall morning in 1949, two riders saddled up at Tipsoo Lake, paused a moment to chat with a friend, and then headed for Crystal Mountain, off to the north beyond Yakima Peak. A few minutes later, one of the pair was sprawled on a narrow ledge with almost every rib in his body broken, the victim of his rearing, falling, rolling horse. Across the continent in Washington, D.C., the United States Supreme Court was suddenly very close to having a vacancy, for it was Justice William O. Douglas who lay on the Cascade cliffside near death.

The jurist had grown up in nearby Yakima—poor, and the victim of polio at an early age. To strengthen his weakened legs, Douglas tirelessly tramped the mountains, pushing himself to hike 20, 30, even 40 miles in a day. He showed the same determination as a scholar, graduating as valedictorian from Yakima High School and as a Phi Beta Kappa from Whitman College in Walla Walla. Douglas then hoboed the trains to Columbia University Law School, arriving with six cents in his pocket; three years later he graduated second in his class. He taught briefly at Columbia, moved on to Yale, and then went to work for the government. Plucked from the Securities and Exchange Commission by Franklin Delano Roosevelt to be an associate justice, Douglas had served on the Court for 10 years by the time of his accident. He had nearly been FDR's pick for vice-president in 1946.

Although his seat remained unoccupied for some time, Douglas eventually recovered from his riding accident and returned to his place on the bench. He spent much of his recuperation writing *Of Men and Mountains*, a paean to the outdoor life and those who lived it.

Douglas became a strong, sometimes strident, voice on the Court, championing individual freedom, protection of wilderness, and civil rights. Twice he survived impeachment attempts by angry conservatives, the first time after granting a stay of execution for convicted spies Julius and Ethel Rosenberg. When he retired in 1975 Douglas had served on the Court for over 36 years, longer than any other justice.

Whether it was reckless horses or removal-minded Republicans, Douglas had withstood it all. They bred them tough in the Cascades.

Enumclaw to Chinook Pass

The pastoral precincts of the White River Valley, long known for their agricultural productiveness, also serve as the northern gateway to Mount Rainier National Park. Departing Enumclaw, State Highway 410 for a time follows the historic Naches Pass emigrant trail, bends south to continue up the White River, and then enters the park. Here the road becomes the Mather Memorial Parkway, making connections with scenic Sunrise Road and with State Highway 123, which leads to Ohanapecosh. The parkway passes lovely Tipsoo Lake while climbing to climactic Chinook Pass, where our wide-ranging route concludes at the park boundary.

Starting at the intersection of State Highway 410 and Griffin Avenue (State Highway 164) on the southern side of Enumclaw, the auto tour follows Highway 410 southeast out of town.

Enumclaw (EE-num-claw)

When Frank and Mary Stevenson arrived at the upper White River in 1879, they found only half a dozen families inhabiting the entire area. Conditions were primitive: Charles Forget built a rough cedar house with a pipe for a chimney and gave a steer horn to his wife. Whenever the roof caught fire (a frequent occurrence), Mrs. Forget "would blow her horn for all she was worth and the men would come running and start a bucket brigade." A similar implement, placed in a tree south of the river, was used to summon James Johnson, the ferry keeper, to pick up travelers from Wilkeson. Anyone who couldn't produce the required sound was left stranded.

The horns kept sounding as the settlers hacked away at the daunting forest that covered the district; the six-foot-diameter firs that were a homesteader's obstacle would soon become a timberman's attraction, but first the region needed to improve its transportation. The initial attempt was the Coal Creek Road from

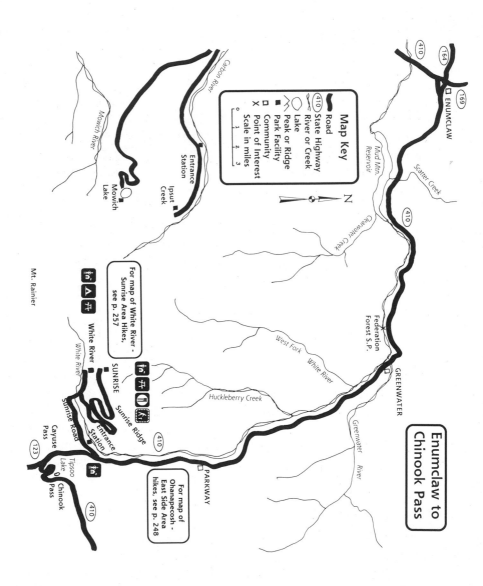

Enumclaw to Chinook Pass

Map Key

━━━ Road

⬡410 State Highway

〰 River or Creek

◯ Lake

◣ Peak or Ridge

■ Park Facility

□ Community

✕ Point of Interest

Scale in miles
0 1 2 3

N

Gabon River

Mowich River

Mowich Lake

Entrance Station

Ipsut Creek

Mud Mtn. Reservoir

Clearwater Creek

Scatter Creek

⬡410

⬡164

⬡169

☐ ENUMCLAW

Federation Forest S.P.

West Fork White River

White River

⬡410

☐ GREENWATER

Greenwater River

Huckleberry Creek

Mt. Rainier

White River

For map of White River - Sunrise Area Hikes, see p. 257

SUNRISE

Sunrise Ridge

Entrance Station

⬡410

Sunrise Road

Cayuse Pass

⬡123

Tipsoo Lake

Chinook Pass

⬡410

☐ PARKWAY

For map of Ohanapecosh - East Side Area hikes, see p. 248

South Prairie in 1884. It was of unusual, but practical, construction: "Trees were cut low to permit wagons to pass over the stumps, but all roots were preserved to avoid the possibility of the drivers becoming sleepy while driving over the route."

A year later came the railroad. To entice the Northern Pacific to put a siding on their property, the Stevensons offered their land for free; the NPRR accepted, and the town had its start. The first building put up was a saloon for the railway workers, followed by a hotel for them to stay in. Frank Stevenson named the new community for a mountain six miles to the north, not knowing, perhaps, that the Indian word "Enumclaw" meant either "thunder and lightning," or, worse yet, "place of the evil spirits."

About this time, the town received an unexpected economic boost, from, of all places, Europe.

Enumclaw Gets Hopping

Salmon, for the local Indians, held an honored place as their main source of food. Settler James Johnson found a different use for the hundreds of great fish that clogged the river near his place—he used them as fertilizer for his hops.

Johnson was one of a number of farmers in the White and Puyallup river valleys who turned to hop growing in the 1880s. Their timing was perfect; a hop blight hit Europe, and prices in the United States, which had been but a few cents a pound, rose to 35 cents and more. Individual harvests brought $10,000 to $60,000 for the year, while one farmer even cleared $100,000. A writer for *Harper's Weekly* described the situation along the Puyallup:

> Bachelors sought out wives, humble ranchers built handsome houses, prosperity blossomed and bourgeoned throughout the length of the valley, and more than one happy couple spent much time ransacking the shops of Tacoma. ("Hop-Picking in Puyallup." *Harper's Weekly* [October 20, 1888], XXXII, 795.)

While the hop boom made fortunes for the farmers, their workers enjoyed the benefit of trickle-down economics; pickers received one silver dollar, cash in hand, per box of hops delivered to the drying house. Indians formed most of the seasonal labor force, arriving in memorable fashion from around Washington state.

Hop pickers

Crossing the Cascades, the Yakimas would arrive "in mile long strings of Cayuse ponies," while members of the coastal tribes

> [i]n their high-powered canoes, each fashioned from a single cedar log and ornamented with barbaric art...[would] navigate the tortuous waters of the Sound and its affluents, and bag and baggage, wives and children, migrate to the hop regions for harvest-work." (Ibid., p. 795)

Picking finished, the season culminated in an all-night dance at the hop kiln. The harvesters then folded their tents and returned to their homes, often taking with them enough silver dollars to last over the winter. The farmers, for their part, took off for another Tacoma shopping spree or merely bolstered their bank accounts. Then, in 1889, an aphid infestation devastated the western Washington fields, and, as quickly as it had come, the hop boom busted. Growing areas east of the Cascades remained unaffected, so that today the Yakima region produces nearly three-fourths of the nation's hops; in Enumclaw, however, the once-profitable product has disappeared completely, and the picturesque hop kilns have followed into oblivion the pickers' "high-powered" canoes and "mile long" processions of Cayuse ponies.

Hopless, but not hapless, the community celebrated 1891's Fourth of July with an Enumclaw pennant flying from the top of

Mount Rainier. Four locals, including future park ranger Oscar Brown, ascended the peak to place the banner there, where it waved from a 23-foot flagpole just beneath Old Glory.

In 1893 an enlarged Enumclaw contained two general stores, two saloons, a drug store, blacksmith shop, market, livery and feed stable, real estate and loan office, and a pair of hotels. Three years later the town saw the start of what soon became its biggest business.

The Green Gold of the
White River Lumber Company

"Tighten up!" called out W. S. Young, and Barney and Jack did just that. The one-ton-plus horses of the lead team promptly took up the slack in the rigging, while Scott, Clyde, and the rest of the other three teams readied themselves for the pull. When he had an extra-heavy turn of logs, Young, who didn't waste words, commanded, "tighten up hard!" Work like this built up big appetites, and by noon, after six hours on the logging road, the teams were ready for the daily special—a gallon of oats and crushed corn, with a flake of hay each for dessert.

Young's eight horses were but the first segment of the White River Lumber Company's transportation system. Barney, Jack, and their cohorts hauled the logs down to the sawmill, which transformed the loads into rough cut timbers, some as large as two feet square. These were then dropped into a flume, where water diverted from Boise Creek washed the wood along a three-mile route to the planing mill at Enumclaw. After a final milling, the finished lumber was loaded onto the railcars of the Northern Pacific and carried to retail lots, with many of the shipments traveling to eastern Washington and the Midwest.

Carl Hanson, his three sons, and a pair of other partners formed the company in 1896, when they bought out an operation whose mill had just gone up in smoke. Six years later, the new outfit had its own fire to contend with; a spark at their logging camp was fanned to flame by high winds, and soon the bunkhouse, cookhouse, and other camp buildings were incinerated. Next to go was the sawmill, where logs in the mill pond burned flat to the water.

Nels Rasmussen, just a day out of the Danish navy, fled the mill with the soles of his boots burning; the flames followed him and the other workers toward Enumclaw, where, at midnight, the planing mill's whistle wailed a warning and all hands turned out to try to save the structure. Merchants did what they could to help, as the general store offered up its stock of shovels and druggist Charlie Newman passed out salve for the men's smoke-sore eyes. By now, the flames were licking at the lumber in the outdoor drying yards.

Buckley's mill let out its men, who rushed over to help fight the blaze. Women stood by their homes, wet gunny sacks in hand, ready to smother embers that landed on their roofs; meanwhile, a train waited at the Northern Pacific station, steam up, prepared to evacuate the town. Sixteen hours later the planing mill and the rest of Enumclaw still stood—the firefighters, although nearly blind from the smoke, had beaten the flames back.

By 1904, Young's horse teams were old news. The company had already used a small, steam-powered "donkey" engine for five years to move logs to the skid road, and now "No. 1" was ready to take over the rest of the hauling. She was a bit bigger than Barney and Jack, weighing in at 25 tons; moreover, the newly arrived Climax locomotive burned wood instead of oats and could pull a much heavier load than the horses. However, getting her from the NPRR's line to the newly built logging railroad on Boise Creek wasn't easy. Every day for a week, company crews laid 50 feet of track, engineer Ed Johnson steamed No. 1 forward, the rails and ties behind the engine were taken up, and then, again and again, the entire process was repeated.

Such persistence paid off. As the logs kept leaving the forest, White River merged with Weyerhauser in 1929 and built an electric powered mill. By 1946 the company maintained 19 retail yards to sell its lumber. The entire operation became wholly owned by Weyerhauser in 1949; twenty-five years later it counted 635 employees. For these modern-era workers mining the green gold of the nearby forests remained a demanding business, but at least there were no more orders to "tighten up hard."

Enumclaw's lumber-led economy was bolstered by a second commodity—dairy products. The area's high-quality cream commanded premium prices, and in 1895 local farmers, many of them

Nova log truck, Enumclaw

Danish, established a cooperative creamery patterned after organizations in their home country. It was the first of several ventures
that by 1909 gave the town more cooperative associations than any
U.S. community of comparable size. In addition to the creamery,
Enumclaw also had a co-op telephone system, a department store
operating under the Rochdale plan, and the Farmers Mutual Insurance Company.

Cooperation...and competition. In 1910 the Chicago, Milwaukee, St. Paul and Pacific built a branch line to Enumclaw, thus challenging the NPRR for the town's rail traffic. Both lines ran several
freights daily, bidding for business from the region's mills and
mines.

The bustling, two-railroad town incorporated in 1913. That
same year saw the start of Heinie Sand's Enumclaw Stage, a popular conveyance whose drivers would pick up passengers at their
homes, sometimes coming in for breakfast while the other riders
waited outside. Always crowded, the five-passenger Fords often
carried up to 12 travelers, their suitcases piled on the hood and the
women seated upon the men's laps.

There were times when Deputy Sheriff Tom Smith could have
used the stage's services. When Smith, a non-driver, needed to pursue a lawbreaker, he would flag down the nearest vehicle, hop in,
and order the startled motorist to catch the culprit. In May 1916,
spotting "an autoist suffering from speed mania," Smith hurried to
the Reliable Garage and commandeered co-owner John Fea and his

Fea's formidable
fleet of Fords

Ford. They chased the car-borne criminal out beyond Enumclaw, where Smith nabbed his quarry when the unsuspecting driver finally slowed down. Hauled back to town and "assessed 14 simoleans," the surprised speed demon remarked, "did you catch me with that—Ford?" This was testimonial enough for the garage, which began selling Fords four months later.

Later years brought changes to Enumclaw—a pickle factory in 1946, an influx of airline pilots, who commuted to SeaTac, in the 1960s—but today the town retains its countrified, cooperative sense of community. It still sees its share of tourists, too, headed for the northern entryway to the park. Mountain-bound motorists who consider speeding through the city streets should, however, first think twice—and look carefully for any nearby Fords.

The highway passes the Weyerhauser (formerly the White River Lumber Company) mill, 2.6 miles, left, and the turnoff for the Mud Mountain Reservoir, mile 5.0, right. Oceanspray, red and blue elderberry, and hardhack then cover parts of the numerous clearcuts in the vicinity of Scatter Creek.

Scatter Creek

Here in 1918 the 53rd Spruce Squadron cut its namesake wood, which was used to build combat airplanes, and sent the logs to the White River Lumber Company mill for sawing. The squadron was part of the War Department's Spruce Production Division, a group of World War I soldiers assigned to saw instead of shoot. Patterned after an army training facility, the squadron's camp featured long wooden barracks, rows of tents set along company streets, and even a parade ground.

Between Enumclaw and Greenwater the highway follows the huge Osceola Mudflow, which rushed down Rainier's northern slopes to fill much of the White River Valley some 6,000 years ago; look for a jumble of various-size rock fragments in roadcuts, such as the one at mile 13.7, left. A patch of old-growth forest precedes the entrance to Federation Forest State Park, 16.6 miles, right.

Federation Forest State Park

History, both human and natural, is the focus at Federation Forest. Trails and interpretive displays showcase the transition zone between coastal and mountain woodlands, while one hiking route follows part of the historic Naches Pass Trail, over which the Longmire wagon train traveled in 1853 on their epic trip to Puget Sound. The property that became the park was purchased by the far-sighted Washington Federation of Women's Clubs, which wanted to preserve a remnant of the impressive old-growth forest that once blanketed the region. In 1925, when a local newspaperman reported on an excursion east of Enumclaw, much of this wondrous woodland was still intact:

> Almost the entire distance the road winds through virgin forests, by high, green mountains, lofty peaks, and along the sylvan banks of silvery mountain streams. Great forest monarchs untouched by the hand of man gird the smooth, winding, but ever climbing roadway; with here a dale, yonder a dell, and just over there a floral mountain meadow forming an Edenlike welkin, the beauty of which is too lofty for language to reach. (Jacobin, *A Glimpse of the Charmed Land*, p. 9)

East of Federation Forest the highway briefly runs beside the White River before bending south to cross the Greenwater River and then enter the village of Greenwater, 18.2 miles.

Greenwater

Just west of town the Greenwater and White rivers meet. The Longmire Party reportedly crossed the former 16 times during their arduous descent from Naches Pass; a stone monument across from the town store commemorates their exploits. In the 1920s, the "nature embowered dell" here already contained a small resort, while up the nearby hill was Captain Dick Crain's Naches Tavern, a rustic structure noted for its Indian curio gallery. Contemporary Greenwater features not only a store, gasoline, dining, lodging, public showers, but also a glossy, modernized version of the tavern.

The conifer-shaded confines of Silver Springs and Parkway, mile 32.0, are followed by the Crystal Mountain resort area turnoff, 33.1 miles, left, and the entrance arch for Mount Rainier National Park, mile 33.2, overhead.

Old Naches Pass Trail,
Federation Forest State Park

Silver Springs Camp and Parkway

A string of cedar cabins, "for rent or sale," lined Silver and Goat creeks in the 1920s. Close at hand was, according to its own advertisement, a "splendid inn." Many of the cabins still repose in well-preserved dignity in the darkening woods.

Bolstered by developments on the northeastern slopes of Mount Rainier, a post office was established at Parkway a few months after the 1931 opening of Sunrise Lodge. The community also contained a small store and a crude collection of "tourist cabins" that each offered a solitary room, no toilet, one dim light bulb, and a wood-burning stove; nearly engulfing the entirety was a shadowy wilderness of tall fir and hemlock. Offered such enticements, most travelers no doubt continued on to the park.

Now the road moves up the steep-sided confines of the White River Canyon, passing at mile 37.3 the Crystal Lakes Trailhead, left. Sunrise Road, 37.8 miles, right, provides access to the White River Entrance Station, White River Campground, and Sunrise (see p. 141). Opposite the turnoff is a sign for the Mather Memorial Parkway.

From Mule Teams to Mountain Scenes: Steve Mather Comes to Run the Parks

Among the hundred or so Sierra Clubbers sojourning at Paradise in July 1905 was an energetic new member from Chicago who had recently recovered from a nervous breakdown. It was a grand gathering, with three other clubs involved, and the Chicagoan, Stephen T. Mather, found plenty of time to rub elbows with some of the country's prime outdoor enthusiasts. The experience took; a decade later, when Mather revisited Paradise, he came as the boss of Mount Rainier—and all the country's other national parks.

Mather had a knack for getting things done. He'd spent part of the 1890s as the publicity man for Francis Marion "Borax" Smith, putting the phrase "20 Mule Team Borax" on the lips of America's housewives and boxes of the product above their sinks. Smith made millions, and Mather then started a competing company that provided him and his partners with their own borax bonanza.

By 1914 Mather was rich but restless. He accordingly toured the West, stopping at several of the national parks. The manner of their management offended his highly attuned business sense, so Mather sent a letter of complaint to his old college chum, Secretary of the Interior Franklin K. Lane. Knowing an opportunity when he saw it, Lane fired off a response to his friend: "Dear Steve," it read, "if you don't like the way the national parks are being run, come on down to Washington and run them yourself."

Which is exactly what Mather did. First as an assistant to Lane, and then, when the National Park Service was established in 1917, as its first director, Mather ran the parks for more than a decade, retiring in 1928 only when a stroke laid him low. His charm, energy, and vision carried the park system from its childhood, as a frail and underfunded foundling, on to an early maturity—a set of expertly staffed, well planned, and easily accessible sites that thrilled thousands upon thousands of tourists while protecting the precious resources in a nearly natural condition.

Even in illness Mather could not let go of the parks. When Horace Albright, his assistant, visited him after his stroke, Albright found Mather had lost his speech and was paralyzed on his right side. Mather tried desperately to speak; Albright bent closer and at last heard his boss form the word "Cascade." Albright understood

Parkway sign,
opposite Sunrise Road

immediately what Mather wanted—information about a project to save the timber along the Cascade Highway then being built through the northeast corner of Mount Rainier National Park.

Albright took over as head of the park service in January, 1929. A year later, Mather, who had seemed to be recovering, suffered a second stroke and died. The Cascade Highway, which had worried him so greatly, was named for Mather after his death. On July 4, 1932, a series of memorial plaques were dedicated in the national parks to commemorate his sixty-fifth birthday. The one at Mount Rainier stands near the Mather Memorial Parkway at Tipsoo Lake; like the others, its inscription reads:

HE LAID THE FOUNDATION OF THE NATIONAL PARK
SERVICE, DEFINING AND ESTABLISHING THE POLICIES
UNDER WHICH ITS AREAS SHALL BE DEVELOPED AND
CONSERVED UNIMPAIRED FOR FUTURE GENERATIONS.
THERE WILL NEVER BE AN END TO THE GOOD THAT
HE HAS DONE.

The highway then climbs past ethereal Ghost Lake, mile 40.9, right, above which is Sheepskull Gap, a high pass in which some 2,000 of the horned ruminants reportedly perished in a snowstorm. Sheep are replaced by ponies at Cayuse Pass, 41.3 miles, where State Highway 123 (see p. 134) branches right on its way towards Ohanapecosh. Our route bears left, soon switchbacking across a huge rockface; penstemon, paintbrush, and larkspur cling to the cliffs, along with woolly sunflower and silverback luina.

Roadcuts here expose the hardened mudflows, now nearly 40 million years old, that carried shattered lava from the sides of submerged volcanoes; the rock is composed of sharp-pebbled breccia and gray-green sandstone. Cutting a roadbed through the three-and-a-half miles of resistant terrain between Cayuse and Chinook passes required 11 years of construction work.

A second switchback showcases avalanche lily, spreading phlox, and crimson columbine; it is followed by the parking lot, mile 44.2, left, for the picnic area at tiny Tipsoo Lake. Located here at the Mather monument is the starting point for two hikes: the Tipsoo Lake loop (see p. 254) and the Naches Peak loop (see p. 254).

Tipsoo Lake

Mather's parkway bends around the lake and makes a final climb to the crest of the Cascades, reaching it and the park boundary at the Chinook Pass entrance arch, 44.8 miles. From here the highway drops into the awesome canyon of the American River's Rainier Fork on its way to the sunny climes of Yakima (see p. 176).

Buckley to Carbon River

Coal gave the Carbon River communities their start, drawing mining operations, hundreds of workers, and the Northern Pacific Railroad into the heavily forested canyon. As logging and sandstone quarrying became secondary industries, a string of company towns sprang up in the vicinity, while alpinists used the rail line and a prospector's trail to approach Mount Rainier. Yet, after an all too brief heyday, the Carbon found its wares either unwanted or unavailable: concrete came to replace sandstone, oil outdid coal, and the timber took its time regenerating. The settlements vanished or diminished, the honeycombed hillsides around them riddled with tunnels that would never open again. Peak-seekers still come up the canyon, bound for either the Carbon River or the Mowich entrance to the park; other visitors now travel only to Wilkeson, or perhaps Carbonado, to see such pieces of the past as time has kept from total ruin. Within the tattered towns, now-silent streets offer a meditation on the impermanence of human enterprise, while eastward, above the river and through the centuries, stands the Mountain.

The auto tour begins on the west side of Buckley, at the "Y" junction of State Highway 410 and State Highway 165.

Buckley

First called Perkins' Landing or Perkins' Prairie, after an early homesteader, the small settlement became White River Siding, a stop on the Northern Pacific's transcontinental line, in 1884. The town was platted four years later by Alexander Wickersham and named for John M. Buckley, division superintendent of the NPRR. The area was big tree country, as a 12.5-foot-diameter stump in the city park attests, and several of the town's early enterprises were mills. One of these, the Buckley Lumber Company, brought about the town's early destruction in 1892, when a fire in its store spread

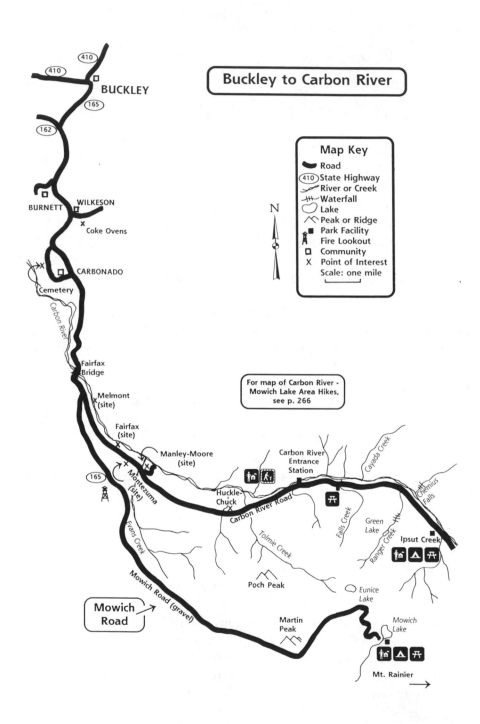

Buckley to Carbon River

Map Key

🐛 Road
(410) State Highway
〜 River or Creek
⊢⊢⊢ Waterfall
◯ Lake
⋀ Peak or Ridge
🔳 Park Facility
🔥 Fire Lookout
□ Community
X Point of Interest
Scale: one mile

N

410

410   BUCKLEY

165

162

BURNETT   WILKESON
                X Coke Ovens

CARBONADO

Cemetery

Carbon River

Fairfax
Bridge

Melmont
(site)

Fairfax
(site)

Manley-Moore
(site)

For map of Carbon River -
Mowich Lake Area Hikes,
see p. 266

Carbon River
Entrance
Station

Cayada Creek

Chenuis
Falls

165

Montezuma
(site)

Huckle-
Chuck

Carbon River Road

Falls Creek

Green
Lake

Ranger Creek

Ipsut Creek

Evans Creek

Tolmie Creek

Poch Peak

Eunice
Lake

Mowich Road (gravel)

**Mowich
Road**

Martin
Peak

Mowich
Lake

Mt. Rainier →

along Main Street and razed eleven businesses and two houses in an hour and twenty minutes.

Buckley rebuilt and soon expanded. By 1904 Main Street was lined with a string of substantial brick buildings, and where the town had featured a mere four saloons before the fire, it could now boast a full dozen. Intensive imbibing was nothing new for Buckley, which had done it big for over a decade.

Main Street, Buckley

When the White River Ran Red: Buckley's Besotted Bucket Brigade

Early Thursday morning, May 22, 1891, found freight train #56 leaving Buckley, heading east. As his locomotive rounded the curve just before the White River, engineer W. E. Shipman stared at an unexpected sight: another train was bearing down on him, already part way across the bridge. Shipman "threw on the air," and then he and his fireman jumped for their lives. On the other train, engineer H. Ingalls and his fireman did likewise, and a moment later the four men heard a terrific crash as a half-mile's worth of rolling stock smashed together.

Buckley's
big wreck

Except for the pair of crushed engines, there was remarkably little damage. Two railcars, one carrying ice and the other grain, had jumped the tracks, and a car filled with hogs had pitched on its side and smashed. One car, telescoped by the tender of engine #56, was more badly mangled; containing some 45 barrels of wine, it appeared badly wounded, its blood-dark liquid oozing ominously into the White River below. Amazingly, a few barrels were thrown free, and they now reposed by the railside, their contents intact.

Word of the wreck reached town within the hour, and soon a stream of bright-eyed Buckleyites was bound for the bridge. As the Buckley *Banner* reported it, "Children forgot to go to school, women deserted their breakfast dishes and men abandoned their positions in the mills which whistled repeatedly to call them but in vain."

When the arrivals sniffed "the peculiar aroma of good California wine," many of the men and boys decided to assist in the salvage work:

> A continual stream of mixed drinks trickled down along the whole length of the side of the car, and tin pans, old cans and every kind of vessel that could be brought into requisition were rapidly filled and drained off, while many began to arrive with buckets and milk pans to obtain a supply to take to their homes....People continued to arrive from both sides of the river

and buckets continued to increase. Section men and members of the steel gang instead of protecting the company's property joined the hoboes and made the most of their opportunity to get full. A number of church members, noted for their piety took an active part in the exercises...

After a while the liquor began to tell upon a goodly number of the bibulous citizens, and not unexpectedly a fight was started ...The contest at this stage of the proceedings between the quietly grunting hogs in one of the wrecked cars and the assembly of American intelligence rioting about the spilled liquor was decidedly in favor of the hogs....

In a subsequent tally, the *Banner* noted that "several women toted away pails full of wine, but some of them only took wheat," and that just three inebriates had been hauled into court; their total fine: $11.

All told, it was a unique event; the only time in the town's history that a train wreck—rather than a fire—brought forth a Buckley bucket brigade.

The city utilized its outstanding soil, known as "Buckley loam," to grow other crops besides tall timber. Hops came early, but were soon supplanted by berries; nurseryman William Schwab produced a new fruit strain known as the "Pacific Gold" peach and Buckley initiated an annual "Peacherino Festival." Meanwhile, eggs and dairy goods also became big-time commodities. Adding to the community's commerce was its position as the trading center for the Carbon River region and its status as a highway hub: in the 1930s Buckley was connected by paved routes with Enumclaw and Seattle to the north; Sumner and Tacoma to the west; and Wilkeson, Carbonado, and Fairfax to the south. The Woman's Musical Club and Literary Club had earlier enhanced the city's budding cosmopolitan air by funding construction of both a municipal library and auditorium. Civic spirit was still strong in 1962, when Buckley won first prize in the Seattle World's Fair beautification contest.

Departing Buckley, the auto tour proceeds some 50 yards southward on Highway 165, turns right at the first intersection, and then runs southwest to a junction, mile 1.6, with State Highway 162. Here our route turns left, continuing on Highway 165, and enters coal country. At mile 2.5 the road passes through Burnett, where a row of weathered houses faces a hulking store.

Burnett

The aging buildings that front Highway 165 (Carbon River Road) are the remnants of Upper Burnett. In the canyon to the west once lay Lower Burnett, the former town of the South Prairie Coal Company. Charles H. Burnett opened the company's mine at the latter site in 1881; accompanied by Hiram and Nellie, his "sure-footed" mules, he supervised the operation until 1906, when the property was acquired by the Pacific Coast Coal Company. The mine produced a high-grade coal favored by the steamers that plied Puget Sound.

In 1891 Lower Burnett consisted of two rows of whitewashed houses, separated by a winding dirt road down whose center ran the rails of the NPRR. The community at the time was divided into "Downtown," "Finntown," and, oddly, "Brooklyn." Finnish and Russian miners predominated; no longer available was Burnett's Chinese workforce, which had numbered some 600 before Tacoma's Knights of Labor, as part of the region's anti-Asian purge, drove them out and set fire to their hillside homes on "Chinaman Slope."

A 1904 tunnel explosion claimed some 15 workers despite the heroics of powerhouse engineer Gus Strand, who made repeated rescue attempts until fumes overcame him, whereupon he was dragged from the mine nearly dead himself. Two years later the Pacific Coast Coal Company bought the Burnett operation; it had its own mine disaster, a 1918 explosion that took a dozen lives.

In 1921 Burnett's mine, like others in the region, endured a bitter strike. The company compelled the miners to vacate their houses, and most of the erstwhile employees never returned. The mine closed in 1927; Lower Burnett was abandoned soon afterward and many of its buildings were moved up the canyon to Carbonado.

Highway 165 then approaches Wilkeson, passing under the town's impressive arch (made from local sandstone) at mile 4.1. A glimpse of the onion-domed Holy Trinity Orthodox Church, mile 4.4, left, precedes the "downtown" business district, mile 4.5. The community offers a gas station, store, and eating establishments.

Holy Trinity Church

Wilkeson

More diversified than other Carbon River communities, Wilkeson at various times produced not only coal but also timber, coke, and sandstone. The coal was first found in 1862, soon forgotten, and then located again in 1874; its rediscovery motivated the Northern Pacific Railroad to put in a branch line three years later. The town, consisting of a depot, store, and post office, was named in honor of Samuel Wilkeson, secretary of the NPRR's board and aide to the rail line's owner, financier Jay Cooke. Mining began in 1879, but by the mid-1880s the community hadn't grown much; a journalist spoke of "the four houses, forming the town of Wilkeson," while noting that a multifaceted Mr. (John Price) Jones combined the duties of station agent, storekeeper, innkeeper, postmaster, express agent, and justice of the peace. The writer, bound for Mount Rainier, took one of the two approved routes of the day (the other was via the Nisqually Valley) by riding the train to Wilkeson and then following the Bailey Willis Trail southeast up the Carbon River Canyon.

Gradually the town and its commerce expanded. The Walker Cut Stone Company started up in 1886, marketing the area's abundant, high-quality sandstone. Two years later Wilkeson became home to the Pacific Coast's first coke ovens, which fueled the Sound's steel industry, and by 1890 the huge St. Paul & Tacoma Lumber Company had a camp in the vicinity.

Mining remained Wilkeson's main activity. At the turn of the century, the miners could still be found walking to and from the tunnels in the dark of night, their way lit by the carbide lamps that also illuminated their workplace; sometimes an entire week would thus pass without the men seeing the light of day. Returning home covered with coal dust, the workers bathed, had supper, and then headed downtown to the saloons and clubs.

It was said that the miner's chief helpers, the "Carbon River" mules, were exceptionally clever. The animals would compliantly pull a string of four loaded coal cars, but if they heard the clink of a fifth car being attached, they would stage a sitdown strike, remaining recumbent until the offending vehicle was removed from the string.

Come 1898 and the bustling burg celebrated the Fourth of July in particularly boisterous fashion. During a barroom altercation Joseph Crotts shot Jack Snell dead amid considerable confusion:

> The saloon was crowded at the time but everyone was drunk and no attempt was made to detain the murderer, who calmly walked out. The curious part of the affair was that but one man was sober enough to be positive as to the identity of the man who fired the shot, and an innocent bystander, Sandy Irish, came near being lynched by the drunken crowd. (Hall, *Dateline: Wilkeson*, p. 3)

The affair was finally cleared up when Crotts surrendered to the Tacoma police. Unchastened by the event, Wilkeson remained a wild place; just two years later came a riot report that sounded as if it belonged on the sports page: "There was a good old fashioned fight in Wilkeson on the previous Sunday—About 200 men took part in it. Rocks, bricks, bats, knives and revolvers were used. No one was killed but several were pretty badly injured."

Wilkeson incorporated in 1909. Soon the city council had civilized the rowdy community by setting a curfew for children, forbidding domestic animals from running loose at night, and prohibiting use of the saloons by women. Only the town's males, who had already established their rectitude in the Crotts-Irish fracas, were exempted from restriction.

The community had two sections; near the mine was uptown, which belonged to the NPRR, while downtown, below the tracks, was privately owned. The latter area had halls for the Finns, Poles,

Wilkeson coke ovens

and Slovaks along with several stores and as many as 13 saloons. Among the town's businesses were the Wilkeson Bottling Works (a manufacturer of soft drinks) and two bakeries, one of which produced "Dickson's Dandy Bread" in quantities of up to 800 loaves a day. Merchant John Kuss maintained a shop where he hand rolled Havana cigars and created enticing advertisements:

> Smoke
> Wilkeson Belle
> Leader Special
> The Cigar That'll Satisfy
> As Good As Any
> And
> Better Than Many
> Anywhere in the District

Twice during the 1910s parts of the town burned. Firefighting efforts had little effect: a series of photos shows store owners calmly removing their goods from several wooden structures, stacking the objects in the street, and then watching as the buildings blazed. Offsetting the losses were several lasting additions, including the $26,985 sandstone school building and the Holy Trinity Orthodox Church, with its blue-hued onion dome and three-barred Slavic cross.

During World War I Wilkeson dealt in superlatives. The International Spar Company brought out some of the largest timbers cut anywhere—sections of Douglas-fir up to 130 feet long for use on four-masted freight schooners. Even more impressive was the operation of the Wilkeson Coal and Coke Company, whose "[o]ne hundred and eighty-five enormous bee-hive coke ovens, blazing night and day as a single battery, proclaim coking to be the biggest industry of Wilkeson."

Yet it was the output of the Wilkeson Sandstone Quarry Company that gave the town its most lasting fame. Besides the community's own school, the quarry provided stone for a number of Washington's most impressive buildings, including the State Capitol and the Temple of Justice in Olympia, several Tacoma high schools, and the Washington State Historical Society Museum. In addition, small pieces of the rock were shaped into cobblestones and used to pave many of Tacoma's streets.

The decade drew to a close with Wilkeson in disarray. In March of 1919 citizens demanded that authorities "clean up" the locale, claiming that bootlegging and gambling flourished openly; by then, Wilkeson was reputedly the roughest mining town west of Butte, Montana. At the end of October came more difficulty when the miners went out on strike. An initial settlement was followed by a rollback in wages that led to a second strike in 1921, which went badly for the workers. Forced to vacate company housing, the miners were eventually "starved out" and lost their union.

By the 1930s the town's mining days were numbered. Demand for coal diminished as oil became the fuel of choice, while Tacoma's smelter now imported its coke from the east via the Panama Canal. The Wilkeson Coal and Coke Company closed in 1936, and by the start of World War II the town was nearly abandoned, with many of the remaining residents "dependent upon relief."

The 1970s found Wilkeson's sole industry its sandstone quarry. The sleepy town had languished so long that when Carl Fabiani, a park ranger, attempted to build a traditionally styled log cabin, the city council was flummoxed; no councilman could recall ever having a *new* building come up for permit review.

At the south end of the business district, unsigned Railroad Avenue, mile 4.6, left, leads past the school and a row of crumbling coke ovens to the site of "uptown" Wilkeson. Only the concrete foundation of a coal bunker, now nearly hidden by the forest, marks the spot.

The highway then leaves Wilkeson and climbs to a clearcut-covered plateau, passing Cemetery Road, 5.8 miles, right, and Carbonado Road, mile 6.8. Both routes lead to Carbonado, a collection of one-time company houses anchored by an imposing brick schoolhouse.

Carbonado (Karh-buhn-AY-doh)

Change came quickly after Robert Wingate located coal here in 1879: within a year a mine opened near the Carbon River, the Northern Pacific Railroad extended its line from Wilkeson to the terrace above the mine site, and a post office was in business. In 1882 rail baron Charles Crocker (of the Central Pacific's "Big Four") and his cohorts acquired the mine and began shipping its coal by steamer to California, where it fueled the locomotives of the CP's sister line, the Southern Pacific.

Crocker had earlier employed Chinese laborers to help build the Transcontinental Railroad, where they had proved impressively industrious; he accordingly brought many of their kinsmen to Carbonado, where they worked the mines and built the "Chinese steps" from the townsite's terrace down to river level. Like their counterparts at nearby Burnett, the adroit Asians were driven from the area in 1886.

Thirteen years later, Carbonado lost another contingent of miners. Intemperance—for tobacco—rather than intolerance was the cause this time.

Benedict Zeidler's Fatal Flame

Saturday, December 9, 1899, came up rainy, but it made little difference to the miners who slogged into Tunnel Number 7 of the Carbon Hill Coal Company; they would spend the entire day deep underground, far away from the weather. The crew passed through the tunnel entrance, where two hours earlier fireman Rees Jones had chalked "No Gas" on the blackboard. The men paid scant heed to the message, for it was always the same; Number 7 never contained any of the explosive methane that was the dread of most miners.

About 8:30 that morning, Benedict Zeidler, a 57-year-old German worker of long experience, decided to take a short break. Out came his tobacco pouch and corncob pipe; smoking was forbidden in the mines, but the rule was often broken and Zeidler was about to break it again. He filled his pipe, tamped down the tobacco, and removed the cover of his carbide lamp to expose the flame.

Some distance away, mule driver James Conway was working near the mouth of the shaft. Suddenly, as if "a ton of dynamite had burst," Conway was thrown to the ground and surrounded by flames. He crawled through the fire on his hands and knees until he reached the tunnel's "lokey," the little railroad engine. "For God's sake, pull out quickly," gasped Conway, as he struggled to breathe.

Tunnel Number 7, the mine's heaviest coal producer, had finally developed a leak of methane gas—and Benedict Zeidler's flame had found it.

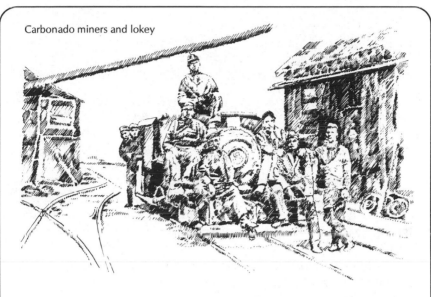
Carbonado miners and lokey

The explosion killed Conway's co-worker, Watt Jones, and snuffed out the lives of Zeidler and his son, Bennie. It caught Rees Jones, the fireman, as he rode out of the mine on a mule cart, throwing him off and killing him instantly. Other workers also died from the blast, but even more perished in the deadly "afterdamp" that followed. Sweeping through the tunnels and shafts, this cloud of smoky, oxygenless gas caught many of the trapped and stunned miners, smothering them where they stood or lay.

As the mine whistle shrieked to summon off-duty workers, the company cut off telegraph communication with Tacoma; officials later claimed they needed to "evaluate" the situation before sending out word of the disaster. At the mine entrance supervisors held back the gathering crowd, which stared in horror as bloodied and choking workers staggered out or were carried from the tunnel. Burn victims were wrapped in cloths soaked in linseed oil and lemon juice; the dead were covered in burlap before being removed from the mine.

The day wore on, word leaked out, and relief parties arrived from Wilkeson and Buckley. At 4:50 P.M. a train left Tacoma filled with officials, including Governor Rodgers, Sheriff Mills, Coroner Hoska, and coal mine inspector Little. Also on board were two reporters from the Tacoma *Daily Ledger*, who would soon provide details absent from the so-far scanty reports of the disaster.

For a time it was feared that most of the shift's 76 workers were dead, but later a procession of battered Finnish miners came down from the top of Wingate Hill, having managed to escape by climbing out of the mine's air shafts. Nearly all of them were burned or otherwise injured.

More victims were located and brought out of the mine as rescuers probed through the poisoned air of the tunnel. At 5:00 A.M. the next morning, Mike Knish was found blindly groping his way through one of the workings; another miner, Peter Merpax, suddenly regained consciousness as his co-workers carried him out for dead. The would-be corpse thought he'd fallen asleep and was now being relieved by the new shift. As he emerged from the tunnel, Merpax slapped himself on the chest and shouted, "Peter's all right; how's my dogs?" The pair were the last men taken from the mine alive; at Carbonado's impromptu morgue, 32 bodies lay in their burlap shrouds.

On December 13, a procession of miners carried 23 coffins west of town on their lengthy journey to the Carbonado cemetery; the caskets were followed the next day by nine more. Most of the

Row of headstones,
Carbonado cemetery

victims were buried alongside each other, in a long row at the edge of the forest. For the living, life, however altered, went on. The wife of Richard Dare, a bride of but a few months and a widow of five days, left on the train, bound for her family in Pennsylvania. Someone came to Rees Jones's room and took away his possessions, which included dozens of books on mining and engineering; the fireman who'd chalked the fateful message on the blackboard had been studying to qualify for a promotion. Daniel Meredith pondered the quirk of fate that spared his life in the blast but later claimed that of his father, Howell, after he entered the tunnel to search for his son.

And, for a time, the workers lit no pipes in the mine.

Unlike Wilkeson, Carbonado was exclusively a company town; employees stayed in company housing and were required to buy their goods at the company store. The latter operation offered no green vegetables or unsalted butter, so residents risked buying these commodities from Sumner farmers, who drove their wagons up to Carbonado's outskirts during the dead of night. Superintendent Lew Davies eased some of the restrictions in the early 1900s, allowing supplies from South Prairie and fresh milk from Wilkeson, but he still strictly enforced the housing regulations, firing William and George Downing for letting another miner, Allen Tweed, board at their house. Tweed promptly returned to the company hotel and the Downings were just as promptly rehired.

As with many mining communities, immigrants made up much of Carbonado's workforce; during World War I some 23 different nationalities were represented. Besides native-born Americans, the largest groups were Italians, Finns, and Austrians, but the far-flung collection also contained Croatians, Dalmatians, Lithuanians, and Bohemians. Benefiting from its cosmopolitan composition, Carbonado claimed the 1928 state soccer championship.

In 1917 the company built a $20,000 "wash and change building." The facility allowed 800 miners to bathe simultaneously, so that "[t]he worker goes home clean in body and refreshed in mind, instead of being depressed and perchance offensive under the sweat and grime of labor." It wasn't enough to satisfy the employees; beset by a rash of accidents that year, they went on strike until their unpopular superintendent was dismissed. A second strike, in 1919, was followed by the region-wide walkout in 1921. After 29 months the stoppage ended; the workers had been evicted and, like others elsewhere, lost their union. More accidents then struck the mines, claiming lives in 1923, 1927, and 1930. A declining coal market and the Depression finally doomed Carbonado, and the mine closed in 1937. Its pumps were turned off on March 17 and immediately water began rising in the shafts. The mine was a menace to the end; on the last work day, April 1, Don Brikett was killed on the final shift.

When the mine closed, its operator, the Pacific Coast Coal Company, gave up ownership and the property reverted to the estate of Charles Crocker, which meant that two schools, Stanford University and the University of California, gained control. Not wanting to be in the mining ghost town business, the universities soon divested themselves of the holdings, destroying unwanted mine buildings and allowing residents to buy company houses for just a few hundred dollars each. Within two years nearly every home in Carbonado was privately owned, but deed restrictions—no new businesses, no digging (including for graves or basements)—caused the town to stagnate. Only in 1966 were the restrictions at last removed, but by then Carbonado had settled into a perhaps perpetual somnolence.

Southeast of the Carbonado turnoff, the highway passes more clearcuts and then runs next to a strip of old-growth forest; a dirt track, right, marks the abandoned right-of-way for the old Northern Pacific rail line. The road narrows as it cuts along the cliffs above the deep Carbon River Gorge, finally crossing the dark chasm on the Fairfax Bridge, 9.7 miles; the aging but recently refurbished structure, officially named the (Robert) O'Farrell Bridge, was completed in 1921. Below the east end of the span, the old railbed leads south to the canyonside site of Melmont.

Melmont

Little is left to mark the whereabouts of Melmont, a coal mining community developed during the early 1900s by a subsidiary of the Northern Pacific Railroad. The mine's coal field ran between that of Carbonado's, on the north, and Fairfax's, to the south; it supplied high grade fuel for the NPRR's locomotives. In Melmont's prime,

Fairfax Bridge

rows of company-owned cottages lined the riverbank, a row for each nationality of workers. Travel was limited, in one form or another, to the railway: "you either rode the train or walked the ties."

After the mine closed, a forest fire destroyed most of the town in the early 1920s. For many years the almost abandoned community consisted of a single reclusive resident and his collection of oversized pets.

Melmont's Montleon

The remains of Melmont were maintained by one Andrew Montleon; generally known only by his last name, he occupied the basement of the Melmont School, adding a roof after upriver resident Steve Poch removed the building's top two stories. Montleon kept to himself while also keeping a few beloved goats, a mule, and a "watch horse," the latter a sort of equine security guard known to attack unsuspecting trespassers. The recluse supplemented his horse's efforts by taking potshots at anyone he believed might harm his livestock. To the area's children, however, he was kindness itself, giving them rides on his horse and mule. Montleon lived with his adored animals until he grew too feeble to care for himself and was taken to a nursing facility. Then, after a lingering life as a hermit's home, Melmont was no more.

A regenerating forest and thickets of berry bushes now cover much of the area. Visitors who walk the leaf-littered railbed will find vestiges of only two structures: a small square of stone walls that was the mine's powder magazine, and a concrete foundation that overlooks the overgrown townsite—the last monuments to little-remembered Melmont.

At the "Mowich Y," mile 10.4, Highway 165 bears right, bound for Mowich Lake (see p. 218). Our way continues to the left on Carbon River Road, which now runs above a broadening section of river valley; second-growth forest, seasonally colored by fireweed, covers the hillslopes. A barricaded road, mile 12.4, left, leads down to the riverside remnants of Fairfax.

Fairfax

Although coal was discovered here in 1892, it took five years for the Western America Company to open a mine and the Northern Pacific to extend a spur line from Carbonado; the community that was then established took its name from another coal-producing area, Fairfax County, Virginia. Within a short time the mine's white workers initiated a labor dispute. They were temporarily replaced, first by blacks and then by Japanese, until an agreement was reached, whereupon the whites returned to work.

In 1907 the Tacoma Smelting Company purchased the mine and its coke ovens; the new owners opened a second mine in 1911. A pretty town developed above the Carbon, with tidy, white-painted homes set along well-planned streets, while a hotel, store, school house, and railroad depot constituted the business district. The big event in Fairfax was the daily arrival of the passenger train; the engine was driven onto a turntable and then laboriously rotated by the engineer and fireman so that it pointed down canyon for the return run to South Prairie. Only in 1921, with the completion of the highway bridge across the Carbon River canyon, did auto transportation at last offer an alternative to the railroad.

By 1915 Fairfax had reached its peak — some 500 residents, 60 coke ovens supplying the Tacoma smelter, a post office that also served nearby Manley-Moore and Montezuma, and a baseball squad in the six-team Valley League. Adding to the town's activity was its function as the jumping-off point for climbers and hikers entering the northwest corner of Mount Rainier National Park; they would come by train to Fairfax and then pack in the rest of the way.

Fairfax's coke ovens shut down in 1929, and the town began a precipitous decline. By the 1940s little was left: both Brehm's store and the mine superintendent's house were torn down for salvage, the hotel had burned, the train depot sat abandoned, and "rusting engines lay along silent tracks..." Today there is even less to see; the townsite, now bereft of its buildings, has been reclaimed by the

Fairfax Hotel

ever-advancing vegetation, although visitors can still trace the old railroad embankment to the south bank of the Carbon and there find vestiges of the NPRR's bridge. Serenely vacant in the summer sunlight, its depot, engines, and tracks long departed, Fairfax is left with only its silence.

Carbon River Road then passes the brush-obscured foundation for the Carbon River School, mile 13.3, left, which itself had occupied the site of the Montezuma store.

Montezuma

A mine and small community were established here in 1901 by the Northern Pacific Railroad. The name was a hopeful allusion to the Aztec emperor's auriferous treasures, but no gold was found and the operators had to settle for coal instead; a sizable seam was located near Evans Creek and its contents washed to Fairfax via a 4,000-foot-long flume. The mine closed in 1909, but the location staged a brief revival after Washington became a dry state in 1916, with "Piggy Joe" Amidaio operating a bootleg saloon in the old company store. Most of Montezuma was dismantled in 1918-19 by a crew of Wilkeson workers, but only in 1991 were the last of the town's buildings finally removed.

The road then crosses Evans Creek and immediately reaches a junction, left, with Manley-Moore Road, which drops to a bridge crossing of the Carbon. Across the river were once the short-lived mining communities of Hillsboro and Olympic.

Manley-Moore

Upriver from Fairfax stood the community of Manley-Moore, which was named for the lumber company that owned it. Also known as Upper Fairfax, the town and its sawmill were built in 1909, and soon the company, using many Japanese workers, was busy cutting old-growth timber purchased from local homesteaders. By 1925 the mill was one of the largest in the state, shipping out between four and ten railcars of lumber each day. Manley-Moore borrowed heavily for expansion, only to be devastated by the Depression; the Eatonville Lumber Company then bought out the operation, but, beset by labor troubles, sold the mill, which finally closed in the late 1930s. Some of the community's buildings lasted until the early 1990s, when the property's owner, the Burlington Northern, removed them. Today a few openings in the forest indicate the townsite.

At mile 15.2 a sign inscribed "HUCKLE-CHUCK" marks a wooded area once homesteaded by a pair of persevering families.

Huckle-Chuck

In the 1890s the Pochs and Zavitskys settled this remote section of the upper Carbon River. Their isolated location offered deep winter snows, springtime floods, and insect-infested summers; supply trips to Wilkeson took two days each way. Both families received a boost in 1909 when they sold their timber rights to the Manley-Moore Lumber Company, which built a logging camp on

Carbon River rain forest

the Pochs' property. In the early 1920s the Pochs bought the Melmont schoolhouse, dismantled and moved it, and then used the material for their new home. Ever enterprising, they set up a small store on the first floor, but it did little business and soon closed. Another school, the Carbon River one near Evans Creek, supplied a later owner of the Pochs' place with hanging lights that still illuminate the building's high-ceilinged rooms. In 1995, a third recycling project found the old guardrails from the Fairfax Bridge transformed into front-yard fencing for the redoubtable residence.

Soon Carbon River Road drops to the bottom of the valley, reaching the boundary of Mount Rainier National Park, 18.2 miles, and then arriving at the park's entrance station.

Carbon River Entrance Station

A rangers' office, self-service entrance station, pay phone, and restrooms are all at the roadside. The Rainforest Loop begins next to the entrance station.

East of here, two mining ventures operated within the park during the 1900s. The Hephzibah Mining Company dug some tunnels and built a short-lived cabin, while the Washington Mining and Milling Company constructed a three-mile-long road to the park boundary, cutting some 28 trees for the right-of-way and then informing park officials that not only other miners but also park rangers were prohibited from using the new route. Both companies ceased operations before doing extensive damage.

The road turns to gravel shortly past the entrance station; the dense rainforest vegetation includes thick-trunked Sitka spruce and thickets of devil's club. On the left at mile 20.2 is the Falls Creek Picnic Area. Nearby once lived an early park resident.

The Squatter's Claim

Some two miles within the present park boundary was the site of a squatter's claim, established opposite the mouth of Cayada Creek in 1895 by W. L. Evans. Although flood and fire destroyed his first two cabins, he had established a five-building compound by 1905, complete with a half-acre garden. Up to then the park had made no attempt to evict him, and Evans conveniently removed himself from any conflict by dying the following year.

Carbon River
Ranger Station

*The Green Lake Trail (see p. 266) departs the road at Ranger Creek,
mile 21.4, right, while the Chenuis Falls Trail leaves from the left at 21.9
miles. After passing the Ipsut Creek Patrol Cabin, mile 23.1, the route
crosses the creek, enters the Ipsut Creek Campground, and then ends, mile
23.3, at a trailhead parking lot. The Carbon Glacier hike (see p. 268) leaves
the upper end of the parking area.*

Ipsut Creek Campground

A park road was completed to within a mile of the Carbon Glacier in 1923, and a campground established at Ipsut (Chinook jargon for "hidden" or "concealed") Creek three years later. The upper three miles of road eventually washed out and were not rebuilt,
so the route now ends at the campground. The facility contains 30
sites, pit toilets, and a picnic area in a moss-festooned old-growth
forest. Across the creek is one of the park's most striking structures,
a handsome patrol cabin constructed in 1933 by CCC workers.

Mowich Road

The upper Mowich River drainage contains some of the park's most striking mid-elevation scenery, with Eunice Lake, Tolmie Peak, Spray Park, and Spray Falls all accessible by day hikes from lovely Mowich Lake. The long drive over gravel Mowich Road (State Highway 165) will soon be forgotten once visitors reach Mowich Lake and its beckoning trailheads. (for map, see p. 196)

The route departs from the Carbon River auto tour (see p. 195) at the Mowich "Y", branching right to continue south on State Highway 165; after climbing on a single lane of pavement from the river canyon, the roadbed turns to gravel at mile 3.3. A short distance beyond the turnoff, 8.0 miles, left, for the Evans Creek ORV area, a stunning vista of Mount Rainier appears ahead. Roadcuts expose sandstone, coal, and shale that originated in the pre-Cascade swamplands of nearly 60 million years ago.

An overlook, mile 10.9, right, offers a view into the deep valley of the Mowich River. Soon a long clearcut line, 11.2 miles, right, marks the Mount Rainier National Park boundary. The Paul Peak Trailhead is on the right at 11.9 miles; adjacent are picnic tables and restrooms. The trailhead parking lot is the site of an erstwhile park entrance arch.

Mowich (MOH-ich) Entrance

The now-vanished arch, which featured a plaque honoring Dr. William Fraser Tolmie, was dedicated on September 2, 1933—a hundred years to the day after the doctor climbed the nearby Mount Pleasant–Hessong Rock ridge. Speaking at the dedication was the physician's son, S. F. Tolmie, who was then Premier of British Columbia. For years the public road ended at the arch; an unfinished final section continued up to Mowich Lake, but it long lacked the funds necessary for its completion and was only opened to the public in 1955.

Mountain Meadows, mile 13.4, right, is followed by a section of the Grindstone (or Bailey Willis) Trail, 14.4 miles, right; pale larkspur and woodland-penstemon, mile 15.2, left, precede a subsequent crossing for the same trail. The roadbanks now display volcanic rock from the Fife's Peak Formation, whose lava flows covered the area some 20 to 30 million years ago. Switchbacks rise uphill to a long parking area, where the route ends at a turnaround, 16.9 miles, at the entrance to the Mowich Lake Campground. The Spray Falls - Spray Park hike (see p. 272) leaves from the campground, as does the Eunice Lake - Tolmie Peak hike (see p. 269); both routes run for a time on sections of the Wonderland Trail. To the left of the campground, a picturesque ranger station sits by the shore of the lake.

Mowich Lake

First called Crater Lake, the ridge-rimmed oval of water early on became a popular hiking stop. Northern Pacific Railroad geologist Bailey Willis opened a horse trail from Wilkeson to the upper Carbon River in 1881 and the next year extended the route south to the

Mowich Lake, with
Castle Peak at rear left

Mowich River, some four miles west of the present park boundary. There Willis constructed "Palace Camp," a collection of four buildings that included a large, barn-like headquarters for his geological exploration. In 1884 Willis pushed his trail east to Mountain Meadows, Crater/Mowich Lake, and Spray Park; over the next few years hundreds of tourists came this way when approaching the northwest side of the mountain. Despite heavy promotion of the area by the NPRR (which hoped to increase passenger use on its branch line), the Carbon-Mowich approach gradually lost popularity as Longmire and Paradise, with better facilities and improved accessibility, became the choice of most visitors. Then, near the turn of the century, miners on the North Fork of the Mowich River began using Willis's trail; a grindstone they placed at pathside for sharpening their tools gave the route its lasting name.

Crater Lake was so designated by Willis in 1883; later he wrote: "The amphitheaters which the young geologist mistook for craters are now known to be glacier basins eroded by ice." The lake was subsequently renamed Mowich ("deer" in Chinook jargon). The Crater Claims mining operation came to occupy the northwest shore; a cabin on the site was confiscated by the park in 1909 and used as a ranger station until it was crushed by snow a decade later. To replace it, a patrol cabin was built on the southeast edge of the lake in 1922. Deemed "an excellent example of rustic architecture," it is still in use.

Section III:
Twenty-Five Favorite Hikes

Although the routes covered in this section represent only a sampling of the myriad trails that spread across the lower and middle sections of the mountain, they include many of the most intriguing pathways found within the park. The hikes were selected to include the following:

1. a wide range of distances, from less than a half mile to over eight miles, but all short enough to be covered during a single day's outing;

2. diverse locations, so that hikers can select routes in any of a half dozen different sections of the park;

3. varying degrees of difficulty, from level terrain to fairly steep climbs;

4. outstanding opportunities to see plants and wildlife, panoramic scenery, and historic sites;

5. places that have touched the spirit and spoken to the heart.

(Note: The hike (and auto tour) descriptions frequently refer to various flowering plants found on and about Mount Rainier. Since bloom times for each species vary from year to year and from location to location, there is no guarantee that a particular flower will be blossoming at a particular time and place. Park staff can often provide current information about what is blooming where.

Hike mileages were computed by the authors while on the trails and then adjusted to conform with official distances recorded and provided by the park. Elevation changes were determined by using USGS topographic maps and are approximate; these measurements represent only the overall difference between a route's lowest point and highest point and do not account for the often frequent gains and losses found along a typical park path.)

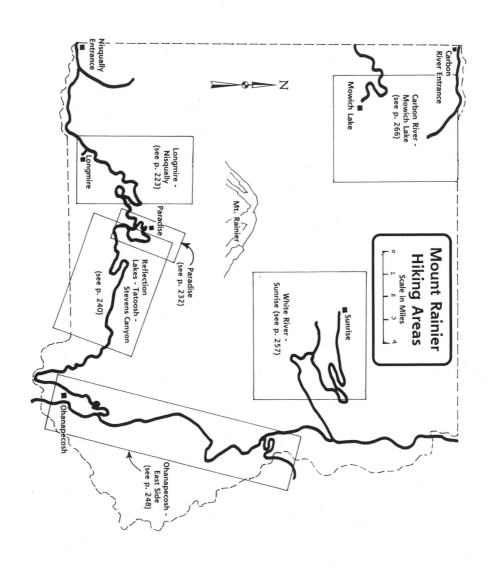

Mount Rainier
Hiking Areas

Scale in Miles

0   1   2   3   4

Nisqually
Entrance

Carbon
River Entrance

Carbon River -
Mowich Lake
(see p. 266)

Mowich Lake

N

Longmire -
Nisqually
(see p. 223)

Longmire

Mt. Rainier

Paradise

Paradise
(see p. 232)

Reflection
Lakes - Tatoosh -
Stevens Canyon
(see p. 240)

White River -
Sunrise (see p. 257)

Sunrise

Ohanapecosh

Ohanapecosh -
East Side
(see p. 248)

Longmire - Nisqually Area Hikes

1. Trail of the Shadows

Highlights: This popular, forested loop passes relics of the pioneer Longmire family's springside resort while circling a meadowy marsh.

Distance: 0.7 mile round trip

Elevation Gain: 100 feet

Trailhead Location: at Longmire, across Nisqually-Paradise Road from the inn

Description: After taking one of the crosswalks from the inn-museum area to reach the Trail of the Shadows, we turn right, commencing our hike on a wide pathway bordered by a pair of split rail fences. Presently a spur route, left, branches a hundred feet to the edge of the marsh. Returning to the main trail, the way bears north through lodgepole pine, red alder, and western redcedar. Soda Springs issues from the center of its surrounding stonework, right.

Scraggly lodgepole pine shades the site of the Longmires' hotel, mile 0.1, right. Constructed in 1890 to accommodate both mountain-bound travelers and users of the springs, the rambling, rough-hewn building served as the area's sole hostelry for 15 years until the far fancier National Park Inn was completed a short distance to the south.

Douglas-fir, western redcedar, and western hemlock promptly engulf the route. Another spur path, left, leads 50 feet to an overlook of several beaver ponds, where the flow from the springs covers the area with a reddish orange scum; the main trail next encounters salal and deer fern in deep forest. The Longmire Cabin reposes in the shadows, mile 0.2, right. Built by James Longmire's son, Elcaine, a couple of years before the hotel, the small, well-weathered structure is now furnished with a table and bedframe of tree limbs. "Iron Mike," a stone-enclosed, rust-stained spring, bubbles by the trailside just ahead, right, feeding the upper end of the Longmire mire. Presently the path crosses a small creek and enters devil's club country; trillium, Scouler's harebell, and twinflower dot the forest floor.

Skunk cabbage scents the drainage of another creeklet, while false hellebore rises from the nearby mud; the trail now runs atop a boardwalk before rising up the hillside. The marsh, left, contains cattail and rush. A short descent leads to a spur route, mile 0.4, left, which follows a boardwalk to Medical Springs; here is more scummy, rusty water, but also a good view of the lower meadow.

223

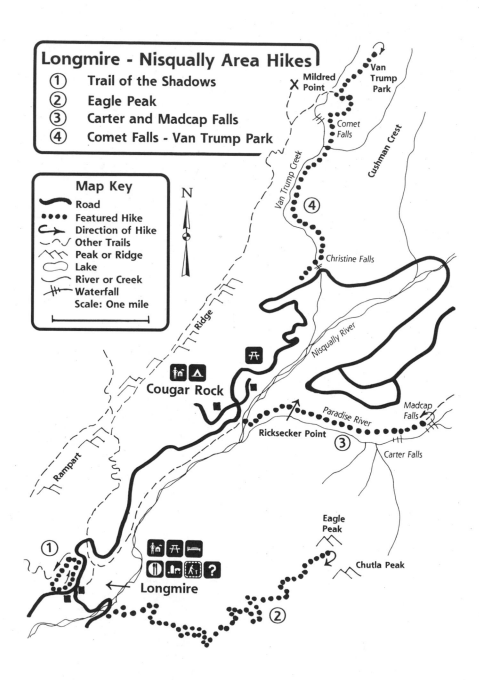

Longmire - Nisqually Area Hikes

1. Trail of the Shadows
2. Eagle Peak
3. Carter and Madcap Falls
4. Comet Falls - Van Trump Park

Map Key

- Road
- Featured Hike
- Direction of Hike
- Other Trails
- Peak or Ridge
- Lake
- River or Creek
- Waterfall

Scale: One mile

N

Van Trump Park

Mildred Point

Comet Falls

Cushman Crest

Van Trump Creek

Christine Falls

Nisqually River

Ridge

Cougar Rock

Rampart

Paradise River

Madcap Falls

Ricksecker Point

Carter Falls

Eagle Peak

Chutla Peak

Longmire

Longmire Museum

The Rampart Ridge Trail then forks to the right. Our route continues left past a series of century-old redcedar stumps, the legacy of the Longmires' logging for building materials. Soon the path levels in an alder-shaded dampness of devil's club, skunk cabbage, and horsetail. After crossing a pair of outlet creeks, the loop concludes at the museum crosswalk, mile 0.7.

2. Eagle Peak

Highlights: First forests, then precipitous parks, and at last a rocky ridgeline—the latter with a stunning view of the mountain and the Paradise River Canyon; a trio of rewards awaits those who assay this steep but mostly shaded route.

Distance: 7.2 miles, round trip

Elevation Gain: 2,900 feet

Trailhead Location: on the access road to the Longmire Community Building, just past of the Nisqually River bridge

Description: To reach the trailhead, hikers should take the paved service road that starts immediately north of the Longmire Museum; the road runs eastward past offices and residences, curves uphill, and crosses the Nisqually on a picturesque suspension bridge. The marked trail leaves the left side of the road about 50 yards beyond the bridge.

Bordered by twinflower and many mossy rocks, the route begins a gradual climb through thick forest. Rattlesnake orchid and Menzies pipsissewa peep up from the pathside at mile 0.3; switchbacks follow, as huckleberry becomes a steady companion.

The route continues zigzagging up the now-steep mountainside, passing one-sided and bog wintergreens, mile 1.0, and the asparaguslike spikes of pinedrops at 1.4 miles; each northern zig ends just before reaching a rollicking creek, whereupon the trail then zags back toward the south. False azalea abounds, mile 1.6, followed by coral-root and, at 2.0 miles, a veritable forest of rhododendron. The path presently crosses a creeklet on a small wooden bridge; rising from the streambanks is clasping twisted-stalk.

Alaska yellow-cedar droops its lichen-laden limbs at mile 2.2, after which Scouler's harebell fringes the pathside. The trail finally leaves the forest, 2.9 miles, and crosses a talus-covered opening. The path cuts back to climb through a steep, rocky, pika-inhabited park, where beargrass, spreading phlox, and rosy spirea seasonally color the slope. Eastward, Chutla (Nisqually for "rock") Peak surmounts another sweeping meadow that clings to the mountainside. Log steps take our route onto a ridgeline of subalpine fir and mountain hemlock; the trail now turns northeast and heads toward Eagle Peak, crossing a parklet of subalpine lupine, broadleaf arnica, and other colorful plants. Although hikers are not likely to see any of the peak's namesake birds, which are seldom sighted in the park, look and listen here for sooty (blue) grouse.

Another steep climb, mile 3.3, arrives at another nearly vertical meadow; more log steps and switchbacks aid the ascent. After the park service completed the trail in 1910 (at a total cost of $239), a visitor could hire a guide and horse to

Suspension bridge over Nisqually River, near Eagle Peak trailhead

First meadow,
Eagle Peak Trail

take him or her up the path for $1.50, but it's doubtful the horses climbed this final stretch. A last, steep pitch leads past both cliff and yellow penstemons before reaching a saddle on the Tatoosh ridgeline. The maintained trail ends here, mile 3.6, with scramble routes heading west toward Eagle Peak and east toward Chutla Peak. (**Warning: use of informal trails may be dangerous.**)

If hikers have any breath left, it will be taken by the view from the saddle—a photographer's panorama of mountain grandeur, ranging from Van Trump Park and Comet Falls on the left, through the Nisqually Glacier and Ricksecker Point in the center, and on to the Paradise Valley on the right. Towering over all is Mount Rainier, which rises toward a glacier-rimmed roundness that seems to fill up the sky. The view back to the south mimics the mountain, for the cones of three Cascadian cousins— Hood, Adams, and St. Helens, can be discerned in the hazy distance.

Having surveyed the striking scenery, we turn round for a welcome downhill run to the trailhead, reached at mile 7.2.

3. Carter and Madcap Falls

Highlights: Cougar Rock campers (or motorists wanting a break on the trip to Paradise) can stretch their legs on this scenic jaunt up the canyon of the Paradise River. Along the way are a crossing of the churning Nisqually and views of the maple-fringed rockfalls below Eagle Peak.

Distance: 2.4 miles round trip

Elevation Gain: 600 feet

Trailhead Location: at mile 8.5 of Nisqually-Paradise Road

Description: Our route bears left on a segment of the Wonderland Trail (right leads downhill to Longmire). In a hundred feet the path reaches the boulder-strewn course of the Nisqually River. Here a series of three bridges, each consisting of a large log (hewn flat on top) and a railing, span sections of the roaring, rumbling torrent of glacial melt; rocks reverberate in the welter of chocolate-colored water as they crash their way downstream. On the right is the towering triangle of Eagle Peak, while the white-topped mound of Mount Rainier glistens up canyon to the left.

At the end of the third bridge, 0.1 mile, the trail climbs out of the canyon on an old roadbed, reaching a nearly level benchland between the Nisqually and Paradise rivers. The colorful palette of plantlife includes black raspberry, red alder, and Pacific silver fir. The roadbed runs through a moss-covered landscape of stately conifers until mile 0.4, where it ends next to a small cleared area, left. Here for over 60 years stood a hydroelectric plant, built in 1920 by the Rainier National Park Company, that lit the lights of Longmire. Through the alder thicket to the right is the Paradise River.

Now the trail, narrower without its roadbed, climbs the north side of the river canyon. Vanilla leaf, mountain boxwood, and vine maple contrast with the gray angularity of a trailside rockfall, left. Visible here is the aging steel-banded, wood-stave penstock that fed water to the powerhouse. Just ahead are false azalea, red elderberry, and wild ginger.

Beside the path is the Paradise River, right, which drops down the canyon in a series of rocky cascades; to the south, the base of Eagle Peak extends a massive talon of talus streamward. In fall the bright gray rock is framed by the flame-colored leaves of vine maple.

At trailside are first oceanspray and Oregon grape, followed by twinflower. Several species of berries find sunlight at a small, rock-covered opening, mile 0.7, as does woodland-penstemon, foxglove and sweet-cicely. The trail rises above the river, meets the penstock, and runs beside it; bog wintergreen, one-sided wintergreen, and huckleberry all grow in the shadows.

Clubmoss and oak fern appear on the forest floor. The trail then steepens in a climaxing climb before leveling near the overlook for Carter Falls, mile 1.1, where the Paradise River drops in a wide wall of foaming white water. Near the falls was once the Short Canyon Lode mining claim, established by Frank Hendricks in 1907. Within seven years Hendricks had erected a blacksmith shop and a high-roofed cabin, dug two tunnels and a shaft north of the river, and excavated several open pits and cuts to the south. However, by

1923 the Short Canyon Lode had come up short; apparently abandoned, the claim was soon declared null and void.

The falls were named for Henry "Steptoe" Carter, who, along with Len Longmire, constructed the trail past them in 1892. The path improved on the previous route to Paradise, which went up the Nisqually River almost to the glacier before climbing out of the canyon on steep switchbacks. The enterprising Longmire clan charged a 50¢ toll for using the new path.

One day, while still working on the trail, Carter encountered Elcaine Longmire and his daughter Maude near the as yet unnamed waterfall. Steptoe asked Maude, "how about naming these falls for me?" and was later abashed to learn she had taken him literally and called them "Carter's Falls." He protested briefly, but then laughingly took up his ax, blazed a tree, and inscribed the name on it.

Now the path climbs past bunchberry to a second overlook, mile 1.2, right. Below is the short, rock-framed cascade of Madcap Falls. Although the trail continues on to such sights as Narada Falls and Reflection Lakes, our route heads back from here, returning to its starting point at 2.4 miles.

4. Comet Falls - Van Trump Park

Highlights: A hard climb, but Comet Falls, a chance to see mountain goats, and an up-front view of Mount Rainier are ample rewards. Summer wildflowers and fall leaf color make this a two-season hike.

Distance: 6.4 miles, round trip

Elevation Gain: 2,200 feet

Trailhead Location: at the Comet Falls trailhead parking lot, mile 10.5 of Nisqually-Paradise Road

Description: A set of steps takes the trail up from the east end of the parking lot. The thick forest shelters Oregon grape, bog wintergreen, and, shortly, one-sided wintergreen. At mile 0.2 is rosy twisted-stalk; beyond a marsh-spanning bridge is false bugbane. A sturdy log bridge then crosses the rocky chasm of Van Trump Creek, 0.3 mile, where a frothing cascade prepares for its impending tumble down Christine Falls. Within the gorge are clasping twisted-stalk, gooseberry, and goatsbeard.

Now the trail angles up the eastern side of the creek canyon, passing through a lovely wooded area before arriving at a rockfall, right. False azalea precedes a patch of vine maple that covers much of the hillside. Left at mile 0.5 is a view of another of the creek's cataracts; the openings ahead blaze with summer color: paintbrush and crimson columbine, tall bluebells and tiger lily. The route then ascends above the gorge. Coralroot and broad-lipped twayblade are followed by a slope full of foamflower, mile 1.0. An opening subsequently offers a view of the mountain; here salmonberry and Sitka alder rise above the smaller plants. Pikas often perch on the forthcoming rockfall, right.

The trail soon runs by spring beauty, fringecup, and fat false Solomon's-seal; soon thin false Solomon's seal also appears. After woodland-penstemon, mile 1.3, comes a small side stream that waters mountain monkeyflower and yellow willowherb. Next to another talus pile is noble fir.

After leveling, the route passes white rhododendron and a bank brimming with avalanche lily, and then crosses the east fork of Van Trump Creek on another substantial bridge, mile 1.6. Upstream is an attractive, two-tiered waterfall, while downstream offers another rocky gorge. After a short climb, Comet Falls comes into view, left; Jeffrey's shooting star and both leatherleaf and brook saxifrages color the trailside.

Switchbacks take us past tall bluebells to a second vista of the falls; a spur path, left, leads to the rocky creekbed below the 320-foot cascade. After another upward pitch, the trail levels and reaches an opening, 1.8 miles, at the base of the falls; the scene here is stunning: a narrow plume of water plunges over the worn rockface in a crystal white spray, spreading slightly at the bottom like the vaporous tracings of an earthbound comet. Hot-day hikers will welcome the cloud of cooling mist that condenses around the viewpoint, perhaps pausing to admire the stream violet and Sitka valerian nestled nearby.

The falls are reward enough for this exerting excursion, but more wonders lie ahead. Now the route turns away from the Comet cascade, running beneath Pacific silver fir, mountain hemlock, and western redcedar. After a creeklet lined with Lewis monkey-flower, mile 2.3, switchbacks traverse a steep-sloped meadow seasonally colored first with avalanche lily and later with subalpine lupine; above, Rainier's peak peeps through the trees. Beargrass and Sitka valerian sit near the top of the meadow, where a glance southward reveals Mount St. Helens, Eagle Peak, and Ricksecker Point. The trail finally levels and reaches a junction, 2.5 miles. Left is the way to Mildred Point and, via Rampart Ridge, Longmire. Our route, right, climbs into a wide-ranging parkland

sprinkled with magenta paintbrush and subalpine lupine.

Soon the path levels. A bench offers a restful view of the mountain, which fills the landscape to the north. Just ahead the trail divides: left leads a short distance to a branch of Van Trump Creek; our route bears right, climbing steeply past creamy cones of beargrass. The maintained trail ends on a knoll, mile 2.8, where a conveniently placed boulder, right, offers views of Cushman Crest to the east and Mounts Adams and St. Helens to the south.

From here a still-perceptible path continues northward into even more striking scenery as mountain-heathers and louseworts spread across the ridge saddle; the ensuing ascent passes tiger and avalanche lilies and western dog violet. A backward glance finds the Nisqually Valley and the Tatoosh Range now in view.

More plantlife lies ahead. First comes fanleaf cinquefoil, then Cusick's speedwell and spreading phlox. The trail crests a hillock, 3.2 miles, where another wide-angled view of Mount Rainier fills the eye; four waterfalls drop from the peak's lower slopes, while the Van Trump and Kautz glaciers whiten the mountainside above.

Here, high up Van Trump Park, hikers can pause for a well-earned lunch, perhaps contemplating the way in which their counterparts, like ranger Kenneth Ashley, made the trip in the 1960s:

> Our procedure is to start up the trail at about four o'clock in the afternoon. On the hike we carry a little more food—generally a steak and the trimmings—that we broil for our supper. A couple of flashlights are included for the late evening walk home. After supper we like to walk up the ridge, in the

Comet Falls

direction of Mt. Rainier, in search of the goats. We have never failed to see anywhere from twelve to thirty-six goats in the vicinity of Van Trump.

The steak suppers may be gone, but the goats remain, often seen climbing the cliffs across the canyon to the northwest. It's an appropriate place for the animals, since they bear a remarkable resemblance to venerable P. B. Van Trump himself. The old climber sported a white goatee in later life, and, decades after his pioneering ascent of the peak, still summered in the high country of Indian Henry's Hunting Grounds, regaling visitors with tales of the mountain that he knew so well and so deeply loved.

A faint track continues up the park, but our route now returns to the trailhead, arriving there at mile 6.4.

Paradise Area Hikes

1. Narada Falls

Highlights: One of the park's loveliest waterfalls lies along this short, shrub-lined pathway.

Distance: 0.4 mile round trip

Elevation Gain: 200 feet on the return

Trailhead Location: at the Narada Falls parking lot, mile 15.5 of Nisqually-Paradise Road

Description: The route begins at the northeast end of the parking lot, immediately crossing a handsome stone bridge that spans the Paradise River. The bridge was built as part of the original auto road to Paradise, which continued a short distance ahead to the base of the mountainside and then zigzagged across a huge rockfall. At the far end of the bridge are restrooms and the Narada-Paradise Trail, both left, and a view up the hillslope of the old road, whose aging, all-but-forgotten switchbacks are still etched upon an enormous pile of scree.

To the right the paved Narada Falls Trail descends into lush vegetation that includes false azalea, goatsbeard, and lady fern. On the bank, left, just before the first overlook, are Mertens saxifrage, alumroot, and a pair of leafy, creeping plants—five-leaved bramble and bedstraw. Soon stink currant and Sitka alder appear at pathside.

Narada Falls fully presents itself at mile 0.1, right, where a second overlook offers a spray-cooled view of the wide cascade as it plunges over dark andesite rock. In August 1893, Arthur F. Knight named the falls for the Narada (Hindu meaning: "uncontaminated" or "pure") branch of the Theosophical Society of Tacoma; to commemorate the event, two of Knight's companions promptly carved the name on a nearby (and previously uncontaminated) tree. The Society's influence also extended up the mountain to Paradise, where the point upon which the visitor center now stands was once known as Theosophy Ridge.

Now the trail turns to dirt, passing salmonberry and tall bluebells; closer to the ground are mountain monkeyflower, marsh violet, and Jeffrey's shooting star. The path levels, 0.2 miles, at a small scree slope, left, near which is clasping twisted-stalk. A short distance ahead the route meets the Wonderland Trail: right descends toward Longmire, passing Madcap and Carter Falls, while left climbs east to Reflection Lakes before dropping into Stevens Canyon. Stink currant mingles with foamflower and devil's club near the junction. Having sampled the splendors of the mountainside, our route now doubles back to regain the parking area, 0.4 mile.

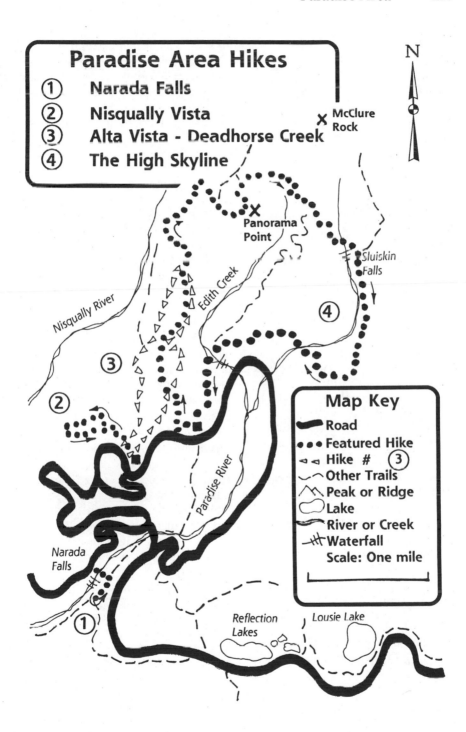

Paradise Area Hikes

1. Narada Falls
2. Nisqually Vista
3. Alta Vista - Deadhorse Creek
4. The High Skyline

McClure Rock

Panorama Point

Sluiskin Falls

Nisqually River

Edith Creek

Paradise River

Narada Falls

Reflection Lakes

Lousie Lake

N

Map Key

— Road
••• Featured Hike
◁◁ Hike # ③
◠ Other Trails
⋀ Peak or Ridge
◯ Lake
↬ River or Creek
⫟ Waterfall
Scale: One mile

Narada Falls

2. Nisqually Vista

Highlights: Small hillside meadows and conifer stands alternate along this short but scenic loop. Several overlooks allow observation of the nearby Nisqually Glacier and the steep canyon it has cut.

Distance: 1.1 miles round trip

Elevation Gain: 200 feet on the return

Trailhead Location: near the north end of the visitor center parking lot, Paradise

Description: Stone steps take the trail uphill from the parking lot; soon they

are replaced by a paved walkway. In 100 feet is a junction: right is the Deadhorse Creek Trail, bound for the upper reaches of Paradise, while left is our route, the Nisqually Vista Loop Trail. Subalpine fir and mountain hemlock cluster intermittently, their dark shapes contrasting with the bloom-filled brightness of the pathside meadows. A flag-colored trio of flowers—creamy white Sitka valerian, magenta paintbrush, and blue-hued subalpine lupine—precedes a concrete bridge that spans Deadhorse Creek. The path runs by a hollow rock, bends around Brewer's mitrewort, and heads downhill, skirting a stellar stand of Jeffrey's shooting star on the descent.

The loop section of the trail begins at a fork, mile 0.2; our route goes right, running by bracted lousewort. A tiny pool, 0.3 mile, right, waters a creekbed filled with more Jeffrey's shooting star. After dropping past a patch of avalanche lily, the trail turns south, reaching a vista point, mile 0.4, right, for the Nisqually Glacier's snout. Marmots prowl the clifftop near the overlook.

Two more overlooks follow; they offer views of the glacier's canyon and, beyond it, of Cushman Crest, the steep ridgeline that separates the Nisqually drainage from Van Trump Creek. The crest commemorates Francis W. Cushman, a Tacoma congressman and early-day champion of the park.

The trail turns east, 0.6 mile, and departs the canyon rim, passing thickets of huckleberry and colorful groupings of paintbrush, tiger lily, and Jacob's ladder; the ragged-topped Tatoosh Range is visible off to the right. Switchbacks take the path uphill, which then levels and completes its loop, mile 0.8. A pair of right turns retraces the start of the route, ending at the parking lot, 1.1 miles.

3. Alta Vista - Deadhorse Creek

Highlights: A pair of Paradise's most scenic paths form a loop featuring hilltop vistas, gracefully sloping meadows, and a brief but brisk bit of climbing (on the asphalt below Alta Vista).

Distance: 2.3 miles, round trip

Elevation Gain: 600 feet

Trailhead Location: at the north side of the Jackson Visitor Center, Paradise

Description: The Alta Vista Loop Trail begins on either of two paved walkways that depart from the northwest and northeast sides of the visitor center; they join after a steep climb of 100 yards, passing Sitka mountain-ash and beargrass along the way. Our route continues uphill, proceeding straight ahead through each of three intersections, while encountering first avalanche lily, next lovage and pasque flower, then Jacob's ladder and currant, and finally cow parsnip and Cusick's speedwell.

At mile 0.5 the trail crests the lip of Edith Creek Basin, which spreads its rocky starkness northward. Guide Jules Stampfler named the creek in 1907 for a woman whose last name he neglected to obtain; at least two contestants have claimed the honor: Edith Corbett Stone, whose credentials included being both the second woman to climb the mountain and the granddaughter of James Longmire, and Edith Maring, who, as a 16-year-old, hiked to Anvil Rock to view the Cowlitz Glacier and then ruined her shoes on the return. Maring's compelling account concludes with her being held upright by Stampfler and Bailey Tremper as the trio glissaded down the mountainslope.

The loop divides at the edge of the basin. Our route bears left to climb the side of the Alta Vista point on switchbacks. To the south Mount Adams's peak peeps up behind the Tatoosh.

In the mid-1890s, the Alta Vista area became home to Paradise's first formal tourist accommodations when a pair of tent camps were established, one on the east shoulder of the point, the other at its southern base on Theosophy Ridge (above the present-day visitor center). Soon Ashford resident John Reese consolidated the two operations at the latter location as the "Camp of the Clouds."

At mile 0.7 the path reaches the crest of Alta Vista. The point's name, which is Spanish for "high view," was bestowed in 1889 by John Hartman, a member of a Tacoma climbing group.

Spreading phlox and woolly pussytoes grow near the ridgetop. The trail levels, narrows, and then descends northward past lousewort, black alpine sedge, and glacier lily. At a rest area, 0.8 mile, our path meets the Skyline Trail, left; hikers can relax on benches while they gaze at the mountain. Here the Alta Vista Loop branches sharply to the right and drops into the basin of Edith Creek, while we now follow the Skyline Trail straight ahead, soon climbing on stone steps into a rock-strewn open area.

At a junction, mile 1.1, our course turns left onto the Deadhorse Creek Trail; a nearby monument commemorates the mountain infantry unit that trained at Mount Rainier during the winter of 1941-42. We now drop down a gently sloping ridgespur, where a row of Sitka mountain-ash presently lines the path. An overlook, right, then offers views of the Nisqually Glacier, Eagle Peak, and the Tatoosh Range. The

Above Alta Vista

trailbed turns to pavement and reaches a spur route, mile 1.5, left, that dips to cross Deadhorse Creek before meeting the Skyline Trail below the west side of Alta Vista; look for marmots among the rocks and flowers. Our way bears right, offering a southward view of Pinnacle Peak before arriving at a junction with the Moraine Trail, right.

We go left, descending on switchbacks past spreading phlox and rosy spirea. After leveling to cross Deadhorse Creek, 1.8 miles, the trail passes a side route, left, and continues down the flower-filled stream canyon: bistort, Sitka valerian, and bracted lousewort are among the many inhabitants. Another side path, left, is followed by the Nisqually Vista Trail, right. A hundred feet farther the Deadhorse Creek Trail ends at the visitor center parking lot. Our route turns left, onto the sidewalk, concluding at the Alta Vista trailhead next to the visitor center, mile 2.3.

4. The High Skyline

Highlights: One of the park's most spectacular hikes, the High Skyline Trail runs past fields of wildflowers, above the Nisqually Glacier, and to the threshold of Rainier's high country. The views down to Paradise and across to the Tatoosh are enthralling.

Distance: 5.7 miles

Elevation Gain: 1,700 feet to the top of the High Skyline; 300 feet on the return

Trailhead Location: just west of the Paradise Ranger Station on the north side of the main Paradise parking lot

Description: Our route begins on a paved walkway next to a large trail map of the Paradise area; we promptly ascend through a steeply sloping meadow colored by rosy spirea, broadleaf arnica, and red mountain-heather. The walkway crosses the Alta Vista Trail, 0.2 mile, and climbs past currant and huckleberry. A spur path branches left, mile 0.5, to meet the Deadhorse Creek Trail; our course continues to the right, passing above the creek while bending around the avalanche-lily-covered side of Alta Vista, right. Watch for marmots.

At a ridgeline rest area, 0.6 mile, the Alta Vista Loop exits from both forks on the right. Our route continues, left, up the ridge; the pavement ends in 50 yards. Stone steps climb past woolly pussytoes, and the trail enters a stretch of rocky tundra. The mountain rises directly ahead.

The upper end of the Deadhorse Creek Trail connects from the left, mile 0.9. We bear right, passing a series of colorful, small-flowered plants: first come partridgefoot and coiled-beak lousewort and then, near another set of steps, pincushion penstemon and bird's-beak lousewort. Ahead at 1.0 miles is a junction with the Glacier Vista Loop, left; our route follows this short alternate, which passes views of the Nisqually Glacier before rejoining the Skyline Trail at a rest area, mile 1.2.

Soon the route reaches the base of a large rockface; to the left are close-up views of Mount Rainier and the Nisqually Glacier. The trail now turns right, climbing up and across the cliff. At 1.6 miles the path levels and meets the turn-off for Camp Muir, left.

Continuing to the right, the Skyline Trail switchbacks past a pair of blue-hued blooms—mountain bog gentian and Jacob's ladder—before reaching Panorama Point at mile 1.9. A short spur, right, leads to a rest and observation area. The point, true to its name, offers a wide-angle view that includes not only the Paradise area and the tattered Tatoosh ridgeline, but also Mounts Adams, Hood, and St. Helens and sundry other peaks and rocks. Resuming our route, we pass the now-closed "Low" Skyline Trail, right, whose dangerous covering of ice and snow render it unsafe for travel.

Taking the "High" Skyline to the left, the way ascends through a marmot zone, passing a restroom and a decaying rock structure, left, and also some pathside yarrow. The trail continues climbing, bending around a striking formation of horizontally bedded rock, right, that is decorated with sky pilot and rusty saxifrage. Just ahead, we meet a connecting path from the Camp Muir route at mile 2.2, left. Our course continues to the right, moving above timberline past alpine lupine and golden fleabane and then arriving at the trail's crest; here a collection of seat-size rocks

On the Skyline

conveniently offers a place for rest and refreshment.

Now the path crosses below craggy McClure Rock. Masses of Davidson's penstemon perch prominently on the cliffside, left, while alpine aster and white mountain-heather maintain a less conspicuous presence. The trail drops on switchbacks into a rockfield dotted with Tolmie's saxifrage; a beautiful boggy area features alpine speedwell. More switchbacks take the route past Fremont's butterweed before we encounter the eastern end of the erstwhile Low Skyline Trail, mile 2.6, right. We bear left, passing a pathside spring. Among the many plants that water themselves here are Lewis and mountain monkeyflowers, sweet coltsfoot, and alpine willowherb.

An overlook then provides a view into the upper Paradise River basin, left. The trail levels, crosses a flower-bordered stream, 2.9 miles, and winds downhill past spreading phlox, huckleberry, and pasque flower. Our route reaches a junction with the Golden Gate Trail at mile 3.2; this shortcut, right, drops on spectacular switchbacks into the Edith Creek Basin, meeting the Skyline Trail above Myrtle Falls. The name Golden Gate apparently derives from a garbled reference to the Pearly Gates: at this spot "the trail on terra firma ended" and hikers stepped into Paradise—or at least into the glacier valley of that name.

Our route continues to the left, running down the escarpment east of the Edith Creek Basin and encountering glacier lily, mountain bog gentian, and beargrass. After a pair of stream crossings the path drops off the scarp, passing over a branch of the Paradise River on a wooden bridge, mile 3.7. A border of beautiful greenery blazes with Lewis monkeyflower; a second branch of the river offers rocks instead of a bridge and no flowers. The trail then climbs out of the valley onto the northern extension of Mazama Ridge, where the Paradise Glacier Trail forks left at 3.9 miles. Our route, right, soon arrives at the Stevens/Van Trump Monument, a rock bench that marks the highest campsite used by the climbers and their guide, Sluiskin, during their 1870 ascent.

The path drops southward; Stevens Canyon falls away to the left, while the Tatoosh Range lies dead ahead. Our route levels and passes glacier lily, sticky currant, and pasque flower. The Lakes Trail departs invitingly to the left, mile 4.3, while we bear right, descending steeply on switchbacks through a garden of glorious flowers; broadleaf arnica, subalpine lupine, and magenta paintbrush contrast their colorful hues with the bright, nearly white blooms of Sitka valerian and avalanche lily. At the bottom of the descent is the Fourth Crossing Trail, mile 4.7, left, which follows the Paradise River down to the Paradise exit road. Our way goes right, continuing the Skyline Trail. A bridge then spans the river, which can be heard off to the right as it rumbles down Sluiskin Falls.

An uphill pitch leads by willow and over another stream crossing. The trail climbs steeply past paintbrush and tall bluebells; a stand of mountain hemlock, Alaska yellow-cedar, and subalpine fir, left, is promptly followed by a pika-populated rockfall, right. After leveling in woods, the route emerges into the Edith Creek Basin, meeting the Golden Gate Trail, mile 5.2, right. We turn left, crossing Edith Creek and passing a spur path, left, that leads a hundred feet to an overlook of Myrtle Falls; the main trail then goes by broadleaf arnica and leatherleaf saxifrage. Approaching the Paradise Inn, we bear left at a junction, cross straight through an intersection, and then turn left at a final intersection to end back at the trailhead, 5.7 miles.

Reflection Lakes - Tatoosh - Stevens Canyon Area Hikes

1. Reflection Lakes - Mazama Ridge

Highlights: One of the loveliest hikes in the park, this looping, shoreline-to-ridgetop ramble offers shimmering lakes and placid ponds, grand vistas, and miles of flower-filled meadows—all without encountering the crowds that flock to the trails of nearby Paradise.

Distance: 5.3 miles, round trip

Elevation Gain: 900 feet

Trailhead location: at the Big Reflection Lake parking lot, mile 1.4 of Stevens Canyon Road

Description: Our route starts at an opening in the rock wall that borders the parking lot; from there an access spur descends some 25 feet to a junction with the Lakes/Wonderland Trail. We turn right, following the lake's south shore past huckleberry, rosy spirea, and pink elephant's head. After crossing several small bridges, the path runs by alpine white marsh-marigold and climbs to Stevens Canyon Road; turning left, we follow the roadside past Little Reflection Lake, passing horsetail and Sitka mountain-ash. At mile 0.3 we take the Lakes/Wonderland Trail as it branches left from the road. The Wonderland then forks right, 0.4 mile, while our way goes left on the Lakes Trail. Cottongrass, alpine aster, and mountain bog gentian color the meadow just ahead; watch, too, for the odd black bear.

Soon the path climbs through huckleberry, crossing an eroded streamcourse and encountering Cascade aster and paintbrush, followed by sickletop lousewort. The trail reaches Faraway Rock, mile 0.9, right, a compelling overlook that surveys not only the entire Tatoosh Range, but also Reflection Lakes, Louise Lake, Bench Lake, and the yawning expanse of Stevens Canyon.

The route turns away from the canyonside, immediately passing placid Artist's Pool, right, and winding past a series of pocket-size meadows. At mile 1.1 is a junction with the Lakes High Trail, left; we go right, soon bending around a pond, left, fringed with alpine aster. The path presently angles upward beneath a rock outcropping colored by scarlet paintbrush. After going past a pair of ponds, right, and Cascade aster, we come out onto the broad, gently rising top of Mazama Ridge.

Mount Rainier and Little Tahoma suddenly appear above a rolling, bumpy meadow, 1.3 miles; fanleaf cinquefoil, subalpine lupine, and red mountain-heather all bloom in the foreground.

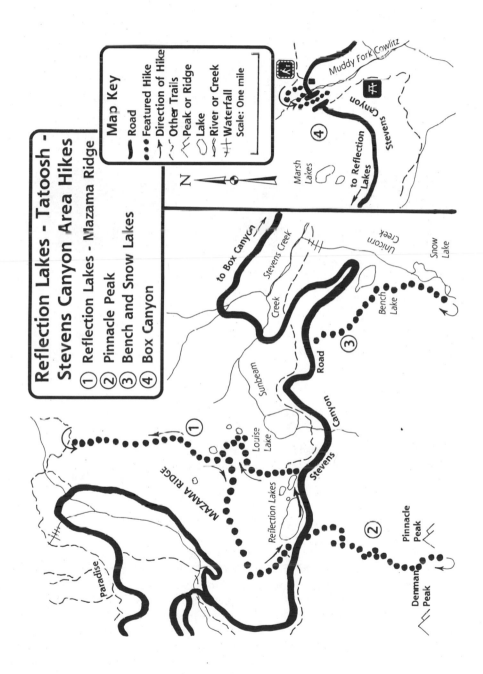

Reflection Lakes - Tatoosh - Stevens Canyon Area Hikes

1. Reflection Lakes - Mazama Ridge
2. Pinnacle Peak
3. Bench and Snow Lakes
4. Box Canyon

Map Key

- Road
- Featured Hike
- Direction of Hike
- Other Trails
- Peak or Ridge
- Lake
- River or Creek
- Waterfall

Scale: One mile

Little Reflection Lake

From the crest of a hummock, mile 1.7, is an equally estimable view southward of the sharp-tipped Tatoosh Range. Next comes scenery to the side: first the trail skirts the rim of Stevens Canyon, which falls away dramatically to the right; then a sloping meadow, left, claims attention with its covering of subalpine lupine and red mountain-heather. Ahead are stretches of Cusick's speedwell, bistort, and pasque flower.

Whether seen in the wildflower-filled profusion of summer or the rich berry-leaf colorings of fall, the meadows of Mazama Ridge amaze with their varieties of beauty, here offering a gathering of plantlife around a small tarn, there sweeping up some rocky hillock that points to the icy whiteness of the mountain—the scenes seem to spring, one after the other, from some vast, perfectly composed picture book, yet the views are so vibrant, so immediate, that they far transcend the makings of any merely human art.

Mount Rainier and Little Tahoma appear again from a low hilltop, mile 2.1. The route then drops into a rolling rockfield, passes a pair of flower-covered hummocks, and meets the Skyline Trail, 2.3 miles, near the northern end of Mazama Ridge. The long landform gained its name from the Mazamas climbing club, which camped here during the summers of 1897, 1905, and 1919, the second time as part of a four-club conclave that also included contingents from the Appalachian, Sierra, and Alpine clubs. Decades earlier, Stevens and Van Trump were led up the ridge by their guide, Sluiskin, while en route to Mount Rainier's summit.

Unencumbered by peak-scaling demands, we reverse direction here, dropping back down the Lakes Trail to mile 3.5, where the Lakes High Trail branches right. We turn onto this narrow, undulating path, following it through small stands of compact conifers and across sloping, flower-dappled meadows. Just past a view, left, of Pinnacle Peak and Reflection Lakes is tiger lily, mile 3.9; Cascade aster then covers a grassy hillslope, while arrowleaf groundsel colors a large opening at mile 4.1. The path descends past huckleberry and sickletop lousewort, mile 4.5, and ends at a junction with the Lakes Trail, 4.7 miles. Our route turns left, dropping past arrowleaf groundsel and avalanche lily before leveling at 4.9 miles. Cottongrass, Jeffrey's shooting star, and mountain bog gentian are found in the damp openings; the wetness is spanned by a boardwalk and several plank bridges. At mile 5.1 is a junction with the Wonderland Trail. Our way turns left, crossing

the outlet from Big Reflection Lake and then following the shoreline to the spur path, right, that returns us to our trailhead, mile 5.3, at the parking lot.

2. Pinnacle Peak

Highlights: Magnificent vistas, plenty of plants, and a short but exhilarating climb make this trek to the Tatoosh ridgeline a memorable hike.

Distance: 2.6 miles round trip

Elevation Gain: 1,100 feet

Trailhead Location: opposite the Big Reflection Lake parking lot, mile 1.4 of Stevens Canyon Road

Description: The trail leaves the south side of Stevens Canyon Road, ascending into woods heavy with subalpine fir, Alaska yellow-cedar, and mountain hemlock. Small meadows break up the congregating conifers; the damp openings feature strawberry and subalpine buttercup. In summer, white rhododendron brightens the nearby forest. The path arcs up to a ridgespur, mile 0.3, that is marked by a large rock, right; nearby are woodland-penstemon and fireweed. The route then bends south, running up the ridgespur. At a crest, 0.5 mile, is a view, right, of Mount Rainier.

Now the trail cuts across the steep slope below Pinnacle Peak. Avalanche lily lines the banks of a small stream, mile 0.6, followed by Jeffrey's shooting star and Brewer's mitrewort. The route then passes through a scattering of scree; watch for perched pikas. White and red mountain-heathers clump in the rocky opening, while to the right are views of both Mount Rainier and Paradise. A short stretch of woods precedes another patch of pika-inhabited talus; returning to forest, the path steepens, passes bracted lousewort, and at mile 0.9 enters a large open area beneath a rockfall, left. A wide chute, right, runs down to the meadowy headwaters of a branch of Tatoosh Creek. Cusick's speedwell speckles the trailside violet-blue.

To the left of the trail an escarpment rises above a huge rockfall, while across the canyon, right, are the steep slopes of Denman Peak. Tacoma attorney Asahel H. Denman was an organizer of the city's chapter of the Mountaineers and a strong "Mount Tacoma" advocate during the long-running name controversy; like A. H. Barnes and Asahel Curtis, he often lectured about the mountain while using "magic lantern" slides.

Small Alaska yellow-cedar and mountain hemlock cluster near the pathside, providing perches for gray jays. The route then switchbacks uphill, mile 1.1, passing Davidson's penstemon and spreading phlox; an impressive rock wall rises above the trail. False hellebore, rusty saxifrage, and Jacob's ladder precede another set of switchbacks.

Newberry's knotweed and crimson columbine decorate the final climb to the saddle. At the Tatoosh ridgeline, mile 1.3, are back-to-back views of mountain grandeur: the ridge falls away to the south, dropping down a steep meadow to the hanging-valley headwaters of Butter Creek; in the distance is the gleaming dome of Mount Adams, while beyond it the haze-softened point of Mount Hood sticks skyward. To the north, Rainier rises above Paradise. East along the ridgeline is the contorted cap of challenging Unicorn Peak.

On August 15, 1870, a trio of tired climbers—Hazard Stevens, Philemon Beecher Van Trump, and their Yakima guide, Sluiskin—crossed over the saddle on their way north to the mountain. They had left the Cowlitz Valley two days earlier, taking the route that Sluiskin insisted on, over the Tatoosh, rather than the Nisqually Valley approach that Stevens favored. Descending from the divide, Van Trump tried fishing Tatoosh Creek; he had no luck, but the party did manage to shoot a grouse for dinner. Two days later, having already tested themselves on the Tatoosh, Van Trump and Stevens made the first ascent of Tacoma/Rainier.

The official park trail ends at the saddle, where the sun-warmed ridgeside provides a prime picnic site. Informal paths lead southwest toward Plummer Peak and to Pinnacle Peak, which bulks high above us to the northeast, but park officials advise against attempting either route without the proper rock climbing training and equipment.

Reversing direction, our route now descends from the divide, returning to Stevens Canyon Road at mile 2.6.

3. Bench and Snow Lakes

Highlights: Hanging below the Tatoosh Range on the rim of Stevens Canyon, an often-burned benchland offers flower-filled meadows to complement a pair of picturesque lakes. At route's end, craggy Unicorn Peak towers over a climactic cirque.

Distance: 2.5 miles round trip

Elevation Gain: 200 feet

Trailhead Location: at a parking area, mile 2.9 of Stevens Canyon Road, east of Reflection Lakes

Description: The trail leaves the east side of the parking lot, ascending into a thicket of Cascade mountain-ash, Sitka

Unicorn Peak

alder, and small conifers. Silvery snags rise spectrally above the second growth trees, monuments to the 19th-century conflagrations that swept through the area. White rhododendron and woodland-penstemon brighten the slowly regenerating forest.

Jeffrey's shooting star and subalpine buttercup are followed by a boardwalk, mile 0.2; northward are views of Mount Rainier and upper Stevens Canyon. After passing willow and red mountain-heather, the trail levels among the barkless, bleached, nearly limbless trunks of more burned trees. Both beargrass and cottongrass dot the benchland, while in late summer mountain

bog gentian opens its inky blue blossoms beside a meandering brook; smallish Alaska yellow-cedar and subalpine fir are scattered across the otherwise open landscape. At mile 0.3 comes a trio of bushes: mountain-ash, white rhododendron, and false azalea.

The trail crests a hillock, mile 0.5, where a short spur, left, leads to an overlook of Bench Lake and its bordering bog; woodland-penstemon colors the ensuing descent. After passing patches of huckleberry, we meet a side path, mile 0.7, left, that leads to Bench Lake. Our route drops to a meadow colored by paintbrush and Gray's lovage, after which plantations of cottongrass cover open areas on both sides of a pebble-bottomed brook. Switchbacks then climb a steep hillslope past stink currant and sticky currant.

More woodland-penstemon brightens the hillcrest; Mount Rainier rises in white-topped resplendence to the north-west. A zigzagging descent arrives at a lovely small stream canyon filled with alpine white marsh-marigold, pink ele-phant's head, and a celestial clustering of Jeffrey's shooting star. Huckleberry and avalanche lily line the trail as it as-cends the next canyonside.

At the top of the grade an access spur, mile 1.0, left, leads around the northern rim of Snow Lake to a pair of campsites. Our route continues right, dropping to an open flat by the upper end of the lake. The maintained trail ends by a small stream, mile 1.2, but a well-worn path, right, continues to a rock-studded ford. The route turns left on the opposite side of the creek, runs downsteam past pasque flower and kalmia, and then reaches a hummock that overlooks the stunning terminus of the canyon.

Punctuated by the exclamation point of Unicorn Peak, the towering Tatoosh ridgeline wraps itself in rocky splendor around the cirque that holds Snow Lake. The great gray cliffs soar skyward, but-tressed by long slopes of scree; together they form a picture of power personi-fied, yet they gently, almost protec-tively, enclose the small, deep-blue bit of water at their base, as if it were the baptistery in some immense, glacier-carved cathedral.

A vague track continues a hundred yards south to a small waterfall, but our route stops at the hilltop viewpoint. The return retraces our approach, reaching the trailhead at mile 2.5.

4. Box Canyon

Highlights: A deep, dark-sided gorge, nearly narrow enough to leap across... more than a hundred feet below, the churning, frothing glacial melt of the Muddy Fork Cowlitz—ever-moving wa-ter and unyielding rock clash daily be-neath and beside Stevens Canyon Road. This short loop trail offers a close look at the dramatic defile as well as providing a striking succession of pathside plants. Fern lovers will delight in finding at least six different species along the route.

Distance: 0.5 mile

Elevation Gain: 100 feet

Trailhead Location: at mile 8.7 of Stevens Canyon Road

Description: Starting from the north end of the crosswalk at the "Box Canyon of the Cowlitz" parking area, the paved walkway leads past pipsissewa, twin-flower, and Douglas maple, reaching a junction with the Wonderland Trail in a hundred yards. Our route turns left, crossing through an open area covered with gently rounded masses of mossy, glacier-scratched intrusive rock. Larks-pur, tiger lily, and woolly sunflower color the grayness, while oceanspray and rosy spirea add their bright blos-soms to the mix; less noticeable but also of interest are stonecrop, serviceberry, and black cottonwood. To the left is the river gorge: a view of the far cliffside, mile 0.1, reveals an Alaska yellow-cedar (right), growing near a western redcedar (left) in close enough proximity to invite comparison of their contrasting foliage.

A wide bridge spans the chasm of the Muddy Fork Cowlitz; 115 feet below, the gravel-gray river roars through the

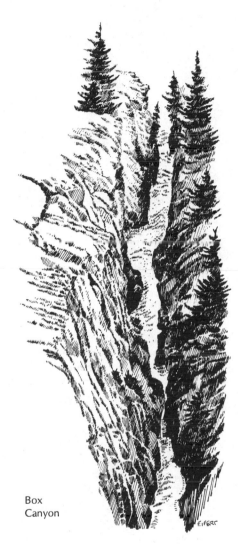

Box
Canyon

conifers. At pathside is a sprinkling of moisture-loving spring beauty.

At mile 0.2 the dirt Wonderland Trail branches right from the paved walkway; hikers on a tight schedule may want to bear left, continuing on the basic loop, but the recommended route follows the Wonderland uphill as it runs past such forest favorites as wild ginger, queen's cup, and trail plant; also present are gooseberry, baneberry, and deer fern. After a single zigzag, the path levels and passes a moss-softened rockface attractively adorned with parsley fern, ground juniper, and western polypody; close at hand are a pair of sunlight seekers— woodland-penstemon and bracken fern. The trail then crosses above the tunnel for Stevens Canyon Road, mile 0.3. Ahead lies a lengthy descent into the depths of Stevens Canyon, so we now reverse course, rejoining the Box Canyon Loop at 0.4 mile; here we turn right to continue our route. Soon we see such shade lovers as devil's club, sword fern, and lady fern, with coast penstemon and fireweed blooming in sunnier spots.

Presently the trail reaches the roadway; a left turn leads across the bridge, where onlookers marvel at the Muddy Fork some 180 feet below. The bridge itself is worth beholding: faced with stone taken from the adjacent tunnel, it was completed in the 1950s and shows the careful craftsmanship of an even earlier era. The loop then concludes at the trailhead, 0.5 miles.

rocky confines. Sitka alder and Douglas maple juxtapose their bright leaves with the darker needles of the cliff-clinging

Ohanapecosh – East Side Area Hikes

1. Silver Falls

Highlights: This low-elevation loop leads through a moss-carpeted forest to plunging, splashing Silver Falls and Stevens Canyon Road, returning by a secluded hillside route that runs above the Ohanapecosh River. Along the way are such additional attractions as Pacific yew, three species of maples, and numerous woodland wildflowers.

Distance: 4.4 miles, round trip

Elevation Gain: 300 feet on the way to Stevens Canyon Road; 200 feet on the return

Trailhead Location: at the rear of the Ohanapecosh Visitor Center

Description: The first section of the route follows the Hot Springs Nature Trail. Leaving the visitor center, our path promptly meets a spur route, left, that crosses a creeklet on a small bridge; we bear right, climbing past western coltsfoot, devil's club, and bunchberry.

After going by maidenhair fern and gooseberry, the trail passes over a shallow creek on stepping stones and joins an old road that ascends from the campground, left. We continue to the right, first meeting Pacific dogwood and evergreen violet, and next dropping past vanilla leaf, bigleaf maple, and fairybell. A pair of boardwalks then spans the runoff from two of the hot springs, right; ahead on the left is the still-visible excavation for the swimming pool that was to have served the early-day Ohanapecosh health resort.

At a junction, mile 0.3, our route, right, picks up the Silver Falls Loop Trail, running along another road remnant past creeping buttercup, vanilla leaf, and vine maple. Beyond a small bridge the path leaves the roadbed and climbs the hillside, passing an old wooden, wire-wrapped water pipe. Near here was the site of the original Ohanapecosh Ranger Station, which sat just north of the first park boundary. The log structure, dating from 1913, was removed in 1965. A family from Vashon Island purchased and disassembled the building, carefully numbering its pieces with a grease pencil to facilitate reconstruction, and took the wood home. Then Washington's moist weather went to work: the grease marks ran into indecipherability, the cabin owners were left with a decaying pile of logs that defied reassembly, and soon the one-time Ohanapecosh station had vanished into Vashon's wet and welcoming earth.

Now the trail follows a moss-lined corridor through the forest, encountering salal and trillium; to the left is the Ohanapecosh River, on the right is the

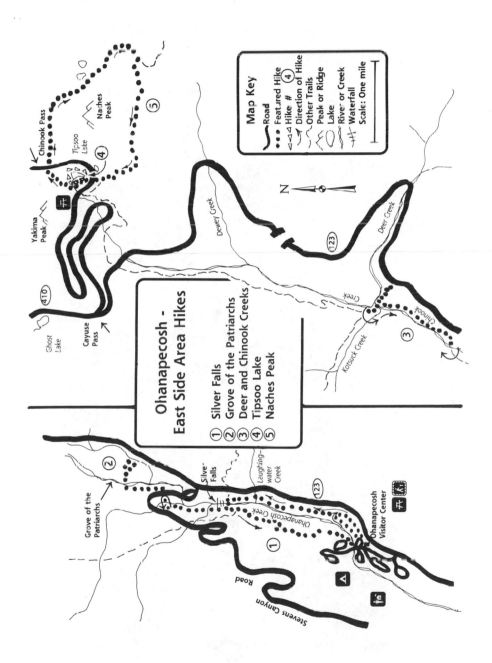

Map Key
Road
Featured Hike
Hike #   4
Direction of Hike
Other Trails
Peak or Ridge
Lake
River or Creek
Waterfall
Scale: One mile

Ohanapecosh -
East Side Area Hikes

1 Silver Falls
2 Grove of the Patriarchs
3 Deer and Chinook Creeks
4 Tipsoo Lake
5 Naches Peak

highway. Skunk cabbage congregates in the damp hollows. Rock-filled Laughingwater Creek chortles its way beneath a long wooden bridge, 1.1 mile; to the right, Pacific yew spreads above both ends of the span. Departing the stream, our route runs by starflower and rises out of the creek canyon, arriving at a junction, mile 1.3, with the Laughingwater Trail. The way right leads uphill to the highway, thus providing motorists with easy access to Silver Falls. Our route turns left, soon dropping on switchbacks to an overlook of the falls. *(Warning: do not approach the falls beyond the trail or overlook.)*

Silver Falls

A bridge spans the roiling river just downstream from the boulder-framed cataract, connecting the mossy cliffs that rise from the gorge. The trail climbs the far bank amid dens of beargrass; we take a spur path, right, that leads 50 yards to another overlook of the falls and then return to the main route. At a junction, 1.6 miles, we make a right turn onto the Eastside Trail. Soon an overlook, right, offers a spectacular view of the rectangular chasm through which the Ohanapecosh flows on its way to the falls. Continuing northward through mossy woods, the path crosses a rocky rill, runs by Smith's fairybell and various ferns, and encounters another stream. A final stretch of lush forest brings us to Stevens Canyon Road, 2.1 miles; across the road are restrooms and the Grove of the Patriarchs Trail.

Our route heads back from the roadway, reaching the Silver Falls Loop at mile 2.6, where we turn right and begin climbing. The Cowlitz Divide Trail forks right, 2.7 miles; our way, left, continues uphill, leveling beneath a mossy cliff. Three ferns—licorice, bracken, and maidenhair—adorn the area, along with alumroot, orange honeysuckle, and woodland-penstemon. A second cliff claims a trio of shrubs: hazelnut and both Douglas and vine maples.

Soon the trail drops into a secluded side canyon whose shade loving residents include white-veined wintergreen, rattlesnake orchid, and coralroot. The open forest is carpeted with moss; an unseen stream softly gurgles somewhere downhill to the right. The quiet spot seems a world away from the rollicking canyon of the Ohanapecosh.

A pair of bogs, 3.5 miles, is bisected by the trail, which levels, climbs briefly uphill, and then undulates. The path,

now high above the Ohanapecosh, drops through thickets of salal to come closer to the river. After passing a spur to the upper campground, right, the route meets the main campground road, mile 3.9, just north of the Ohanapecosh bridge. Our course turns left and crosses the river, immediately arriving at a junction with the "B" Loop. Hikers in a hurry can continue along the main campground road, right, to promptly reach the visitor center; our route, however, provides additional scenery: we turn left onto the "B" Loop and a short distance ahead make another left at the Silver Falls Loop trailhead, mile 4.0.

We now follow the bed of an old road that led to the Ohanapecosh Hot Springs; lining the way are false lily-of-the-valley, snowberry, and trail plant. Soon we encounter a large boulder, right, that is home to sword and licorice ferns. Red alder and bigleaf maple then shade the way. After passing the site of the hot springs lodge and bath house, the route arrives at a junction with the Hot Springs Nature Trail, right. We take this path, which formed the first section of our hike, back to the visitor center, concluding our trip at mile 4.4.

2. Grove of the Patriarchs

Highlights: On an island in the Ohanapecosh River grows a grove of ancient, oversized conifers; this short excursion circles through the center of the stand.

Trailhead Location: at mile 19.0 of Stevens Canyon Road, just north of the Stevens Canyon Entrance Station

Distance: 1.1 miles, round trip

Elevation Gain: 100 feet

Description: A paved walkway leaves the northern end of the grove parking lot, immediately passing a shaded set of restrooms. In a hundred yards the walkway meets the dirt Eastside Trail, which our course now follows to the right as it drops downhill through thick woods. At mile 0.1 the trail levels beside the Ohanapecosh River; foamflower borders the pathside. Twinflower, devil's club, and hazelnut also line the way, which, at 0.2 mile, reaches a rock outcropping whose seams are stippled with saxifrage and crisscrossed by snow bramble.

Oak fern, trail plant, and maidenhair fern precede a junction, mile 0.3, where the Eastside Trail branches left. Our route runs right, descending on switchbacks past piggy-back plant to the river; the banks here blush wine in autumn with the tint of vine maple. An impressive wood and steel suspension bridge, 0.4 mile, crosses to the island, where a stand of Pacific silver fir lies just beyond the bridge. Just ahead is the patriarchal collection of conifers, but first comes an

On the Grove trail

assemblage of red alder—itself a worthy, leafy matriarchy.

Vine maples form a corridor at the Grove's entrance. Then, at mile 0.5, the trail divides; our route, right, passes a succession of huge logs and roots. A spur path, right, runs 50 feet to "Big Cedar," a behemoth western redcedar. Nearby, huge western hemlock and Douglas-fir tower above a carpeting of oak fern. In this damp, fertile environment, regeneration is rapid and opportunistic: seedlings sprout from "nurse" logs, the youngsters often growing in a row called a "colonnade." The new trees sometimes send out long roots that wrap themselves around the logs; the nurses eventually decay, leaving large openings under the roots of what have then become "octopus" trees.

After passing various nurses and octopi, the loop completes its circuit, mile 0.6, and the route then retraces itself to the parking lot, concluding at mile 1.1.

3. Deer and Chinook Creeks

Highlights: This descent into a heavily forested creek canyon features full-sized conifers, a bevy of berries, and three wonderful waterfalls.

Distance: 2.5 miles round trip

Elevation Gain: 400 feet on the return

Trailhead Location: at mile 11.5 of Highway 123

Description: A pullout 50 yards south of the trailhead provides parking for the hike; the route begins on the west side of the highway where a sign marks the trail but gives it no name. Immediately the path drops down the hillside into forestland filled with huge western hemlock and scatterings of bunchberry.

After switchbacking past foamflower, dwarf bramble, and twinflower, the route arrives at the fenced overlook, mile 0.2, right, for Deer Creek Falls, whose multiple ribbons of water splash down a narrow chute of reddish rock. Large Douglas-fir shades a blanket of moss moistened by the falls' spray.

More switchbacks lead to a junction, 0.3 miles, with the Eastside Trail. Our route branches right, promptly crossing Deer Creek and then almost as quickly reaching Chinook Creek. Here, just above the bridge crossing, is a small, picture-perfect waterfall framed by fallen logs; crystal clear water courses brightly down the creek. Until 1931, this area (along with the rest of our route) lay outside the park. The boundary was a half mile west at appropriately named Boundary Creek until an extension pushed the line eastward to the Cascade crest.

Ahead lie the trails to Owyhigh Lakes and Chinook Pass; having seen the scenic mini-falls, however, our route reverses course, going back to the trail junction and then turning right onto the Eastside Trail. In 75 yards the path passes Deer Creek Camp, whose several shaded sites sit on the hillside, left. Huckleberry and queen's cup are regular campground occupants.

Now the trail makes a gradual descent down the canyon of Chinook Creek, passing wood rose and a congregation of oak fern, deer fern, and lady fern; full-size hemlock rises overhead. A lovely, rambling stretch of trail runs beneath a mix of Pacific silver fir and more hemlock, crosses a shallow defile, 0.9 mile, and arrives at a collection of devil's club. Nearby, Pacific silver fir shades maidenhair fern. The trail then bends west and drops to Chinook Creek, 1.3

miles. Here a stout wooden bridge spans a sublime gorge: mossy rocks, sparkling pools, and an "S"-shaped chute all lie near the crossing. A dipper may even add her bobbing, bent-legged dance to the display.

Woodland-penstemon colors the far end of the crossing, tempting hardy hikers to continue downstream to Stafford and Ohanapecosh Falls. Our route saves these splendors for another day, turning round to regain the trailhead at mile 2.5.

4. Tipsoo Lake

Highlights: Wildflower-fringed Tipsoo Lake provides an idyllic respite from the rigors of travel on the park's East Side. The lake-encircling loop is both level and short, but it will loosen the kinks of motorists long confined to their cars.

Distance: 0.6 mile, round trip

Elevation Gain: negligible

Trailhead Location: at the Tipsoo Lake picnic area parking lot, on State Highway 410 (Mather Memorial Parkway) between Cayuse and Chinook passes

Description: Starting from the left side of the Mather plaque at the upper end of the parking lot, the rock-bordered path runs east toward the lake. Pasque flower and rockslide larkspur brighten the meadow area, while mountain-ash and huckleberry rise above them; mountain hemlock and subalpine fir form scattered islands of forest. The trail promptly bears right at a junction with the northern end of the Naches Peak Loop and proceeds to a fork, mile 0.1, in front of the lake. Our route turns left, encountering fan-leaf cinquefoil and aster.

"Tipsoo" in the Chinook jargon means "grassy or hairy," and the lakeshore is appropriately fringed with greenery. A glacially sculpted tarn, Tipsoo sits in a cirque beneath the Cascade divide, with Yakima Peak rising to the left and Naches Peak to the right. The trail heads toward the latter landmark and then bends to the right, passing arrowleaf groundsel, subalpine lupine, and magenta paintbrush. After reaching the south end of the lake, 0.3 mile, the route meets the first of two spurs, left, that connect with the southern end of the Naches Peak Loop. False hellebore, red mountain-heather, and huckleberry border the shore.

At one time a road circled through the fragile meadows that surround the lake; photos from the time show a host of picnickers among the wildflowers, their dark, high-cabbed autos parked nonchalantly upon the suffering vegetation. During the 1930s an "improvement" project threatened to do even more damage, but a proposed ranger station, picnickers' kitchen, and 200-car parking lot were never built, and the restroom and small picnic/parking facilities that were constructed have had limited impact upon the site.

At Tipsoo's outlet (Chinook Creek), the loop reaches another junction, 0.5 mile; our route turns left, skirting the edge of a small pond and passing, left, another connection with the Naches Peak Loop. After crossing a bridge over the outlet, the trail concludes at the parking lot, mile 0.6, just south of the Mather plaque.

5. Naches Peak

Highlights: Only about half of this peak-encircling loop lies within Mount Rainier National Park, but the balance, which follows the Pacific Crest Trail

Yakima Peak from
the Naches Peak loop

through the William O. Douglas Wilderness, shows that spectacular scenery doesn't end at the park boundary—as hanging valleys, north slope flower fields, and dazzling Dewey Lake all admirably attest.

Distance: 3.4 miles round trip

Elevation Gain: 600 feet

Trailhead Location: at the Tipsoo Lake picnic area parking lot, on State Highway 410 (Mather Memorial Parkway) between Cayuse and Chinook passes

Description: We start at the northern end of the parking area on the left side of the Mather memorial plaque; our route runs east 50 yards to a junction just opposite a small pond. The way right continues to Tipsoo Lake, while our course turns back sharply to the left, climbing through meadows alive with aster, Sitka valerian, and pasque flower. The trail enters a stand of conifers, mile 0.1, and starts zigzagging uphill; it crosses a small meadow notable for its false hellebore, huckleberry, and mountain-ash, 0.2 mile, and then reaches the ridgeline. Here the route joins the Pacific Crest Trail, bearing right to cross the Mather Memorial Parkway on a path atop the park entrance arch. The trail moves into the Wenatchee National Forest, which spreads north and east across the deep drainage of the Rainier Fork of the American River.

Now the route runs across the shaded northern slope of Naches Peak, passing subalpine lupine, Sitka valerian, and both red and white mountain-heathers. White rhododendron rises from the mountainside, preceding our entrance, mile 0.6, into the William O. Douglas Wilderness Area. Supreme Court Justice Douglas, who grew up in Yakima, tramped the trails south and east of here as a youth, strengthening legs stricken by polio in early childhood.

After encountering mountain hemlock, the route passes a hanging valley, left, that hangs above the Rainier Fork; at 0.8 mile a rocky cascade moistens Lewis monkeyflower, leatherleaf saxifrage, and fringed grass-of-Parnassus. The trail crosses the top of the valley and climbs past Alaska yellow-cedar, subalpine lupine, and false hellebore. Naches Peak rises steeply to the right.

More creek chutes and more Lewis monkeyflower lie ahead; the plant's pink-purple petals are favored by the local pikas as an ingredient in their sun-dried bouquets. After passing a lovely tarn, mile 1.2, left, the path runs beneath a stretch of gray-rock cliffside, right, and then climbs gently past huckleberry. Look and listen for elk.

A switchback, 1.5 miles, leads to a small promontory, left, that provides a northward view of the ridgeline near Crystal Mountain. The trail then crests the Cascade Divide and soon drops to a landmark-loaded overlook, left. Visible are: Goat Rocks on the horizon, Dewey Lake in the valley below, and Seymour Peak above the lake on the right. The latter landform was named for William W. Seymour, mayor of Tacoma from 1911 to 1914, and who, under the guidance of Henry "Steptoe" Carter, climbed Mount Rainier in 1892.

A junction, mile 1.7, allows the Pacific Crest Trail to descend, left, on its way toward Dewey Lake and White Pass; our loop route turns right and then runs across the southern flank of Naches Peak. Rosy spirea and ground juniper cover sections of the hillside.

Presently the path reenters the national park, and, rounding a bend, presents a stunning vista of Mount Rainier beyond a long, sloping, storybook meadow. Pasque flower, bistort, and subalpine lupine speckle the grassland, which also supports scattered stands of subalpine fir, mountain hemlock, and whitebark pine. The trail skirts a small teardrop tarn, right, and then crests a ridgespur, 2.1 miles. The slopes ahead are a colorful mixture in fall: yellowed false hellebore, red-purple huckleberry, yellow-green grass, and inky green conifers; also tinting the hillside are beargrass, rosy spirea, and mountain-ash. The Chinook Creek drainage drops away dramatically to the left.

A view of Mount Adams, left, precedes another round-the-bend sighting of Rainier at mile 2.7, as the sharp serrations of Governor's Ridge rise raggedly in front of the park's namesake peak; white rhododendron and huckleberry cluster near trailside. Now the route winds downhill, reaching an intersection, 3.1 miles. To the right is a spur trail to a small tarn, while on the extreme left is the start of the Eastside Trail, bound downhill towards Chinook Creek and, eventually, Ohanapecosh. The middle path continues our route, which promptly crosses the highway and approaches Tipsoo Lake. Our course turns left at all the remaining junctions, first cresting a hillock, next passing the south side of a small pond, and then crossing the lake's outlet (Chinook Creek) before finishing back at the Mather plaque, 3.4 miles.

White River – Sunrise Area Hikes

1. Owyhigh Lakes

Highlights: After zigzagging up a conifer-shadowed hillside, this easy ascent reaches serene and scenic Owyhigh Lakes, the skyline behind them cut by the incisors of sharp-toothed Governors Ridge.

Distance: 8.2 miles, round trip

Elevation Gain: 1,700 feet

Trailhead Location: at mile 3.6 of Sunrise Road.

Description: The broad pathway leaves the south side of the road, rising gently through mixed forest. A succession of plants appears at trailside: first twinflower and northwestern twayblade; next bunchberry, clasping twisted-stalk and fringed grass-of-Parnassus; then skunk cabbage; also lining the way is the glowing green foliage of oak fern and vanilla leaf. The route now gradually climbs the lower slopes of Tamanos (Chinook jargon for "guardian spirit") Mountain, passing at 0.3 mile western teaberry and both bog and one-sided wintergreens. A switchback, 0.5 miles, provides a view, left, of the log- and rock-filled bed of Shaw Creek. The wide-spreading stream, which drains the Owyhigh Lakes, was named for Tacoma school teacher and principal Carrie Shaw Rice, the first woman to serve on the Washington State Board of Education. Her poem, "Tacoma, the Rose of the West," was set to music and sung at the 1910 dedication of Stadium Bowl.

Continuing to zigzag up the mountainside, the trail passes white-veined wintergreen and Oregon grape, mile 1.1, and then bog-orchid at a stream crossing, 1.2 miles. Alaska yellow-cedar shades a subsequent recrossing of the creek, near which are horsetail and mountain bells. The switchbacks and streams continue: false azalea, mile 2.0, and huckleberry, 2.5 miles, are frequently found trailside shrubs. We cross Tamanos Creek on a log bridge and promptly reach a junction, mile 3.0, with the spur to Tamanos Creek Camp, left.

The main trail then runs along a forested hillside before entering a large meadow, 3.4 miles; upslope to the right is Tamanos Mountain, while Governors Ridge rises across the canyon to the left. Brightening the grassland are first wandering daisy, bistort, and arrowleaf groundsel, then pasque flower and Cascade aster. At mile 3.6 a gathering of false hellebore marks a vista, left, of the two Owyhigh Lakes. The name (usually spelled Owhi) honors the Yakima chief who summered nearby in the area now

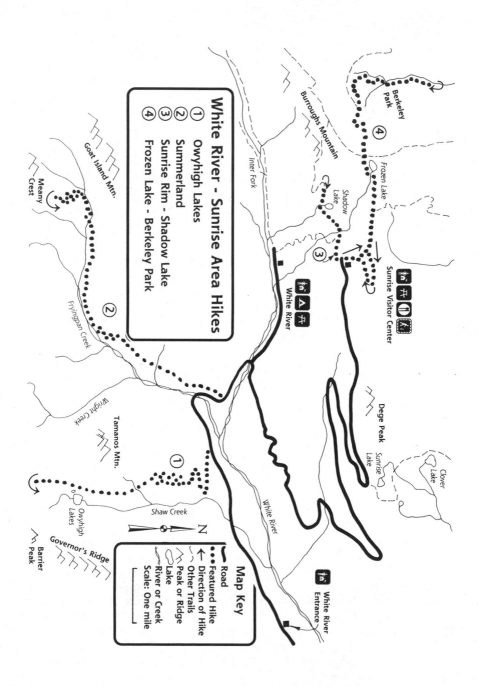

White River - Sunrise Area Hikes

① Owyhigh Lakes
② Summerland
③ Sunrise Rim - Shadow Lake
④ Frozen Lake - Berkeley Park

Map Key

•••• Road
•••• Featured Hike
→   Direction of Hike
---- Other Trails
⋏   Peak or Ridge
◯   Lake
      River or Creek
―――   Scale: One mile

Owyhigh Lakes and Governors Ridge

called Sunrise. The jagged row of peaks rising behind the lakes was named Governors Ridge by early-day Park Superintendent Ethan Allen "for all men who have held that office or may hold it in the future," a proclamation that failed to anticipate Dixie Lee Ray.

Crimson columbine colors the pathway as the route passes above the southern, smaller lake and winds uphill through a mix of meadow and woods; subalpine lupine, magenta paintbrush, and fanleaf cinquefoil provide deep-hued decoration in the openings. At mile 4.0 the trail crests the divide at Kotsuck Pass. Barrier Peak rises to the left, while the Cowlitz Chimneys fill the distance to the right; remnants of volca-

nic plugs, both landforms contain rock from the ancient Ohanapecosh Formation. Our way then drops gently to arrive at a narrow gap, mile 4.1, where the headwaters of Kotsuck Creek, right, form for their descent into the valley of the Ohanapecosh. Here the hike reverses course, finishing at the trailhead, 8.2 miles.

2. Summerland

Highlights: Magnificent meadows, mountain goats, and the arresting proximity of alpine high country make this semi-steep trek a rewarding route.

Distance: 8.3 miles, round trip

Elevation Gain: 2,200 feet

Fryingpan Creek

Trailhead Location: at mile 4.3 of Sunrise Road

Description: The trail leaves the south side of Sunrise Road a hundred feet west of the Fryingpan Creek bridge; the wide pathway climbs gently through mixed conifers, meeting the Wonderland Trail at mile 0.1. Our way goes left, moving onto the side of a hillslope. At pathside is first one-sided wintergreen, then starflower and salmonberry; pinesap surfaces in the shade of deeper forest, 0.7 mile. As we continue up the gradual grade, vanilla leaf and devil's club precede a stretch of Pacific silver fir and very large Douglas-fir. The craggy Cowlitz Chimneys are visible at 1.0 mile, left.

Several switchbacks, starting at mile 1.4, offer vistas of Fryingpan Creek, left, and the Cowlitz Chimneys, above. White rhododendron, 2.1 miles, and then northwestern twayblade line the trail, while thimbleberry and Sitka alder congregate at a subsequent opening. A trio of creek crossings, 2.7 miles, features white rhododendron and brook saxifrage.

Mountain boxwood and willow now line the gently rising stream corridor. Presently the path crosses rocky Fryingpan Creek, mile 3.1; in the streambed is Lewis monkeyflower. A switchback takes us past arrowleaf groundsel, tall bluebells, and crimson columbine, after which the trail enters a long, sloping meadow filled with false hellebore and mountain-ash. Our route enters forest and begins zigzagging up an abrupt mountainslope, 3.6 miles, encountering mountain-heather and Jacob's ladder; a flower-filled opening at mile 4.0 offers subalpine lupine, magenta paintbrush, and Sitka valerian. The switchbacks end at the edge of the rolling, bright green park known as Summerland. The conifer-fringed meadow and its alpine backdrop seem straight out of *Heidi*: a soft, inviting carpet of grass and flowers, dotted with tufts of rosy-hued mountain-heather and bounded by a scattered spread of rocks and boulders that leads the eye upward, first to the snow and ice, and then to the rising ridgeline—two-peaked Meany Crest, the ragged pyramid of Little Tahoma, and the shining white top of the mountain.

Spur paths leading to a restroom and stone shelter branch left shortly after 4.1 miles. The main trail continues to the right on its way up to Panhandle Gap; along the way is an attractive stretch of alpine tundra that features such hardy, handsome flowers as rosy pussytoes, spotted saxifrage, and pussypaws. However, an intervening ice field causes us to turn back at Summerland's scenic meadow.

Hikers who pause before their return may find mountain goats picking their way up the side of aptly named Goat Island Mountain, which rises above the canyon to the right. The history-minded might contemplate Meany Crest, named for Edmond S. Meany, a longtime president of the Mountaineers hiking club, editor of the *Washington Historical Quarterly*, and UW history professor. Whatever their interest, nearly everyone will find something to savor at Summerland.

Retracing our steps, we reach the trailhead at mile 8.3.

3. Sunrise Rim - Shadow Lake

Highlights: Some of Sunrise's prettiest wildflowers, grand vistas of the mountain, and shimmering Shadow Lake lie along this nearly level route.

Distance: 2.6 miles, round trip

Elevation Gain: 200 feet on return

Trailhead Location: at the south side of the Sunrise parking lot, across from the restrooms

Description: A wide dirt path descends gradually to a ridgeside flat, entering a mixture of forest and meadow. The Emmons Vista/Silver Forest Trail forks left, mile 0.1, while our course turns right, soon providing views of Mount Rainier, the White River Valley, and Little Tahoma; subalpine lupine, Gray's lovage, and Cascade aster are among the more prominent plants. The route runs above the ridgeslope, passing a lovely mini-meadow with its wandering daisy and arnica, and then meets the Wonderland Trail on its ascent from White River, 0.5 mile, left. We continue to the right.

Soon a squeaky log bridge spans a small creek; in the streambed are bistort and Lewis monkeyflower. More vistas of alpine scenery are followed by trail-side displays of coiled-beak lousewort, sandwort, and spreading phlox. At mile 0.9 a large, nearly level park opens to the right, while its lower end drops away down the canyon to the left. Scatterings of subalpine lupine now tint the grasslands a purplish blue. Rounding a rocky outcropping, Mount Rainier springs into view; closer at hand, pine-mat manzanita, lace fern, and ground juniper decorate the cliff face.

Presently the trail cuts through a meadow that contains both subalpine *and* alpine lupine, mile 1.2. To the right of a wooden bridge is tree-lined Shadow Lake; its placid but not noticeably shaded waters are occasionally rippled by the strokes of a hardy swimmer. Beyond the bridge is a spur path to the lake, right; near the junction is woolly pussytoes. Our route then levels and enters a small basin, 1.3 miles, where it meets an aging road. In the woods to the right is a section of the Sunrise Camp; its relict log restroom sits on a hummock to the immediate right. Bistort, spreading phlox, and pincushion penstemon color the surroundings, while in the background the bare bulk of Burroughs Mountain looms high above.

The series of three peaks was named (by a committee of the Mountaineers) for New York naturalist and author John Burroughs. The austere, rounded ridgeline bears little resemblance to the grandfatherly, bewhiskered Burroughs, who visited Mount Rainier in the days before it became a national park.

From the campground, the recommended route doubles back over the same course, reaching Sunrise at mile 2.6. An alternate return is via the access road that departs to the right, which is 0.2 mile shorter but also less scenic. Alpine adventurers can consider, as a longer but lovelier option, a loop over wildflower-speckled Burroughs Mountain (if the icepack has melted to allow a safe crossing of the north slope); hikers should check with park staff regarding trail conditions before attempting the circuit. The Burroughs route runs through an enchanting alpine rock garden, wherein grows not only mountain sorrel, northern goldenrod, and golden fleabane, but also Davidson's and pincushion penstemons, smelowskia, and moss campion; an added bonus is the probable presence of mountain goats.

4. Frozen Lake - Berkeley Park

Highlights: Alpine tundra, several sightings of the mountain, and a magical flower garden lie along this wide-ranging route. Day hikers will wish they'd brought their overnight gear when they arrive in beautiful Berkeley Park.

Distance: 8.0 miles round trip

Elevation Gain: 400 feet on the way to Berkeley Park; 1,200 feet on the return

Trailhead Location: on the north side of the Sunrise parking lot, between the restrooms and the lodge

Description: The hike leaves the parking area on the paved loop road for the Sunrise picnic area, bearing right in 50

feet when the loop splits. At mile 0.1 our way turns right, heading onto the start of the gravel-surfaced Sourdough Ridge Nature Trail. After passing sandwort and dwarf hulsea the path divides, mile 0.2. We go left, climbing briskly past Newberry's knotweed, subalpine lupine, and alpine buckwheat.

Arriving at a ridgetop junction, 0.3 mile, the nature trail turns right. We proceed left, soon passing an overlook, right, that offers a vertiginous view into deep Huckleberry Basin. The path then runs along the southern slope of the ridge, showcasing additional scenery: Shadow Lake on the benchland below and Mount Rainier looming large above it; look for Cascade aster among the mix of flowers. Stunted conifers cluster on the mountainside at mile 0.6, while tongue-leaved luina and ground juniper diversify the groundcover. A gap in the ridgeline offers another view northward just before a junction with the Huckleberry Creek Trail, which branches right. Our route continues to the left past Cascade mountain-ash and whitebark pine, which are followed by Englemann spruce and northern goldenrod.

At mile 0.8 the trail cuts across an immense talus slide; a pair of penstemons, pincushion and Davidson's, are prominent. Here a lengthy stone wall attempts to stabilize the slipping scree slope, as parsley fern peeps from the rock crannies. At the far end of the wall, 1.1 miles, is a cluster of infrequently found elmera; look and listen for pikas. The trail passes pussypaws and descends to cross a creeklet below the dam, right, that impedes the ice of Frozen Lake. Switchbacks climb out of the stream canyon, as both white and yellow mountain-heathers spread across the rock-studded landscape.

A spur path, mile 1.2, left, leads to an overlook of the Sunrise camping area. The trail now levels, running above the south side of Frozen Lake and providing a view of Burroughs Mountain to the west; dotting the stone-strewn tundra are first golden fleabane, alpine lupine, and cliff paintbrush, followed by Drummond's cinquefoil, kinnikinnik, and spreading phlox. Beyond the lake is a major intersection, 1.4 miles, that offers four options: to the far left, the Wonderland Trail descends to the Sunrise campground; a slight left climbs up onto Burroughs Mountain; a slight right continues the Wonderland Trail to the west; a sharp right leads to the Mount Fremont Lookout. Our route goes slight right, descending through an austere alpine landscape on the Wonderland Trail.

No trees here, but some interesting, long-named plants: first three-forked artemisia and diverse-leaved cinquefoil; next yellow, red, and white mountain-heathers; then smelowskia. Watch for marmots. Brightening the gray-brown rockfields is Newberry's knotweed, followed by fan-leaf cinquefoil and kalmia, 1.6 miles, and then shrubby cinquefoil with its sunny, summertime yellow blossoms at mile 1.8.

Now the trail winds through a nearly level valley, after which a quartet of conifers—mountain hemlock, whitebark pine, subalpine fir, and Englemann spruce—announce the drop below timberline; farther on, a stand of stolid subalpine fir forms a compact circle like a herd of defensive muskoxen. The path meanders downward through rocky barrens, reaching a junction at 2.1 miles. Here the Wonderland Trail continues to the left, bound for Carbon River country; we turn right, following the Northern Loop Trail on its descent into Berkeley Park. A panorama of peaks presents itself: south is Burroughs Mountain, with Mount Rainier towering over its right shoulder; to the northwest, out across Berkeley Park, Skyscraper Mountain abrades the atmosphere, while northward the ridgeline of Mount Fremont rises to similar heights.

Below the junction, the wide, steeply sloping park falls away to the north, cutting between the rocky bulks of Skyscraper Mountain and Mount Fremont; the keen eyed may discern mountain goats on either or both of the peaks. The path now drops through a broad meadow fringed by clusters of inky dark conifers.

Soon the trail is within a wonderland of wildflowers; alpine aster and pussytoes rise from the grass, followed by the white spikes of bistort. A waterfall glints from the foliage far below in the park.

The path angles down the mountainside, mile 2.4, descending into the canyon of Berkeley Park. Partridgefoot mingles with bird's-beak lousewort, an attractive combination, followed shortly by coiled-beak lousewort.

In late summer the many-hued wildflowers glimmer like a galaxy upon the hillslope; one, however, shines more brightly than the rest—at a switchback, mile 2.6, the sparkling cascade of Lodi Creek, left, waters Lewis monkeyflower, whose plump, brightly pink petals are more dazzling than the daylight.

Now the trail turns north, following Lodi Creek and its accompanying meadow as they descend into the canyon; after a patch of pasque flower comes a slope full of subalpine lupine, magenta paintbrush, and Sitka valerian. The stream sinks out of sight, returning

at mile 2.9, left, among a blaze of pink-purple and yellow monkeyflowers. The path then crosses a series of side creeks that descend the mountainside, right; monkeyflowers cover the streambanks, flowing down the steep slopes in colorful, eye-catching cascades.

Lodi Creek drops away from the trail, splashing through a series of gentle falls; soon a pair of springs are surrounded by yet more monkeyflower. Tall bluebells blooms near a rockfall, mile 3.3, right, while mountain and Lewis monkeyflowers join groundsel on an island in the creek. Nearby, yellow willowherb lines the streamsides.

The canyon widens and levels: stalks of green-gold false hellebore stick up from the open flat, while low-growing mountain bog gentian rims a creeklet with its blue-purple blossoms; white rhododendron hides nearby in a shadowy thicket of subalpine fir. On the right a large rockfall, courtesy of the Mount Fremont ridge, offers a home to peeking pikas. Cottongrass and then alpine white marsh-marigold brighten the trailside.

The effect by now is overwhelming. No matter how determined the hiker, the feet must slow and then surely stop; it is a time for the eyes to travel—up and down the streamcourse and across the canyonsides, past the glinting waterfalls and the wildflower-filled hillslopes, beholding a universe of beauty from a single spot.

A stand of conifers shelters Berkeley Park Camp, mile 3.7. On the right is an outhouse; a short distance to the left is Lodi Creek. The stream received its name from prospectors who hoped to find ore in the area: two claims, the Lodi #1 and #2, were invalidated before they

Antler Peak

did much damage, leaving only a small cabin and an 18-foot-deep tunnel in their wake. When the Mazamas climbing club came up through here in 1914, they noted the real wealth of the area, calling the wildflower-filled creek canyon "the prettiest place they had ever seen."

We reluctantly head back from the camp. The return trip bears left at the Wonderland Trail junction, mile 5.2, and then arrives at the big intersection, 5.9 miles. From there our course takes a slight left, retracing our way past Frozen Lake, turning right at the junction with the trail to Huckleberry Basin, and arriving at the Sourdough Ridge Nature Trail, mile 7.0; here we go left to complete the Nature Trail loop (by turning right, hikers in a hurry can cut 0.6 mile from the remainder of their trip). Newberry's knotweed, pasque flower, and aster decorate the ridgeline route, which aims eastward toward angular Antler Peak. At a junction, 7.5 miles, we turn sharp right to continue the loop, dropping past bracted lousewort and wandering daisy. A look downslope toward Sunrise Lodge reveals a gridlike scarred area, the lingering imprint of a summer-cabin splurge that placed some 200 structures on the fragile meadow in the 1930s.

The way bears left at the last two junctions, finishing, mile 8.0, at the Sunrise parking lot.

Carbon River - Mowich Lake Area Hikes

1. Ranger Falls - Green Lake

Highlights: Secluded Ranger Falls and mountain-enclosed Green Lake reward this gradual ascent through thick forest.

Trailhead Location: at mile 21.4 of the Buckley–Carbon River auto tour, 3.1 miles east of the Carbon River Entrance Station

Distance: 3.5 miles, round trip, including the side trip to Ranger Falls

Elevation Gain: 1,100 feet

Description: Departing the south side of Carbon River Road, the trail climbs into dense, mossy woods; western hemlock and large Douglas-fir shade a varied quartet of ferns—lady, deer, oak, and sword—along with numerous woodland wildflowers. Switchbacks at mile 0.4 take the path under an enormous "nurse" log covered with baby hemlocks. A series of wide-spaced log steps is followed by a thicket of Scouler's corydalis, 0.7 mile; next comes evergreen violet, then rattlesnake orchid and more full-size Douglas-fir. Our route bears left onto a spur path, mile 0.9, dropping briefly past bunchberry to reach an overlook of Ranger Falls. The log-strewn cascade splits in two in mid-descent, moistening a mass of devil's club below the falls; nearby is Hooker's fairybell.

The creek and falls apparently derive their name from the first Carbon River Ranger Station, which was located north of the trailhead near the confluence of the creek and river. One of the earliest structures in the park, it was completed in 1911 and stood until 1962, when it burnt. An early ranger at the remote station was Jimmy Brantner, whose only companion was his big bay horse, Bud. The ranger treated the animal like an equal, seldom riding him; when packing, Jimmy carried his own gear and walked, while Bud followed behind bearing only his saddle and saddlebags.

Leaving the falls, our route doubles back to the main path, climbing past queen's cup and pipsissewa, mile 1.1, on a trailbed beset by numerous roots. After leveling, the path runs through huckleberry, 1.6 miles, and then crosses Ranger Creek on a one-rail log bridge.

A final pitch leads over a low ridge-spur and then down to Green Lake, mile 1.8. The isolated, placid pond is framed by Rust Ridge, right, and Gove Peak, left. A slope of dark conifers descends to the far shore, while our side of the lake is brightened by the leafy greenness of

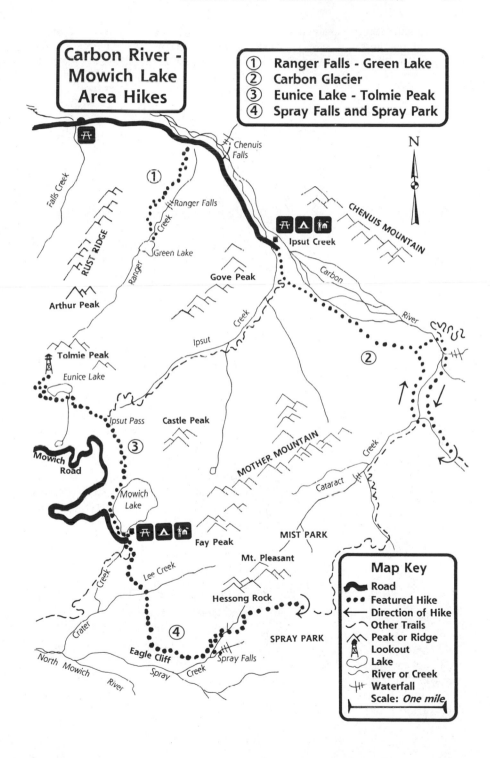

**Carbon River -
Mowich Lake
Area Hikes**

① Ranger Falls - Green Lake
② Carbon Glacier
③ Eunice Lake - Tolmie Peak
④ Spray Falls and Spray Park

N

Chenuis
Falls

Falls Creek

RUST RIDGE

①

Ranger Falls

Creek

Green Lake

Ranger

Arthur Peak

CHENUIS MOUNTAIN

Ipsut Creek

Gove Peak

Carbon

River

Ipsut

Creek

②

Tolmie Peak

Eunice Lake

Ipsut Pass

Castle Peak

③

Mowich
Road

MOTHER MOUNTAIN

Creek

Mowich
Lake

Cataract

Fay Peak

MIST PARK

Mt. Pleasant

Lee Creek

Hessong Rock

SPRAY PARK

④

Eagle Cliff

Spray   Creek

Spray Falls

Crater

North Mowich   River

Map Key

〰 Road
••• Featured Hike
← Direction of Hike
‿ Other Trails
⋀ Peak or Ridge
Lookout
Lake
River or Creek
Waterfall
Scale: *One mile*

Pacific ninebark and Sitka alder. The return to the trailhead is by the same route, minus the side trip to Ranger Falls, concluding at 3.5 miles.

2. Carbon Glacier

Highlights: A close-up look at the lowest-elevation glacier in the Lower 48 accents this river canyon loop hike. Crossing the Carbon River suspension bridge on a windy day will add excitement to an otherwise easygoing ramble. (*Note: hikers should check with park staff to determine if the seasonal bridges are in place on the lower crossing of the river before attempting that part of the route.*)

Distance: 7.2 miles, round trip

Elevation Gain: 1,300 feet

Trailhead Location: at the upper end of the parking lot just beyond the Ipsut Creek Campground, at the end of Carbon River Road

Description: After following an aging roadbed for a hundred feet, the route reaches a map display, turns right, and promptly plunges into deep woods. Masses of moss testify to the Carbon River Canyon's wetness, covering logs, rocks, and much of the ground. Pacific yew, queen's cup, and bunchberry reside beneath an overstory of western hemlock, Douglas-fir, and western redcedar. The spur for Ipsut Falls branches right, mile 0.2, while our route continues left, climbing the hillslope. Below to the left is a leafy tapestry of salmonberry, Scouler's corydalis, and devil's club; closer to the trail are deer fern and baneberry. At 0.3 mile is a junction with the Wonderland Trail: right leads to Ipsut Pass and Mowich Lake, while our way goes left, passing piggy-back plant and leveling to meet the floor of the river canyon.

The trail comes close to the Carbon, mile 0.6, left, and soon picks up another stretch of old roadbed. During the early 1920s the park built an eight-mile auto route up the canyon, from the park entrance to Cataract Creek. Plans were then made for a 15-mile extension that would tunnel beneath Ipsut Pass to reach the North Mowich River; eventually an expanded thoroughfare was to link White River with the west side of the park as part of a proposed "Around-the-Mountain" road. The Ipsut Pass section proved impossible to engineer, however, and conservationists persuaded the park service to scuttle the mountain-encircling loop, partly to preserve the Carbon/Mowich region's remoteness. Eventually the river came to wash out portions of the upper road, which was finally abandoned above the Ipsut Creek trailhead. Those segments still intact became part of the hiking trail.

Cow parsnip, large-leaved avens, and thimbleberry line the roadbed, which subsequently vanishes at a cliff above the river, only to return just ahead, where the bright fronds of oak fern shine from the forest floor. The trail climbs away from the road and enters an open area, 1.2 miles, passing patches of Scouler's corydalis and vine maple; a flank of Mother Mountain descends from the right. Pacific bleeding heart then announces a brief forested interlude, after which another opening, mile 1.6, is filled with a colorful mixture of red alder, black gooseberry, and red elderberry. Hooker's fairybell, both fat and thin false Solomon's-seals, and Siberian candyflower follow.

At 2.0 miles the loop section of our route divides: our way goes left to reach the lower crossing of the river. (*Note: if this crossing is made in the morning it will reduce the chance for encountering high water later in the day due to increased runoff from the glacier.)* Log bridges seasonally span the braided streams of the Carbon, taking us toward the trail's continuation on the far bank. From there the conifer-shaded path climbs past pipsissewa before reaching a junction, mile 2.4, with the Northern Loop. Left leads towards Lake James and Berkeley Park, while our way, right, follows a contour upstream above the Carbon, passing twinflower and starflower.

An impressive rockface, 2.6 miles, left, precedes the crossing of boulder strewn Spukwush (Klickitat for "a large number of small streams") Creek. The trail then cuts through a near-jungle of Scouler's corydalis as it moves away from the river onto a wide benchland. After climbing gently through a huckleberry-filled mixed forest, the route reaches a junction, mile 3.5. Right is the upper crossing of the loop trail, which we will use presently; for now, though, our way is left, continuing up the canyon. A talus-filled opening offers not only thimbleberry, coast penstemon, and orange agoseris, but also such rock-lovers as stonecrop, common harebell, Davidson's penstemon, and possibly a few pikas; oceanspray rises from crevices in the cliff face high above.

The trail then approaches the snout of the Carbon Glacier, climbing around its left nostril. At mile 3.9 the path narrows; a large flat rock at trailside serves as an overlook: the glacier's blue-white ice is crisscrossed with the gray-red tracings of numerous debris falls—from time to time a bit of rock will drop from the top of the snout, crashing down onto the ice below. *(Warning: do not approach the glacier.)*

We reverse course here, returning to the loop junction, 4.2 miles, where a left turn leads across the long, impressively situated suspension bridge; sturdy but easily swayed, the structure may remind Tacoma old-timers of "Galloping Gertie," should they attempt to cross on a gusty day. The Carbon churns below, while upstream to the left is the still-close glacier. At mile 4.3 the Spray Park Trail branches left, while our way, right, passes stink currant, crosses Cataract Creek on a log bridge, and picks up the huckleberry-bordered old roadbed. A subsequent spur path, left, is for Carbon River Camp.

We now follow the decaying road as it clings to the canyonside above the river; aster, woodland-penstemon, and devil's club become prominent wayside plants. After passing mountain boxwood and Pacific bleeding heart, we meet the lower loop, mile 5.2, right. Here our course bears left to retrace the first part of the hike, turning right at the remaining two junctions before reaching the trailhead at 7.2 miles.

3. Eunice Lake - Tolmie Peak

Highlights: Lovely Eunice Lake, shoreside meadows, and a far-ranging ridgetop panorama are all found along this delightfully diverse route. The view of Mount Rainier from the Tolmie Peak Lookout is one of the finest in the park.

Distance: 6.6 miles, round trip

Elevation Gain: 1,000 feet on the way to the lookout; 300 feet on the return

Trailhead Location: at Mowich Lake Camp, at the end of Mowich Road

Description: Our route commences at the camp entrance, bears left across the tenting area to a sign for the Wonderland Trail, and then follows a rail fence alongside the outlet for Mowich Lake. A spur path, mile 0.1, right, leads to the rustic lakeside ranger station, while our way takes the main trail to the left, crossing the lake's outlet (Crater Creek) on a plank bridge and winding above the shore. At mile 0.2 a spur descends from the parking lot, left; we turn right, wandering through a mix of huckleberry and wildflowers. Several side routes subsequently branch either toward the shore or the parking area. Beyond Mowich's deep blue bowl is the rectangular mass of Castle Peak.

After passing white rhododendron, we bear right at a junction with the final

Trailside cliffs
south of Eunice Lake

Mount Rainier and Eunice
Lake from Tolmie Peak

access spur from the parking lot, mile 0.5. The path crosses through thick forest before climbing away from the lake to crest a ridgeline, 0.8 mile. In the vicinity was once the Crater Claims, a short-lived mining operation of the early 1900s. The trail descends past avalanche lily to run beneath a series of cliffs; coloring the stony surroundings is woodland-penstemon. An uphill pitch offers a view, mile 1.0, left, of Mountain Meadows far below. Our route cuts across the side of a steep forested slope, reaching a junction, 1.5 miles: right continues the Wonderland Trail, rising in 50 yards to Ipsut Pass; we go left, dropping on switchbacks to cross below another series of cliffs. Openings offer Sitka valerian and coast penstemon, followed at 1.7 miles by tiger lily. After a steep climb comes pale larkspur, mile 2.0; a side path, left, then leads a few feet to the base of a small waterfall. The main trail, often crisscrossed by roots, continues uphill through a mix of forest and small openings.

Huckleberry and beargrass, mile 2.3, precede the start of a large meadow that features false hellebore. As the trail crests the hillslope, Eunice Lake appears to the right; the rocky ridgeline of Tolmie Peak forms a rugged backdrop, its columnar cliffs buttressed by long scree slopes that angle into the dark water. Named for Eunice Gilstrap of Tacoma, who frequently visited the Mowich area with her husband, the lake nestles in the confines of a small, glacier-scoured basin. Several spur paths, right, reach the shore, crossing through subalpine lupine, rosy spirea, mountain-heathers, and other delicate flowers; hikers should protect the meadow by staying on established routes.

Now the main trail runs above the south side of emerald-blue Eunice, dropping, mile 2.5, to cross the outlet creek. After reaching the west end of the lake, the path begins climbing through subalpine fir, 2.8 miles, passing beargrass, huckleberry, and tiger lily; a flower-filled opening features common harebell and woodland-penstemon, followed by orange agoseris, spreading phlox, and stonecrop. At mile 3.1 the route comes out onto the Tolmie Peak ridgeline, offering views, left, of the clearcut-ravaged Carbon River drainage. After cresting a hillock, mile 3.3, the official trail ends at the wooden fire lookout. Ground juniper, crowberry, and common harebell all grow nearby, while Davidson's penstemon clusters at the base of the building.

The view from the lookout is vast and varied, with Glacier Peak and even Mount Baker visible to the north; most striking, though, is the southeasterly sight of Eunice Lake, and, rising majesti-

cally beyond it, the Mountain. Eastward runs more of the rocky ridgeline, which was mistakenly named for Dr. William Fraser Tolmie in the belief that he had climbed it. Tolmie, the Scottish physician who approached Mount Rainier from Fort Nisqually in 1833, apparently ascended the Hessong Rock–Mount Pleasant ridge (which lies southeast of Mowich Lake) instead.

A scramble trail continues along the ridgeline, but our route turns back at the lookout, returning to the Mowich Lake Campground at mile 6.6.

4. Spray Falls – Spray Park

Highlights: After crossing the forested slopes above the Mowich River, this wide-ranging route reaches spectacular Spray Falls and then climbs through a series of scenery-packed parklands. The hike follows the final section of trail constructed by geologist Bailey Willis in the 1880s.

Distance: 8.0 miles round trip

Elevation Gain: 1,300 feet on the way in; 400 feet on the return

Trailhead Location: at Mowich Lake Camp, at the end of Mowich Road

Description: Starting from the turnaround at the end of Mowich Road, the route runs some 50 yards through the campground, bearing right to a trailhead sign, and then drops down the path into mixed forest; on the descent are clasping twisted-stalk and Siberian candyflower. At 0.3 mile the Wonderland Trail branches to the right while our way, left, continues toward Spray Park. Scouler's corydalis subsequently masses below the trail in leafy greenery, and soon the purple petals of pale larkspur poke above the surrounding plants. A small meadow, mile 0.8, is adorned with leatherleaf saxifrage, mountain bog gentian, and rosy spirea; the banks of Lee Creek are covered with more corydalis.

The route returns to forest, climbs briefly, levels, and then goes by queen's cup and twisted stalk at mile 1.0. After passing rusty saxifrage, another climb leads to another level stretch, this one punctuated by a spur path, 1.6 miles, right, that descends a hundred feet to the Eagle Cliff overlook: the vista above is of the mountain, that below of Spray Creek. In 1908 the "Mountain View" mines were active in the canyon below the cliffs; shortly thereafter the claims were voided, and soon the weather and plantlife began their work. By 1970, the

Spray Falls

sawmill, blacksmith shop, and other buildings were no more than brush-covered piles of rotten wood.

Now the trail runs past a trio of shade-loving saprophytes: coralroot, pinesap, and pinedrops. After dropping slightly, 1.9 miles, we pass the access path, right, to Eagle's Roost Camp. At mile 2.0 is the junction, right, with the spur to Spray Falls. We take the spur, promptly crossing Grant Creek on a log bridge before reaching the base of the falls; tall bluebells, woodland-penstemon, and crimson columbine color the approach. A scramble trail, left, leads up to a more complete view of the compelling cascade: a broad, flashing flow of water whitens the dark rockface, dropping in two plunges to the rocky gorge below. The spray from the aptly named falls dampens Lewis and mountain monkey-flowers, yellow willowherb, and stink currant. *(Warning: approaching close to the falls or attempting to cross Spray Creek can be hazardous.)*

After doubling back to the main trail, 2.2 miles, the route climbs on switchbacks, passing an opening at mile 2.8 that reveals the stump-filled hillside below Hessong Rock, left; the peak was named for James L. Hessong, a photographer from nearby Kapowsin who visited the area in 1915. Just ahead, red mountain-heather and subalpine lupine brighten the pathside. The trail then crosses Grant Creek on a footlog and enters a grassy bog via a boardwalk; mountain bog gentian and wandering daisy are followed by alpine aster. Now the way winds uphill through a mix of openings and forest, leveling somewhat, 3.2 miles, upon entering the lower end of one of the major meadows of Spray Park. Jeffrey's shooting star, bird's-beak lousewort, and avalanche lily are among the host of flowers that fill the gently sloping expanse. On the left, the grassland sweeps upward to the ridgeline of Hessong Rock and Mount Pleasant; to the right, the tarn-dotted landscape leads toward the mountain.

A series of semi-steep climbs culminates at a nearly level, final section of park, 3.8 miles, where fanleaf cinquefoil and alpine pussytoes decorate the meadow. To the west and north is a peak-filled ridgeline panorama that begins with Mount Pleasant on the left, continues past Fay Peak, and ends with the rocky crenelations of Mother Mountain. A spur path, mile 3.9, left, leads a hundred yards to an overlook of verdant Mist Park and the deep drainage of Cataract Creek. The main trail then passes black alpine sedge and rises into rocky tundra colored by alpine lupine and mountain-heathers. After sampling this austere but admirable landscape, the route turns back, mile 4.1, bypassing the Spray Falls side trip on its return and ending at the Mowich Lake Camp, 8.0 miles.

Section IV:
A Quick Guide to the Park

Visitors to Mount Rainier National Park will find a multitude of features and facilities, services and schedules, rules and regulations, that—if fully understood and appreciated—should greatly enhance a vacation at the mountain. Park staff are available at the various visitor centers to answer questions and provide a selection of helpful handouts; the following "Quick Guide" collects much of this information in one place, summarizing the essentials for the Mount Rainier sojourner.

(Note: readers can locate additional descriptions of the park's many offerings by consulting the index: headings such as "campgrounds," "camps, backcountry," "entrance stations," "picnic areas," and "visitor centers" may prove especially helpful.)

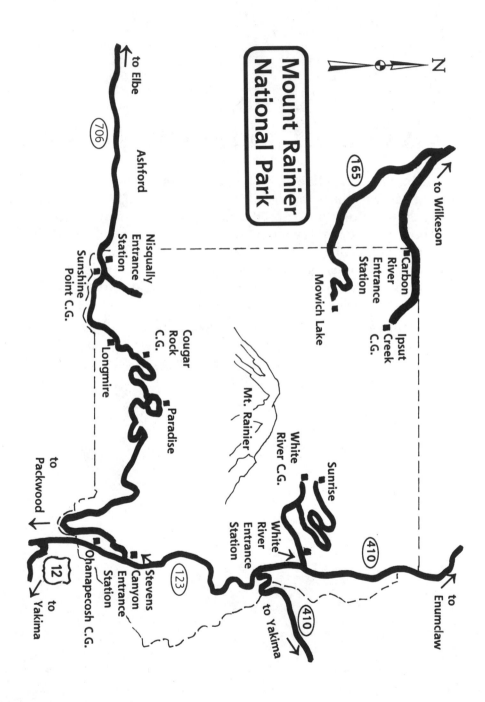

Mount Rainier
National Park

N

to Elbe

706

Ashford

165

to Wilkeson

Nisqually
Entrance
Station

Carbon
River
Entrance
Station

Sunshine
Point C.G.

Mowich Lake

Ipsut
Creek
C.G.

Longmire

Cougar
Rock
C.G.

Paradise

Mt. Rainier

White
River C.G.

Sunrise

to
Packwood

White
River
Entrance
Station

410

to
Enumclaw

Stevens
Canyon
Entrance
Station

123

to Yakima

410

Ohanapecosh C.G.

12

to
Yakima

Visiting the Park:
What, When, and Where

Park Address and Phone Numbers

Superintendent
Mount Rainier National Park
Tahoma Woods Star Route
Ashford, WA 98304

(360) 529-2211

(360) 569-2177 (TTD)

911 (Emergency)

Entrance Stations

Nisqually Entrance: on State Highway 706, 5.8 miles east of Ashford

Stevens Canyon Entrance: on Stevens Canyon Road, 0.1 mile west of State Highway 123, 1.8 miles north of the Ohanapecosh Campground

White River Entrance: on Sunrise Road, 1.4 miles southwest of State Highway 410

Carbon River Entrance: on Carbon River Road, 13.8 miles southeast of Wilkeson

Visitor Centers

Longmire Museum: on the Nisqually-Paradise Road, 6.5 miles east of the Nisqually Entrance

Henry M. Jackson Memorial Visitor Center, Paradise: on Nisqually-Paradise Road, 18.2 miles northeast of the Nisqually Entrance, 0.2 mile west of the Paradise Inn

Ohanapecosh Visitor Center: on the campground access road 0.2 mile west of State Highway 123, 3.7 miles north of the park's southern boundary

Sunrise Visitor Center: at the end of Sunrise Road

Carbon River Ranger Station: on Carbon River Road, at the Carbon River Entrance Station, 13.8 miles southeast of Wilkeson

Hiker Information Centers

Longmire: in the administration building (mid-June through September); in the museum (October until mid-June)

White River: at the White River entrance ranger station (summer only)

Food and Lodging

Longmire National Park Inn: lodging, dining, and outdoor (summer only) snack bar; for reservations call Mount Rainier Guest Services (360) 569-2275; open year round

Longmire General Store: gifts and limited supply of groceries and beverages; located next to the National Park Inn; open year round

Paradise Inn: lodging, dining, cocktail lounge, snack bar, and gift shop; for reservations call Mount Rainier Guest Services (360) 569-2275; open summer only, but reservations accepted year round

Henry M. Jackson Memorial Visitor Center, Paradise: food service and gift shop; open summer only

Sunrise Lodge: food service and gift shop; open summer only

Showers

Paradise: located in the basement of the Henry M. Jackson Memorial Visitor Center; towel and soap available for fee in the gift shop

Outside the park: at Morton, Eatonville, Ashford, Packwood, and Greenwater

Note: park campgrounds **do not** have showers.

Miscellaneous Services

Gasoline is not available in the park; nearby service stations are in Ashford, Packwood, White Pass, Cliffdell, Greenwater, and Wilkeson. **Post offices** are located in the park at the Paradise Inn (summer only) and at the National Park Inn in Longmire (year round). **Banking services** are available in Eatonville, Enumclaw, and Morton. **Hospitals and dentists** can be found at Enumclaw, Morton, and Puyallup.

Nisqually Entrance Station

Vehicle Camping

The park's five automobile-accessible campgrounds offer sites on a first come, first served basis. All camp areas have running water, flush or pit toilets, and individual sites with table and fireplace; group sites (available only at Ipsut Creek and Cougar Rock) are designed for tent camping only. Stays at all sites are limited to 14 days in July and August and 30 days the rest of the year. Contact the park for details regarding fees and group reservations. A free handout containing campground regulations is available, to insure a pleasant camping experience it should be requested, read, and followed. Campgrounds are located at:

Sunshine Point: on Nisqually-Paradise Road, 0.4 mile east of the Nisqually Entrance; 18 sites, none for groups; open year round

Cougar Rock: on Nisqually-Paradise Road, 8.6 miles northeast of the Nisqually Entrance; 200 sites, five group sites; open during summer and fall until mid-October

Ohanapecosh: 1.3 miles north of the park's southern boundary via State Highway 123 and a paved access road; 205 sites, none for groups; open during summer and fall until late October

White River: 5.1 miles west of the White River Entrance Station via Sunrise Road and a paved access road; 117 sites, none for groups; open during summer and fall through mid-September

Ipsut Creek: at the end of Carbon River Road; 29 sites, two group sites; open from May through October; no fee and no treated water after early September

Note: Mowich Lake Camp, although designated as a backcountry camping area, is located directly adjacent the end of Mowich Road and can be reached by a short walk from the Mowich Lake parking lot.

Wilderness and Backcountry Camping

Subject to certain regulations, backpackers may camp overnight in the park's wilderness and backcountry; a free permit is required year round. Permits are available on a first come, first served basis at hiker information centers, ranger stations, and visitor centers. Camping is limited to 14 consecutive days. Open fires are not allowed in any part of wilderness or backcountry areas; portable stoves may be used instead. Request the park's "Wilderness Trip Planner" (no charge) for detailed information and a map of campsites.

Picnic Areas

Sunshine Point: on Nisqually-Paradise Road, 0.4 mile east of the Nisqually Entrance

Cougar Rock: on Nisqually-Paradise Road, 8.6 miles northeast of the Nisqually Entrance, opposite the Cougar Rock Campground

Paradise: at mile 17.7 and mile 18.1 of the Nisqually-Paradise Road, southwest of the Jackson Memorial Visitor Center

Ohanapecosh: across the road from the Ohanapecosh Visitor Center at the campground entrance

Tipsoo Lake: on Highway 410 (the Mather Memorial Parkway), 0.6 mile southwest of the Chinook Pass entrance

Box Canyon: at mile 8.2 of the Stevens Canyon Road, west of the tunnel next to Box Canyon

Visitor center, Paradise

Sunrise: behind the Sunrise Visitor Center

Falls Creek: on the Carbon River Road, 1.9 miles east of the Carbon River Entrance Station

Ipsut Creek: at the end of Carbon River Road, 4.9 miles east of the Carbon River Entrance Station

Mountain Climbing and Guide Service

Climbers must register with a park ranger before climbing and must check out upon their return. Guided summit climbs, climbing instruction, and equipment rentals are provided by Rainier Mountaineering, Inc., located at the Guide House, Paradise. Phone (360) 569-2227 (summer) or (206) 627-6242 (winter).

Hiking

Dozens of trails, totaling more than 300 miles in length, spread across low- and mid-elevation areas of the park. Short, self-guided nature trails depart from Longmire, Paradise, Sunrise, near the Stevens Canyon Entrance Station, Ohanapecosh, and the Carbon River Entrance Station; the 93-mile Wonderland Trail encircles the peak.

Note: Meadows and alpine tundra are **extremely** fragile; travel in such locations must be limited to trail use only. A single misplaced bootprint can be a disaster, destroying years of soil building and plant development, crushing rocks and flowers, and leaving the landscape filled with foot-shaped pock marks. Avoid taking such drastic steps; keep your feet on the trail and follow the path of righteousness.

Winter Sports

Snowshoeing and cross-country skiing are popular wintertime activities in the park. The Paradise area, which has year round road access, is the main center for winter sports. Limited rental equipment is offered at Longmire. Snowmobiling is allowed **only** on certain designated roadways when these routes are closed by snow to other forms of traffic. Snowmobiles may **not** use other areas of the park. A map of approved roads is available.

Fishing and Boating

Fishing is permitted in most of the park; no license is required; non-motorized boating is allowed on some lakes. A handout containing complete information is available.

Horses

Horses are permitted on almost 100 miles of trails, but are restricted from using most other areas of the park. Four trail camps accommodate horses; they are located at Deer Creek, Mowich River, North Puyallup River, and Three Lakes. A horse trail map is available.

Other Activities

Bicycling is permitted on public park roads and campground roadways, but is **not** allowed on any park trails. **Roller skating and skateboarding** are **not** allowed in the park.

Pets

Pets are not allowed on trails, in amphitheaters, or in buildings. When elsewhere in the park they must be caged, leashed, or under other physical restraint at all times. A pet exercise loop is located at Sunrise; a kennel is available in Eatonville.

Ranger Programs

Rangers help reveal Mount Rainier's many wonders through a regular series of guided walks and interpretive programs. Current information is available in the park's seasonal newspapers and at the museum and visitor centers.

Handicapped Access

Most park restrooms and buildings are accessible or accessible with help. Both the Longmire National Park Inn and the Paradise Inn have accessible overnight accommodations. All picnic grounds and campgrounds except Sunshine Point have accessible sites and toilets.

Books and Maps

The Northwest Interpretive Association provides various park-related books and maps for sale in outlets at park ranger stations and visitor centers. For a catalogue of Mount Rainier publications, contact the Mount Rainier Branch, Northwest Interpretive Association, Longmire, WA, 98397; (360) 569-2211 ext. 3320. Relevant books and maps are also available in the concession-operated gift shops at the Sunrise Lodge, Paradise Visitor Center, Paradise Inn, and Longmire General Store.

Seasonal Road Access

Nisqually-Paradise Road: open year round, with nighttime closures at Longmire during the winter

Stevens Canyon Road: open Memorial Day through early November

Golden Lakes Patrol Cabin

Highway 123 and Highway 410 via Cayuse Pass: usually open from late April to December

Highway 410 across Chinook Pass: opens in early June and closes in November

Sunrise Road: open as far as the White River Campground by mid-June and to Sunrise by July 1st; closed in late September or early October

Note: Snowfall may intermittently close higher stretches of park roads in fall before their final winter shut down. Dates for spring openings and winter closures are subject to change due to weather-related influences.

Plants Mentioned in Text: A Species List

Trees:

alder, red	*Alnus rubra*
cottonwood, black	*Populus trichocarpa*
dogwood, Pacific	*Cornus nuttallii*
Douglas-fir	*Pseudotsuga menziesii*
fir, noble	*Abies procera*
fir, Pacific silver	*Abies amabilis*
fir, subalpine	*Abies lasiocarpa*
hemlock, mountain	*Tsuga mertensiana*
hemlock, western	*Tsuga heterophylla*
maple, bigleaf	*Acer macrophyllum*
pine, lodgepole	*Pinus contorta*
pine, western white	*Pinus monticola*
pine, whitebark	*Pinus albicaulis*
redcedar, western	*Thuja plicata*
spruce, Engelmann	*Picea engelmannii*
spruce, Sitka	*Picea sitchensis*
yellow-cedar, Alaska	*Chamaecyparis nootkatensis*
yew, Pacific *or* western	*Taxus brevifolia*

Shrubs:

alder, Sitka	*Alnus sinuata*
azalea, false (rusty leaf)	*Menziesia ferruginea*
blueberry—see huckleberry	
boxwood, mountain	*Pachistima myrsinites*
bramble, dwarf	*Rubus lasiococcus*
bramble, five-leaved (rubus, trailing)	*Rubus pedatus*
bramble, snow	*Rubus nivalis*
bunchberry	*Cornus canadensis*
crowberry	*Empetrum nigrum*
currant, red-flowering	*Ribes sanguineum*
currant, sticky	*Ribes viscosissimum*
currant, stink	*Ribes bracteosum*

Shrubs, continued:

currant	*Ribes* spp.
devil's club	*Oplopanax horridum*
elderberry, blue	*Sambucus caerulea*
elderberry, red	*Sambucus racemosa*
goatsbeard	*Aruncus dioecus*
gooseberry, black	*Ribes lacustre*
gooseberry	*Ribes* spp.
hardhack (steeplebush)	*Spiraea douglasii*
hazelnut	*Corylus cornuta*
honeysuckle, orange	*Lonicera ciliosa*
huckleberry, Alaskan	*Vaccinium alaskaense*
huckleberry, Cascade	*Vaccinium deliciosum*
huckleberry, evergreen	*Vaccinium ovatum*
huckleberry, grouseberry	*Vaccinium scoparium*
huckleberry, oval-leaved	*Vaccinium ovalifolium*
huckleberry, red	*Vaccinium parvifolium*
huckleberry, thin-leaved	*Vaccinium membranaceum*
huckleberry, western	*Vaccinium occidentale*
juniper, ground	*Juniperus communis*
kalmia (bog-laurel)	*Kalmia microphylla*
kinnikinnik	*Arctostaphylos uva-ursi*
manzanita, pinemat	*Arctostaphylos nevadensis*
maple, Douglas	*Acer glabrum*
maple, vine	*Acer circinatum*
mock-orange	*Philadelphus lewisii*
mountain-ash, Sitka	*Sorbus sitchensis*
mountain-ash, Cascade	*Sorbus scopulina*
mountain-heather, Alaskan	*Cassiope stellariana*
mountain-heather, white	*Cassiope mertensiana*
mountain-heather, red	*Phyllodoce empetriformis*
mountain-heather, yellow	*Phyllodoce glanduliflora*
ninebark, Pacific	*Physocarpus capitatus*
oceanspray (creambush)	*Holodiscus discolor*
Oregon grape	*Berberis nervosa*
raspberry, black	*Rubus leucodermis*
rhododendron, white	*Rhododendron albiflorum*
rose, wood	*Rosa gymnocarpa*
salal	*Gaultheria shallon*
salmonberry	*Rubus spectabilis*
serviceberry	*Amelanchier alnifolia*
snowberry, creeping	*Symphoricarpos mollis*
spirea, rosy *or* subalpine	*Spiraea densiflora*
teaberry, western	*Gaultheria ovatifolia*
thimbleberry	*Rubus parviflorus*

Shrubs, continued:

twinflower	*Linnaea borealis*
willow	*Salix* spp.

Ferns and Fern Allies:

clubmoss	*Lycopodium* spp.
fern, bracken	*Pteridium aquilinum*
fern, deer	*Blechnum spicant*
fern, lace	*Cheilanthes gracillima*
fern, lady	*Athyrium filix-femina*
fern, licorice	*Polypodium glycyrrhiza*
fern, maidenhair	*Adiantum pedatum*
fern, oak	*Gymnocarpium dryopteris*
fern, parsley	*Cryptogramma crispa*
fern, sword	*Polystichum* spp.
horsetail	*Equisetum* spp.
polypody, western	*Polypodium hesperium*

Flowers:

agoseris, orange	*Agoseris aurantiaca*
alumroot	*Heuchera* spp.
arnica, broadleaf *or* mountain	*Arnica latifolia*
artemisia, three-forked	*Artemisia trifurcata*
aster, alpine *or* purple	*Aster alpigenus*
aster, Cascade *or* tall leafybract	*Aster ledophyllus*
aster, leafy	*Aster foliaceus*
aster	*Aster* spp.
avens, large-leaved	*Geum macrophyllum*
baneberry	*Actaea rubra*
beargrass	*Xerophyllum tenax*
bedstraw	*Galium* spp.
bistort	*Polygonum bistortoides*
bleeding heart, Pacific	*Dicentra formosa*
bluebells, tall (mertensia)	*Mertensia paniculata*
bog-orchid	*Platanthera* spp.
buckwheat, alpine (dirty socks)	*Eriogonum pyrolifolium*
bugbane, false	*Trautvetteria caroliniensis*
buttercup, creeping	*Ranunculus repens*
buttercup, subalpine	*Ranunculus eschscholtzii*
butterweed, Fremont's	*Senecio fremontii*
candyflower, Siberian	*Claytonia sibirica*
cinquefoil, diverse-leaved	*Potentilla diversifolia*
cinquefoil, Drummond's	*Potentilla drummondii*
cinquefoil, fanleaf	*Potentilla flabellifolia*

Flowers, continued:

cinquefoil, shrubby	*Potentilla fruticosa*
coltsfoot, sweet	*Petasites frigidus* var. *nivalis*
coltsfoot, western	*Petasites frigidus* var. *palmatus*
columbine, crimson or red	*Aquilegia formosa*
coralroot, spotted	*Corallorhiza maculata* ssp. *maculata*
coralroot, striped	*Corallorhiza striata*
coralroot, western	*Corallorhiza maculata* ssp. *mertensiana*
corydalis, Scouler's	*Corydalis scouleri*
cow parsnip	*Heracleum lanatum*
daisy, wandering	*Erigeron peregrinus*
elephant's head, pink	*Pedicularis groenlandica*
elmera	*Elmera racemosa*
fairybell, Hooker's	*Disporum hookeri*
fairybell, Smith's	*Disporum smithii*
fireweed	*Epilobium angustifolium*
fleabane, golden (golden daisy)	*Erigeron aureus*
foamflower (sugar scoop)	*Tiarella trifoliata*
foxglove	*Digitalis purpurea*
fringecup	*Tellima grandiflora*
gentian, mountain bog or explorer's	*Gentiana calycosa*
goldenrod, northern or mountain	*Solidago multiradiata*
grass-of-Parnasus, fringed	*Parnassia fimbriata*
groundsel, arrowleaf	*Senecio triangularis*
groundsel, western	*Senecio integerrimus*
harebell, common (bluebell)	*Campanula rotundifolia*
harebell, Scouler's	*Campanula scouleri*
hellebore, false	*Veratrum* spp.
hulsea, dwarf	*Hulsea nana*
Jacob's ladder	*Polemonium pulcherrimum*
knotweed, Newberry's	*Polygonum newberryi*
larkspur, rockslide	*Delphinium glareosum*
larkspur, pale or tall	*Delphinium glaucum*
lily, avalanche	*Erythronium montanum*
lily, glacier	*Erythronium grandiflorum*
lily, tiger or Columbia	*Lilium columbianum*
lily-of-the-valley, false	*Maianthemum dilatatum*
lousewort, bird's-beak	*Pedicularis ornithorhyncha*
lousewort, bracted	*Pedicularis bracteosa*
lousewort, coiled-beak	*Pedicularis contorta*
lousewort, sickletop (parrot's beak)	*Pedicularis racemosa*
lovage, Gray's (meadow parsley)	*Ligusticum grayi*
luina, silverback	*Luina hypoleuca*
luina, tongue-leaved	*Luina stricta*
lupine, alpine or dwarf mountain	*Lupinus lyallii* or *L. lepidus* var. *lobbii*

Flowers, continued:

lupine, subalpine	*Lupinus latifolius* var. *subalpinus*
marsh-marigold, alpine white	*Caltha leptosepala*
mitrewort, Brewer's (bishop's caps)	*Mitella breweri*
monkeyflower, Brewer's	*Mimulus breweri*
monkeyflower, chickweed	*Mimulus alsinoides*
monkeyflower, Lewis	*Mimulus lewisii*
monkeyflower, mountain	*Mimulus tilingii*
monkeyflower, seep-spring	*Mimulus guttatus*
mountain bells	*Stenanthium occidentale*
mountain-sorrel	*Oxyria digyna*
orchid, rattlesnake	*Goodyera oblongifolia*
paintbrush, cliff	*Castilleja rupicola*
paintbrush, harsh	*Castilleja hispida*
paintbrush, magenta or small-flowered	*Castilleja parviflora*
paintbrush, scarlet or common red	*Castilleja miniata*
partridgefoot	*Luetkea pectinata*
pasque flower, western	*Anemone occidentalis*
pearly everlasting	*Anaphalis margaritacea*
penstemon, broad-leaved	*Penstemon ovatus*
penstemon, cliff	*Penstemon rupicola*
penstemon, coast or Cascade	*Penstemon serrulatus*
penstemon, Davidson's	*Penstemon davidsonii*
penstemon, meadow	*Penstemon rydbergii*
penstemon, pincushion	*Penstemon procerus*
penstemon, shrubby	*Penstemon fruticosis*
penstemon, yellow	*Penstemon confertus*
phlox, spreading	*Phlox diffusa*
piggy-back plant	*Tolmiea menziesii*
pinedrops	*Pterospora andromedea*
pinesap	*Hypopitys monotropa*
pipsissewa	*Chimaphila umbellata*
pipsissewa, Menzies	*Chimaphila menziesii*
pussypaws	*Calyptridium umbellatum*
pussytoes, alpine	*Antennaria alpina*
pussytoes, rosy	*Antennaria microphylla*
pussytoes, woolly	*Antennaria lanata*
queen's cup	*Clintonia uniflora*
sandwort	*Arenaria* spp.
saxifrage, brook	*Saxifraga arguta*
saxifrage, leatherleaf	*Leptarrhena pyrolifolia*
saxifrage, Mertens	*Saxifraga mertensiana*
saxifrage, red-stemmed	*Saxifraga lyallii*
saxifrage, rusty	*Saxifraga ferruginea*
saxifrage, spotted	*Saxifraga bronchialis*

Flowers, continued:

saxifrage, Tolmie's	*Saxifraga tolmiei*
shooting star, Jeffrey's	*Dodecatheon jeffreyi*
skunk cabbage	*Lysichiton americanum*
sky pilot (skunky Jacob's-ladder)	*Polemonium elegans*
smelowskia	*Smelowskia* spp.
Solomon's-seal, fat false or branched	*Smilacina racemosa*
Solomon's-seal, thin false or star	*Smilacina stellata*
speedwell, alpine	*Veronica wormskjoldii*
speedwell, Cusick's	*Veronica cusickii*
spring beauty	*Montia* spp.
starflower	*Trientalis* spp.
stonecrop	*Sedum* spp.
strawberry	*Fragaria* spp.
sunflower, woolly	*Eriophyllum lanatum*
sweet-cicely	*Osmorhiza* spp.
trail plant (pathfinder)	*Adenocaulon bicolor*
trillium, white	*Trillium ovatum*
twayblade, broad-lipped	*Listera convallarioides*
twayblade, northwestern	*Listera caurina*
twisted-stalk, clasping	*Streptopus amplexifolius*
twisted-stalk, rosy	*Streptopus roseus*
valerian, Sitka	*Valeriana sitchensis*
vanilla leaf	*Achlys triphylla*
violet, evergreen	*Viola sempervirens*
violet, marsh	*Viola palustris*
violet, stream or pioneer	*Viola glabella*
violet, western dog or early blue	*Viola adunca*
wild ginger	*Asarum caudatum*
willowherb, alpine	*Epilobium anagallidifolium*
willowherb, yellow	*Epilobium luteum*
wintergreen, bog	*Pyrola asarifolia*
wintergreen, one-sided	*Orthilia secunda*
wintergreen, white-veined	*Pyrola picta*
woodland-penstemon	*Nothochelone nemorosa*
yarrow	*Achillea millefolium*

Grasslike Plants:

cattail, common	*Typha latifolia*
cottongrass	*Eriophorum* spp.
rush	*Juncus* spp.
sedge, black alpine	*Carex nigricans*

Wildlife: A Species List

Birds:

blackbird, red-winged
chickadee, mountain
creeper, brown
dipper, American
finch, gray-crowned rosy
flicker, northern
flycatcher, western
grouse, sooty or blue
hawk, red-tailed
hawk, rough-legged
hummingbird, rufous
jay, gray
jay, Steller's
junco, dark-eyed
kestrel, American
kinglet, golden-crowned
nutcracker, Clark's
nuthatch, red-breasted
pigeon, band-tailed
pipit, water or American
raven, common
robin, American
sapsucker, yellow-bellied
siskin, pine
swallow, barn
swallow, violet-green
swift, Vaux's
thrush, hermit
thrush, varied
vireo, warbling
wood peewee, western
wren, winter

Mammals:

bat, big brown
bat, hoary
bat, lump-nosed or western big-eared
bat, silver-haired
bear, black
beaver
bobcat
chipmunk, Townsend
chipmunk, yellow pine
cougar (mountain lion)
coyote
deer, mule
elk, Rocky Mountain
ermine
flying squirrel, northern
fox, red
ground squirrel, golden-mantled
hare, snowshoe
jumping mouse, Pacific
marmot, hoary
marten
mink
mole, Pacific
mole, Townsend
mountain beaver (aplodontia)
mountain goat
mouse, deer
myotis, long-legged
myotis, Yuma
pika
pocket gopher, northern
porcupine
raccoon

Mammals, continued:

redback vole, boreal
shrew, dusky
shrew, masked
shrew, northern water
shrew, Pacific water
shrew, Trowbridge
shrew, vagrant *or* wandering
shrew-mole
skunk, spotted
skunk, striped
squirrel, Douglas
vole, creeping *or* Oregon
vole, heather
vole, long-tailed
vole, Townsend
vole, water
weasel, longtail
woodrat, bushy-tailed

Reptiles, Amphibians, etc.:

boa, northern rubber
ensatina
frog, Cascade
frog, northern red-legged
frog, tailed
garter snake, northern
garter snake, Puget Sound
garter snake, valley
lizard, northern alligator
newt, northern rough-skinned
salamander, brown
salamander, long-toed
salamander, Pacific giant
salamander, Van Dyke's
salamander, western redbacked
slug, banana
toad, western
treefrog, Pacific

Selected Sources

General Information:

Kirk, Ruth. *Exploring Mount Rainier*. Seattle: University of Washington Press, 1968.

Schmoe, Floyd. *Our Greatest Mountain: A Handbook for Mount Rainier National Park*. New York: G. P. Putnam's Sons, 1925.

Guidebooks:

Plumb, Gregory A. *Waterfalls of the Pacific Northwest*. Seattle: The Writing Works, 1983.

Spring, Ira, and Harvey Manning. *50 Hikes in Mount Rainier National Park*, 2d ed. Seattle: The Mountaineers, 1978.

Weldon, Robert K. and Merlin K. Potts. *A Guide to the Trails of Mount Rainier National Park*. Longmire, WA: Mount Rainier Natural History Association, 1966.

Human History — General:

Hitchman, Robert. *Place Names of Washington*. N.p.: Washington State Historical Society, 1985.

Morgan, Murray. *Puget's Sound: A Narrative of Early Tacoma and the Southern Sound*. Seattle: University of Washington Press, 1979.

Reese, Gary Fuller. *Origins of Pierce County Place Names*. Tacoma: Friends of the Tacoma Public Library, 1989.

Human History — Indians:

Carpenter, Cecelia Svinth. *Where the Waters Begin: The Traditional Nisqually Indian History of Mount Rainier*. Seattle: Northwest Interpretive Association, 1994.

Clark, Ella E. *Indian Legends of the Pacific Northwest*. Berkeley: University of California Press, 1953.

Curtis, Edward S. *The North American Indian*. Vol 7. N.p., 1911. Reprint. New York: Johnson Reprint Corporation, 1970.

Deloria, Vine, Jr. *Indians of the Pacific Northwest: From the Coming of the White Man to the Present Day*. Garden City, NY: Doubleday & Company, Inc., 1972.

Eckrom, J. A. *Remembered Drums: A History of the Puget Sound Indian War*. Walla Walla, WA: Pioneer Press Books, 1989.

Haeberlin, Hermann, and Erna Gunther. *The Indians of Puget Sound*. Seattle: University of Washington Press, 1930.

Keyes, E. D. *Fifty Years' Observation of Men and Events*. New York: Charles Scribner's Sons, 1884.

Ruby, Robert H., and John A. Brown. *Indians of the Pacific Northwest: A History*. Norman, OK: University of Oklahoma Press, 1981.

Schuster, Helen H. *The Yakimas: A Critical Bibliography*. Bloomington IN: Indiana University Press, 1982.

Smith, Marian. *The Puyallup-Nisqually*. New York: Columbia University Press, 1940.

Human History—Local Communities:

Calton, Cindy. "Burnett Items 1891-1965." Photocopy.

Clevinger, Woodrow R. "The Appalachian Mountaineers in the Upper Cowlitz Basin." *Pacific Northwest Quarterly* 29:2 (April 1938): 115-134.

———."Southern Appalachian Highlanders in Western Washington." *Pacific Northwest Quarterly* 33:1 (January 1942): 3-26.

Engle, Pearl, and Jeannette Hlavin. 1954. "History of Tacoma Eastern Area." Eatonville, WA: Eatonville Public Schools. Mimeo.

Erickson, Kenneth A. *Lumber Ghosts: A Travel Guide to the Historic Lumber Towns of the Pacific Northwest*. Boulder, CO: Pruett Publishing Company, 1994.

Gossett, Gretta Petersen. *Beyond the Bend: A History of the Nile Valley in Washington State*. Fairfield, WA: Ye Galleon Press, 1979.

Hall, Nancy Irene. *Carbonado Centennial 1880-1980*. Carbonado, WA: 1980.

———. *Carbon River Coal Country*, edited edition. Orting, WA: Heritage Quest Press, 1994.

———. *Dateline: Wilkeson*. South Prairie, WA: Meico Associates, 1984.

———. *In the Shadow of the Mountain: A Pioneer History of Enumclaw*. Enumclaw, WA: Courier-Herald Publishing Co., Inc., 1983.

———, and Steve Meitzler. *Buckley, 1892*. Orting, WA: Northwest Heritage, 1992.

History Committee, Packwood Community Study Program. 1954. "Packwood on the March: 1854–1954 — 100 Years of Progress." Mimeo.

Jacobin, Louis. *A Glimpse of the Charmed Land*. N.p.: Community Publishing Co., 1925. Reprint. South Prairie, WA: Meico Associates, Inc., 1983.

———. *Old King Coal: The Pierce County Coal Mining District in late 1917*. Wilkeson, WA: 1917. Reprint. South Prairie, WA: Meico Associates, Inc., 1983.

Kirk, Ruth, and Carmela Alexander. *Exploring Washington's Past: A Road Guide to History*. Seattle: University of Washington Press, 1990.

Nadeau, Gene Allen. *Highway to Paradise: A Pictorial History of the Roadway to Mount Rainier*. Tacoma, WA: N.p., 1983.

Panco, Betty. *Look behind You through a Window to the Past*. N.p., 1989. (Packwood area)

Pierce County Department of Planning and Community Development. *Pierce County Cultural Resource Inventory*. Vol. II, *Rainier Planning Area*. N.p., 1982.

———. *Pierce County Cultural Resource Inventory*. Vol. III, *Tapps and Clearwater Planning Area*. N.p., 1982.

Poppleton, Lousie Ross. *There is Only One Enumclaw*. Enumclaw, WA: 1981.

Ramsey, Guy Reed. *Postmarked Washington: Lewis and Cowlitz Counties*. Chehalis, WA: Lewis County Historical Society, 1978.

———. *Postmarked Washington: Pierce County*. Tacoma: Washington State Historical Society, 1981.

Sparkman, LaVonne M. *The trees were so thick there was Nowhere to Look But Up!: Early Settlers of Morton and Mineral Washington*. N.p.: A Maverick Publication, 1989.

Washington: A Guide to the Evergreen State, revised ed. Portland, OR: Binfords & Mort, 1950.

Human History—Mount Rainier and the Park:

Circular of General Information Regarding Mount Rainier National Park Washington. Washington: GPO, 1928.

Haines, Aubrey L. *Mountain Fever: Historic Conquests of Rainier*. Portland, OR: Oregon Historical Society, 1962.

Hough, Emerson. "Made in America: Mount Rainier National Park." *Saturday Evening Post*, 6 November 1915, 19ff.

Kendall, Carpenter. "Motoring on Mount Rainier." *Sunset*, September 1916, 304-309.

Laing, Hamilton M. "On Barking Betsy to the Mountain: A Motorcycle Run to Rainier National Park." *Sunset*, September 1916, 21ff.

Martinson, Arthur D. "Mountain in the Sky: A History of Mount Rainier National Park." Ph. D. diss., Washington State University, 1969.

——. "The Story of a Mountain." *American West* 8, no. 2:34-41.

——. *Wilderness above the Sound: The Story of Mount Rainier National Park.* Flagstaff: Northland Press, 1986.

McCoy, Genevieve. " 'Mount Tacoma' vs. 'Mount Rainier': The Fight to Rename the Mountain." *Pacific Northwest Quarterly* 77:4 (Oct. 1986): 139-149.

McNeill, Virginia C., and William L. Worden. "Mountain Rescue Man." *Saturday Evening Post*, 12 November 1949, 28ff.

Meany, Edmond S., ed. *Mount Rainier: A Record of Exploration.* New York: The Macmillan Company, 1916.

Molenaar, Dee. *The Challenge of Rainier.* Seattle: The Mountaineers, 1971.

Mt. Rainier National Park Washington: The Throne Room of the Monarch Mountain. Chicago, Milwaukee & St. Paul Railway, n.d.

Muir, John. "Washington and Puget Sound." In *West of the Rocky Mountains*, edited by John Muir. Philadelphia: Running Press, 1976.

Schmoe, Floyd. *A Year in Paradise.* New York: Harper & Brothers, 1959.

Schullery, Paul, ed. *Island in the Sky: Pioneering Accounts of Mount Rainier 1833–1894.* Seattle: The Mountaineers, 1987.

Shankland, Robert. *Steve Mather of the National Parks.* 3d ed., rev. Alfred A. Knopf, 1970.

Thompson, Erwin N. *Mount Rainier National Park, Washington: Historic Resource Study.* Department of the Interior. National Park Service. 1981.

Tolbert, Caroline Leona. *History of Mount Rainier National Park.* Seattle: Lowman & Hanford Co., 1933.

Williams, John H. *The Mountain That Was God.* 3rd ed. Seattle: Lowman & Hanford Co., 1932.

Natural History — General:

Mathews, Daniel. *Cascade-Olympic Natural History: A Trailside Reference.* Raven Editions, 1988.

Saling, Ann. *The Great Northwest Nature Factbook.* Anchorage: Alaska Northwest Books, 1991.

Whitney, Stephen. *Western Forests.* New York: Alfred A. Knopf, 1985.

Natural History — Geology:

Alt, David D., and Donald W. Hyndman. *Roadside Geology of Washington.* Missoula, MT: Mountain Press Publishing Company, 1984.

Chronic, Halka. *Pages of Stone: Geology of the Western National Parks and Monuments.* Vol. 2, *Sierra, Cascades, & Pacific Coast.* Seattle: The Mountaineers, 1986.

Crandell, Dwight R. *The Geologic Story of Mount Rainier.* Pacific Northwest National Parks & Forests Association, 1983.

Mueller, Marge, and Ted Mueller. *A Guide to Washington's South Cascades' Volcanic Landscapes.* Seattle: The Mountaineers, 1995.

National Research Council. *Mount Rainier: Active Cascade Volcano.* Washington, DC: National Academy Press, 1994.

Natural History — Plants:

Brockman, C. Frank. *Flora of Mount Rainier National Park.* U.S. Department of the Interior. National Park Service. Washington: GPO, 1947.

Clark, Lewis J. *Wildflowers of the Pacific Northwest: from Alaska to Northern California.* Sidney, B.C.: Gray's Publishing Limited, 1976.

Fries, Mary A., Bob Spring, and Ira Spring. *Wildflowers of Mount Rainier and the Cascades.* Seattle: The Mount Rainier Natural History Association and The Mountaineers, 1970.

Haskin, Leslie L. *Wild Flowers of the Pacific Coast.* 2d ed. Portland, OR: Binfords & Mort, 1970.

Hitchcock, C. Leo, and Arthur Cronquist. *Flora of the Pacific Northwest.* Seattle: University of Washington Press, 1973.

Manning, Harvey, Bob Spring, Ira Spring. *Mountain Flowers of the Cascades & Olympics.* Seattle: The Mountaineers, 1979.

Moir, William H. *The Forests of Mount Rainier National Park: A Natural History.* Seattle: Pacific Northwest National Parks and Forests Association, 1989.

Mosher, Milton M. *Trees of Washington.* Pullman, WA: Washington State University Cooperative Extension, 1992.

Niehaus, Theodore F., and Charles L. Ripper. *Pacific States Wildflowers.* Boston: Houghton Mifflin Company, 1976.

Peatty, Donald Culross. *A Natural History of Western Trees.* Boston: Houghton Mifflin Company, 1953.

Petrides, George A., and Olivia Petrides. *Western Trees.* Boston: Houghton Mifflin Company, 1992.

Pojar, Jim, and Andy MacKinnon, eds. *Plants of the Pacific Northwest Coast.* Redmond, WA: Lone Pine Publishing, 1994.

Sharpe, Grant and Wenonah Sharpe. *101 Wildflowers of Mt. Rainier National Park.* Seattle: University of Washington Press, 1957.

Strickler, Dee. *Wayside Wildflowers of the Pacific Northwest.* Columbia Falls, MT: The Flower Press, 1993.

Taylor, Ronald J., and George W. Douglas. *Mountain Plants of the Pacific Northwest.* Missoula, MT: Mountain Press Publishing Company, 1995.

Natural History—Wildlife:

Anthony, H. E., ed. *Animals of America.* Garden City, NY: Garden City Publishing Co., Inc., 1937.

Burt, William H., and Richard P. Grossenheider. *A Field Guide to the Mammals,* 3rd ed. Boston: Houghton Mifflin Company, 1976.

Cahalane, Victor H. *Mammals of North America.* New York: The Macmillian Company, 1961.

Christensen, James R., and Earl J. Larrison. *Mammals of the Pacific Northwest: A Pictorial Introduction.* Moscow, ID: The University Press of Idaho, 1982.

Dawson, William Leon, and John Hooper Bowles. *The Birds of Washington,* 2 vols. Seattle: The Occidental Publishing Co., 1909.

Hoffman, Ralph. *Birds of the Pacific States.* Boston: Houghton Mifflin Company, 1927.

Peterson, Roger Tory. *Western Birds.* Boston: Houghton Mifflin Company, 1990.

Schamberger, M. L. *Mount Rainier's Mammals.* Longmire, WA: Mount Rainier Natural History Association, n.d.

Other Sources:

Additional information came from the following:

pamphlet and newspaper clipping files at local libraries, including those at Buckley, Eatonville, Enumclaw, Packwood, Tacoma, Wilkeson, and Yakima;

computer diskettes containing various articles and excerpts compiled by the Tacoma Public Library;

numerous articles in various early issues of *Mazama, Mountaineer,* and *Sierra Club Bulletin;*

bound copies of "Nature Notes," oral interview transcripts with park "old-timers," and clipping and pamphlet files; all at the Mount Rainier National Park Library, Longmire;

interviews with local residents and park personnel.

Index

In recent years, hikers at Mount Rainier often beheld a strange sight: a dark-haired woman crouched by the trailside, studying a small plant with a hand lens, while a bearded man stood nearby, busily transcribing his partner's comments into a small notebook. Although few observers knew it, they had just seen the Rohdes, hard at work on their guidebook for the park.

Gisela and Jerry first met in the San Bernardino Mountains of Southern California in 1972. Since then, they have toured much of the United States and parts of Canada, learning all they can about what they see, and, for the last six years, putting their gleanings into guidebooks. After writing two books about the redwood parks of California's North Coast, the Rohdes returned to a locale frequented by Gisela in her childhood, creating this guide to Mount Rainier and its surroundings.

Each of their books takes about two years to complete. Gisela, a self-taught naturalist, studies the local plants and wildlife, while Jerry, an avid historian, collects information about the area's past. Additional research, along with writing and editing, is done at the Rohde's home in the woods of Northern California's Humboldt County.

Larry Eifert's art is featured in some of the country's premier natural places. His murals adorn the visitor centers of such national parks and monuments as Yosemite, Redwood, Badlands, Crater Lake, Mammoth Cave, Joshua Tree, Bryce Canyon, Devil's Tower, and Mount Rainier; the latter, which is on exhibit at Ohanapecosh, provides a detailed depiction of a Pacific Northwest old-growth forest. Larry's other work includes commissions from the U.S. Fish and Wildlife Service, the Nature Conservancy, and the Sierra Club. His paintings and drawings are frequently featured as prints, posters, post cards, calendars, and even jigsaw puzzles.

The son of noted author-artist-photographer Virginia Eifert, Larry was trained from early childhood not only to express himself through art but also to appreciate nature. His father, the education curator of the Illinois State Museum, stressed the learning value of visual displays. Larry's work continues to reflect these influences.

For many years Larry owned and operated his own art gallery in the historic village of Ferndale, California. Larry and his partner, Nancy Cherry Martin, now live, tour, and paint aboard "Rumpy," a 44-foot classic Monk bridgedeck cruiser based in Port Ludlow, Washington.

Help us make better books:

We are constantly trying to improve the form and content of our guidebooks. It you have corrections, comments, and/or suggestions, please share them with us. To show our appreciation, we'll send you a coupon good for $5.00 off your next order from **MountainHome Books**.

Write to us at:

MountainHome Books
1901 Arthur Road
McKinleyville, CA 95519

Thank you,
Jerry & Gisela Rohde

Order direct from **MountainHome Books**:

Mount Rainier National Park: Tales, Trails, & Auto Tours
by Jerry & Gisela Rohde $17.95

Redwood National & State Parks: Tales, Trails, & Auto Tours
by Jerry & Gisela Rohde $15.95

Humboldt Redwoods State Parks: The Complete Guide
by Jerry & Gisela Rohde $15.95

Shipping: one book — $3.00; each additional book — $1.00
California residents add 7.25% state sales tax.